RADIO CITY

SPECTACULAR

A PHOTOGRAPHIC HISTORY OF THE ROCKETTES AND CHRISTMAS SPECTACULAR

PHOTOGRAPHS BY

MSG ENTERTAINMENT

JAMES PORTO

Interior design by Kathleen Burchell

Photographs supplied by James Porto, David James, MSG Entertainment, and George Kalinsky for Madison Square Garden

Printed on acid-free paper

Library of Congress Cataloging-in-Publication Data is available upon request.

ISBN 13: 978-0-06-156538-0

23 SCP 10 9 8 7 6 5 4

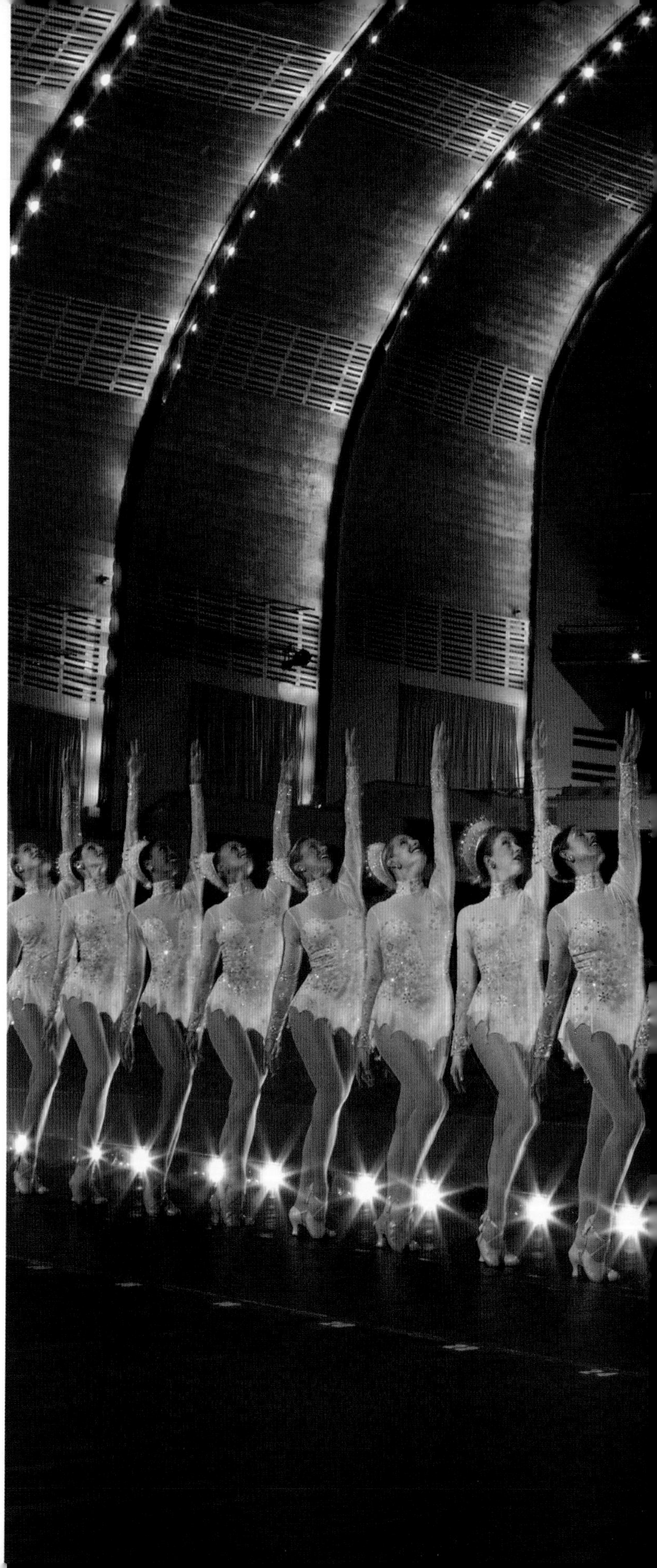

RADIO CITY

SPECTACULAR

A PHOTOGRAPHIC HISTORY OF THE ROCKETTES AND CHRISTMAS SPECTACULAR

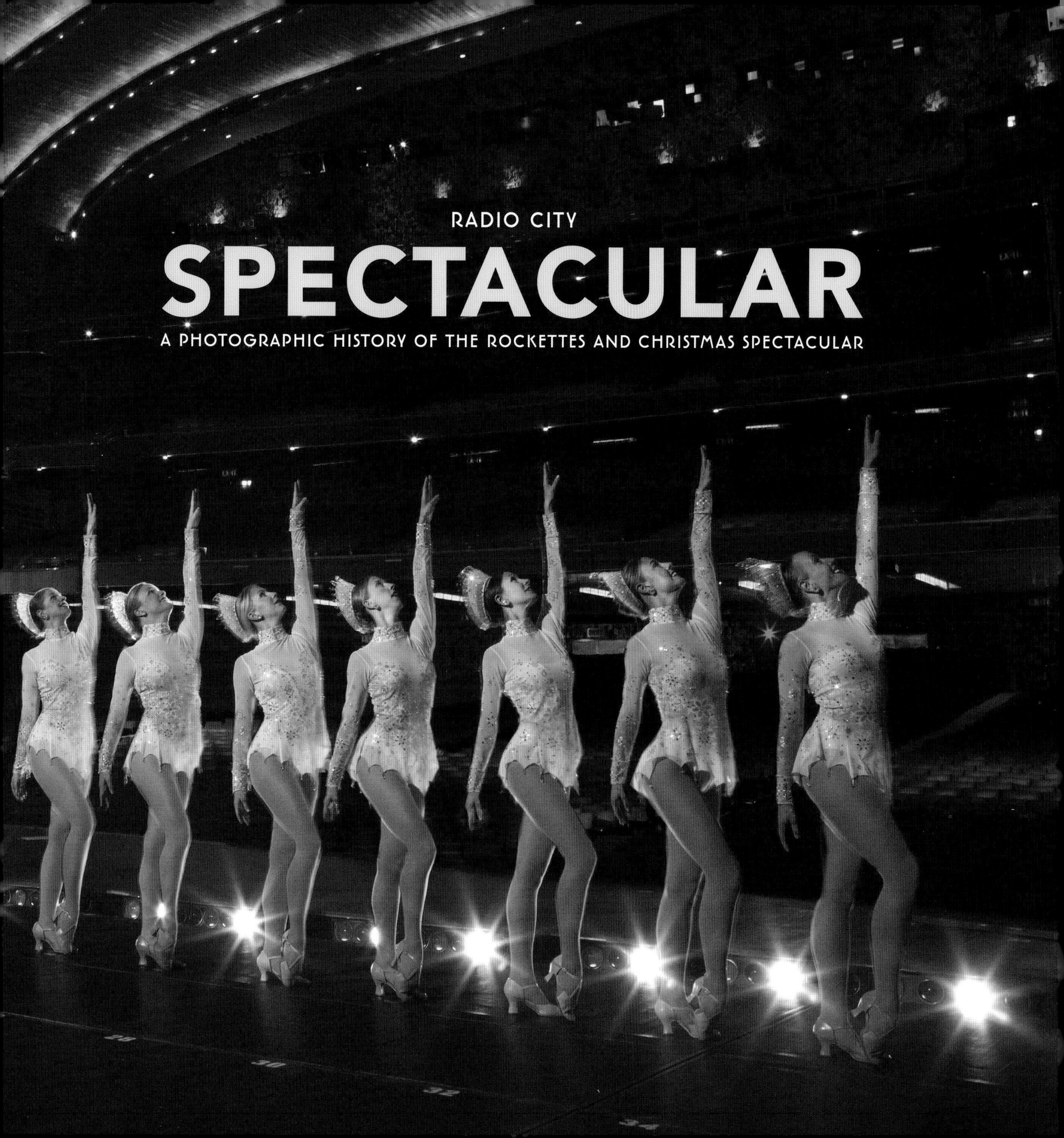

CONTENTS

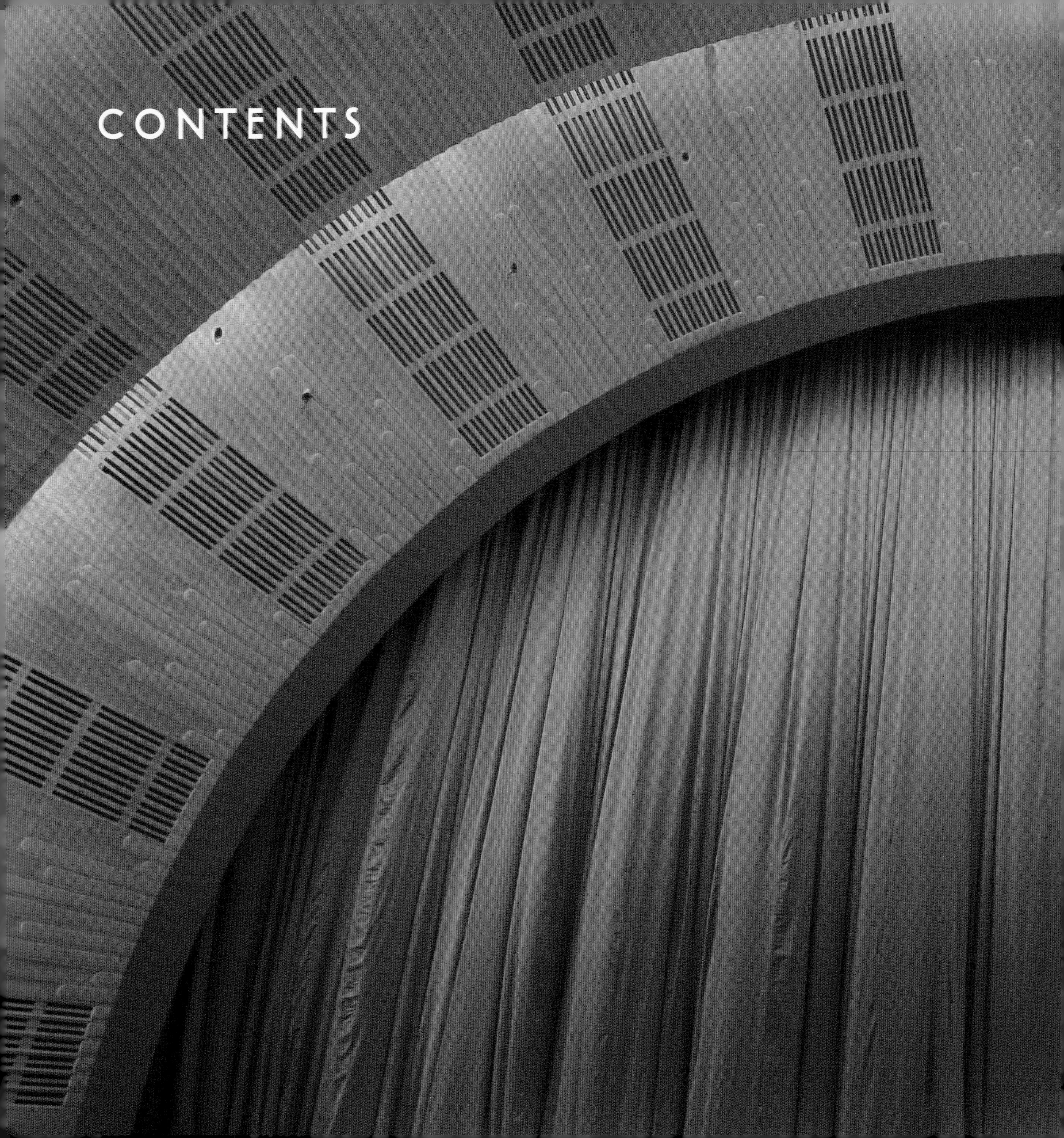

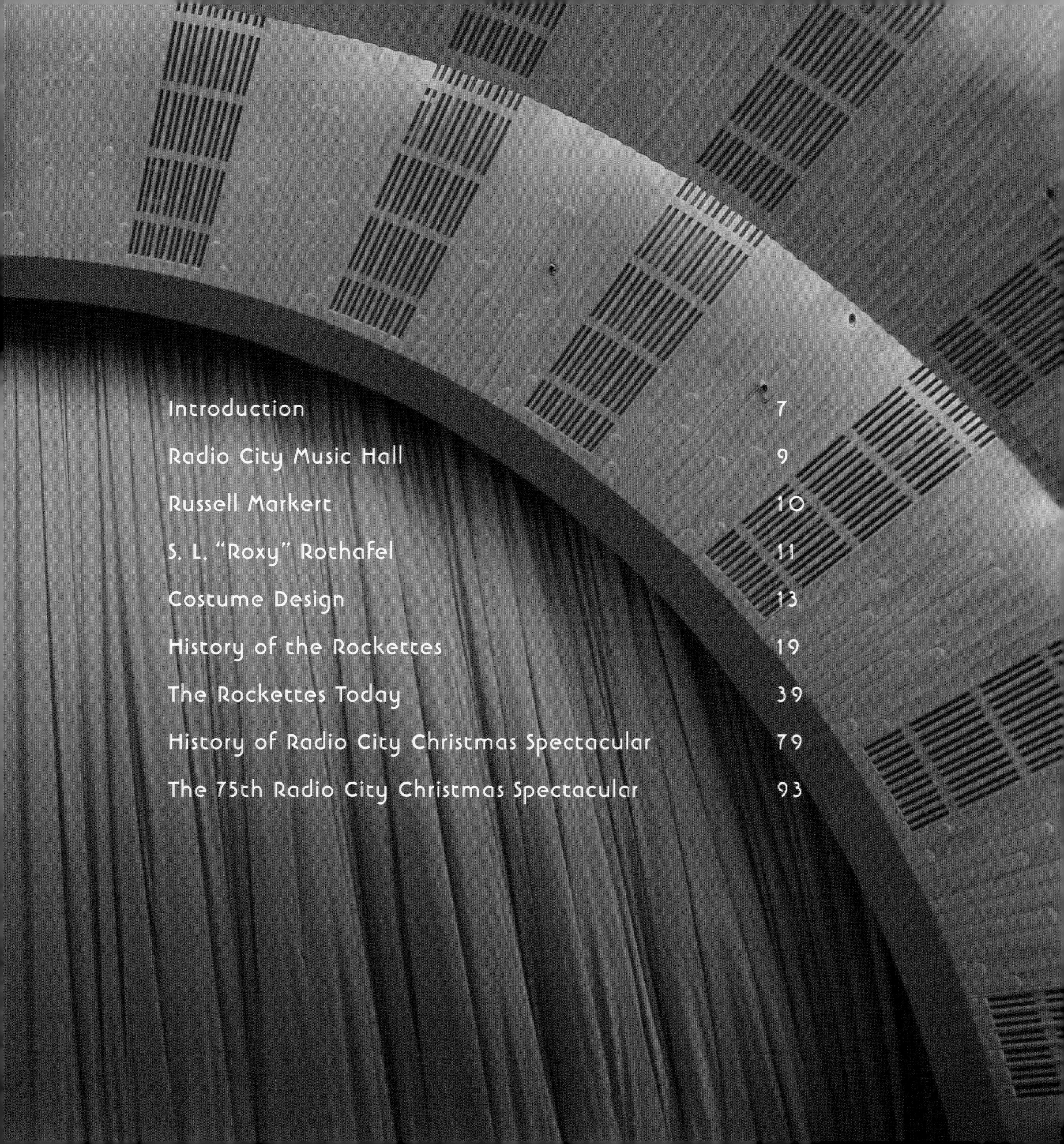

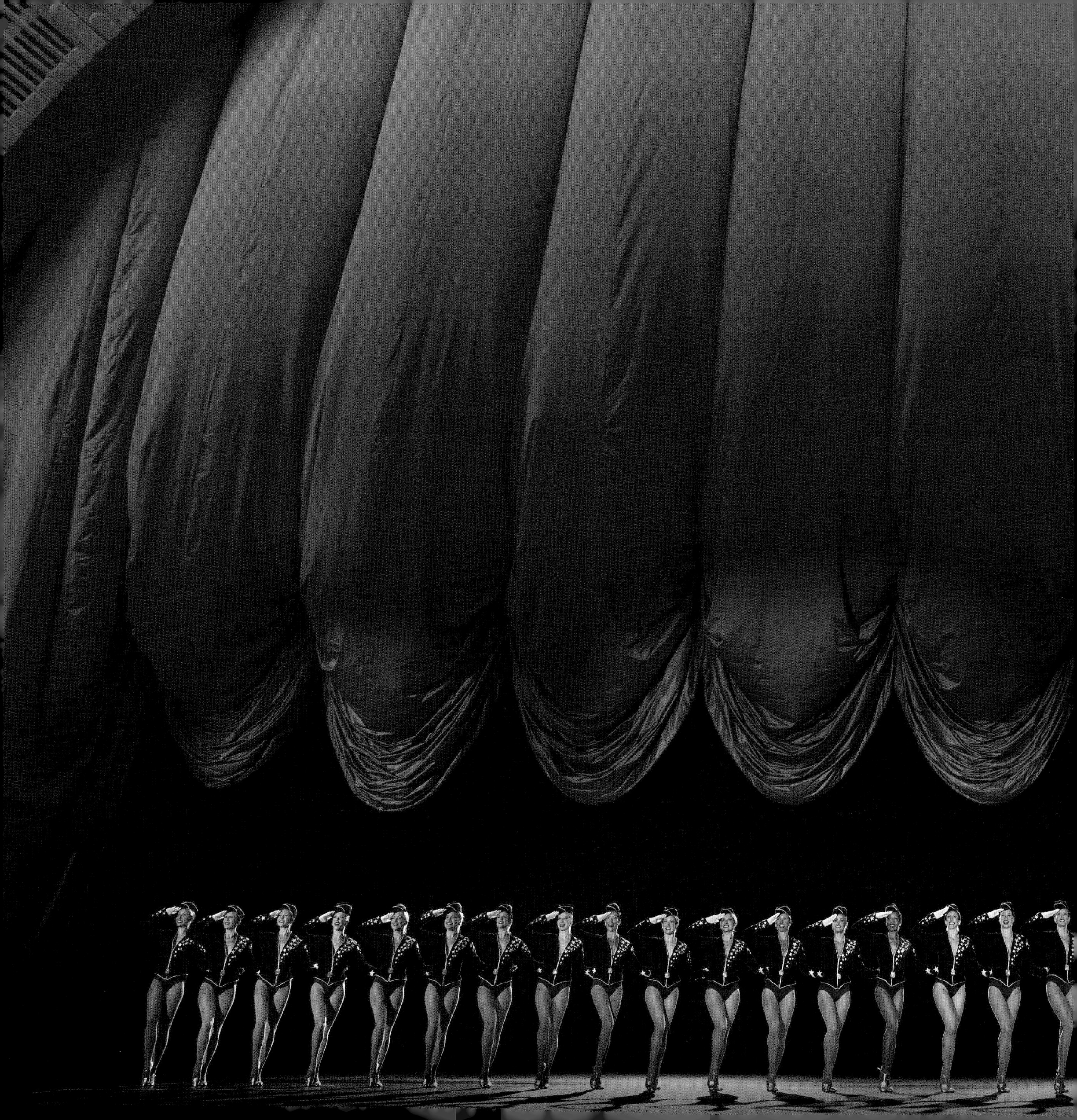

Introduction

Capturing the energy and elegance of the American treasures, the *Radio City Christmas Spectacular* and the Rockettes, was a difficult task. Add to that the challenge of explaining the depth of this holiday institution and the famed Rockettes. The best vehicle proved to be a mix of the old and the new. By combining the modern photography of James Porto with historical photographs, we aim to share these collections of photos and memories that audiences can cherish as keepsakes.

The Radio City Rockettes, the stars of the *Christmas Spectacular,* appeared in hundreds of stage spectaculars that accompanied the greatest Hollywood films and premieres of the day. They performed four shows a day, twenty-eight shows a week, three hundred and sixty-five days a year for more than fifty years. The Rockettes participated in many historic and memorable events. They won the grand prize at the "Paris Exposition de Dance" in 1936, starred in USO tours during World War II, and performed their show-stopping eye-high kicks at the 1988 Super Bowl Halftime Show. They also appear annually in the Macy's Thanksgiving Day Parade and the Rockefeller Center Tree Lighting in New York City.

The main event which draws people from all over the world is the *Radio City Christmas Spectacular*. The *Radio City Christmas Spectacular* creates wonderful memories for more than one million patrons each year and has been seen by approximately 62 million people since its inception in 1933, when it was originally performed as a holiday "gift" between movie screenings. The *Christmas Spectacular* has long since become part of the holiday tradition and draws people from far and wide who want to experience a quintessential New York City Christmas.

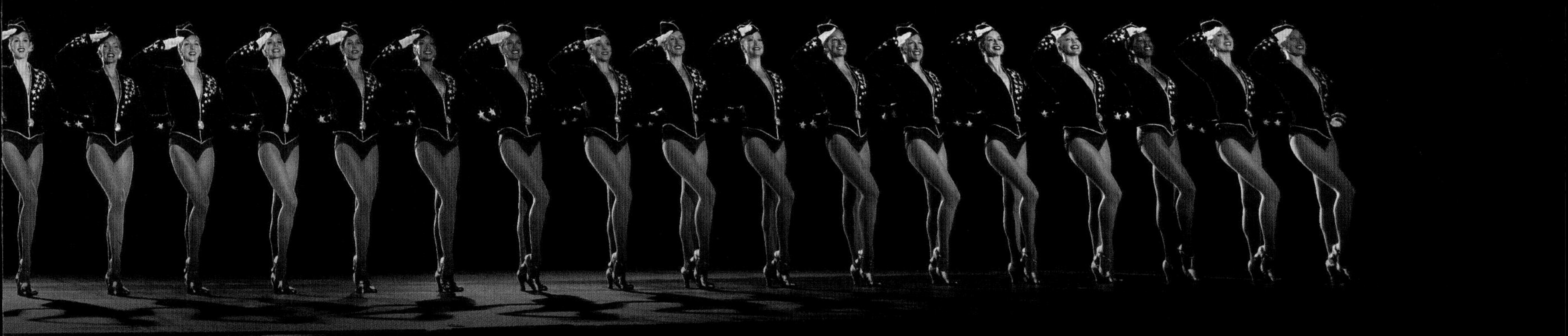

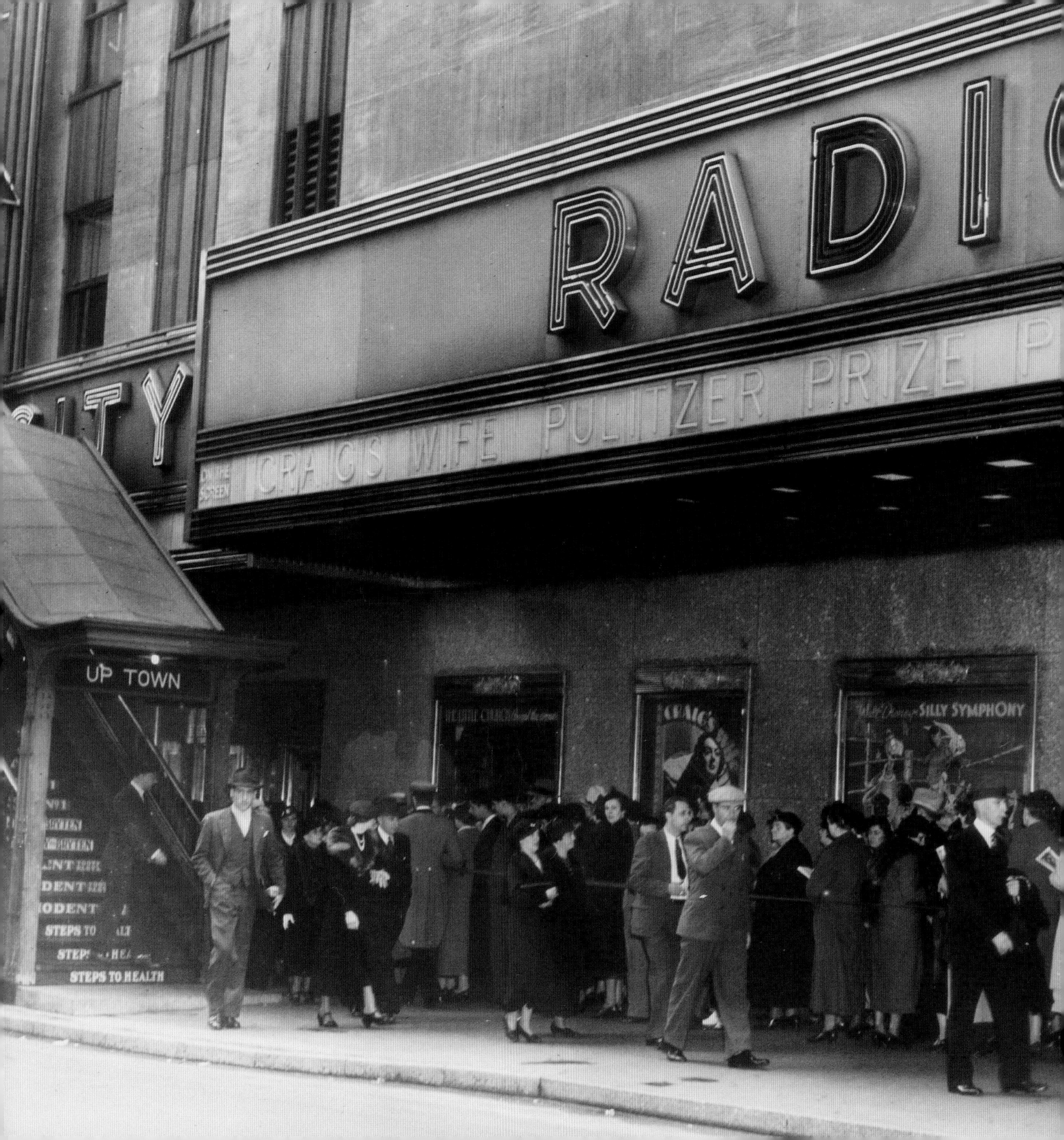
RADI
CRAIG'S WIFE PULITZER PRIZE
ON THE SCREEN
UP TOWN
SILLY SYMPHONY
STEPS TO HEALTH

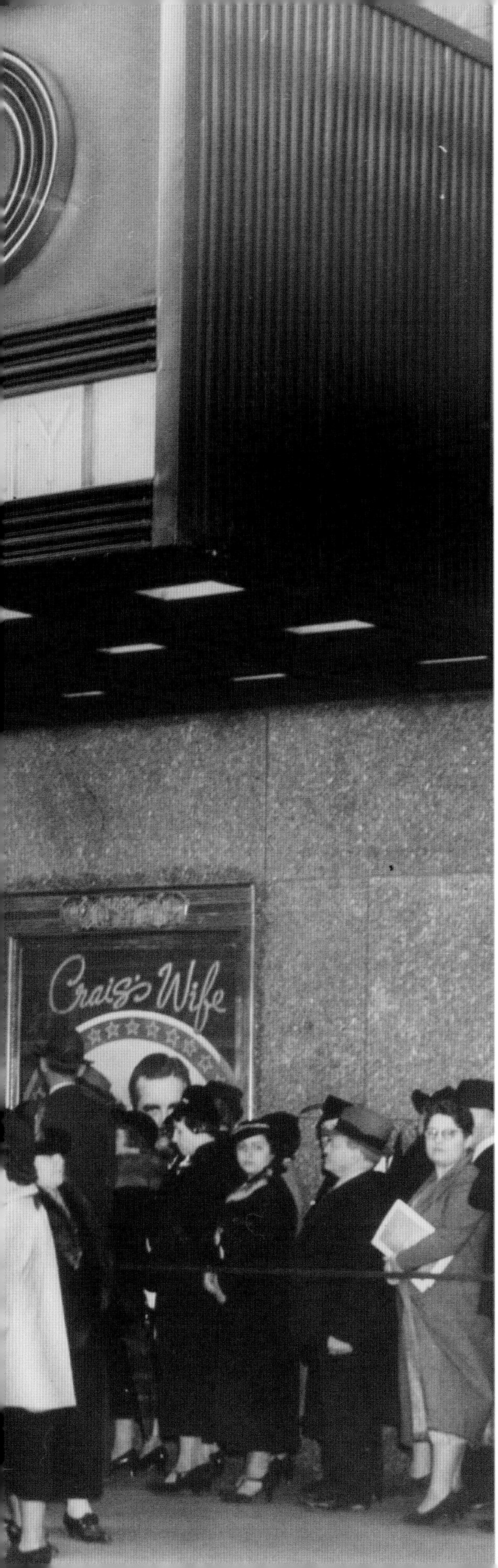

RADIO CITY MUSIC HALL

When the stock market crashed in 1929, most people tried to hold on to whatever money they had left. Contrary to public sentiment, John D. Rockefeller made the bold decision to build an entire complex of buildings.

Rockefeller's financial power and Radio Corporation of America's media might were joined by the impresario S. L. "Roxy" Rothafel. Roxy had earned a reputation as a theatrical genius by employing an innovative combination of vaudeville, movies, and razzle-dazzle décor to revive struggling theatres across America. Together they realized a fantastic dream—a theatre unlike any in the world. It was a palace for the people, a place of beauty offering high-quality entertainment at prices ordinary people could afford. It was intended to entertain and amuse, but also to elevate and inspire. It was Radio City Music Hall.

A contest was held to select the designer for the Music Hall's interior. Donald Deskey wasn't the most celebrated designer in the competition; in fact, he was relatively unknown. Deskey's designs chose elegance over excess, grandeur above glitz. He designed more than thirty separate spaces, including eight lounges and smoking rooms, each with its own motif. Art was an integral part of the design. Fine artists created murals, wall coverings, and sculptures; textile designers developed draperies and carpets; craftsmen made ceramics, wood panels, and chandeliers. Everything about it was larger than life. Although it was built in 1932, the Art Deco style of the Music Hall is still fresh today.

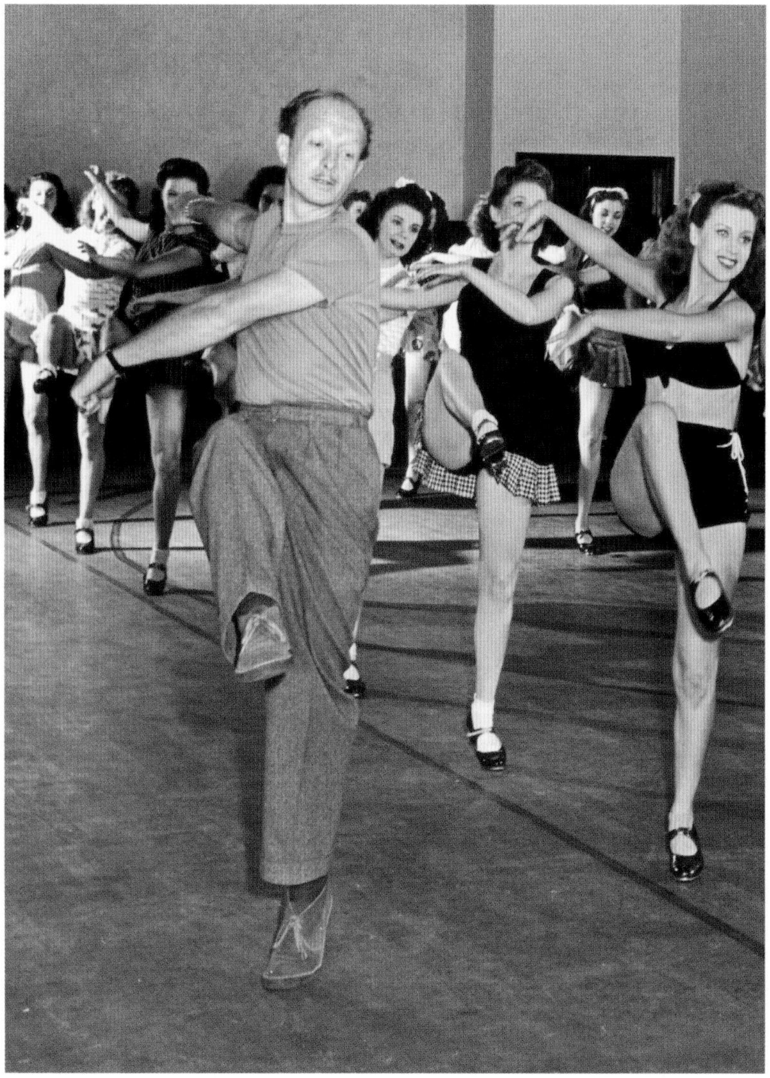

Russell Markert

Russell Markert created the exemplary American chorus line—an exciting precision dance company with great style, flair, and glamour. His inspiration was the John Tiller girls of the 1922 Ziegfeld Follies.

Markert's stringent requirements never varied, and he continued to stage and choreograph productions at the Music Hall until his retirement in 1971.

His concept of the dance line was to achieve absolute precision and ultimate uniformity in the movements of the dancers. The audience saw thirty-six Rockettes perform intricate routines, but always moving as "one dancer." Everything—from the costumes to the specific steps—was kept completely identical. The illusion of uniform height has always been maintained by having the tallest dancers in the center of the line and placing dancers of gradually decreasing height on either side, with the shortest women at both ends of the line.

S. L. "Roxy" Rothafel

The Missouri Rockets were in New York City rehearsing to perform in the Broadway show *Rain or Shine* when they were discovered by consummate showman S. L. "Roxy" Rothafel. Their New York debut was in the Roxy Theatre on 50th Street and Seventh Avenue. "The Rockets" were so much of an instant hit that Rothafel was loathe to let them leave. He pleaded with Russell Markert to form another line to replace the departing Rockets.[1] There were actually three separate Rocket dance troupes performing in New York at the time.

Rothafel moved two of the troupes to Radio City Music Hall for opening night in 1932. He first dubbed them the "Roxyettes." In 1934, the Roxyettes officially became the Radio City Music Hall Rockettes.

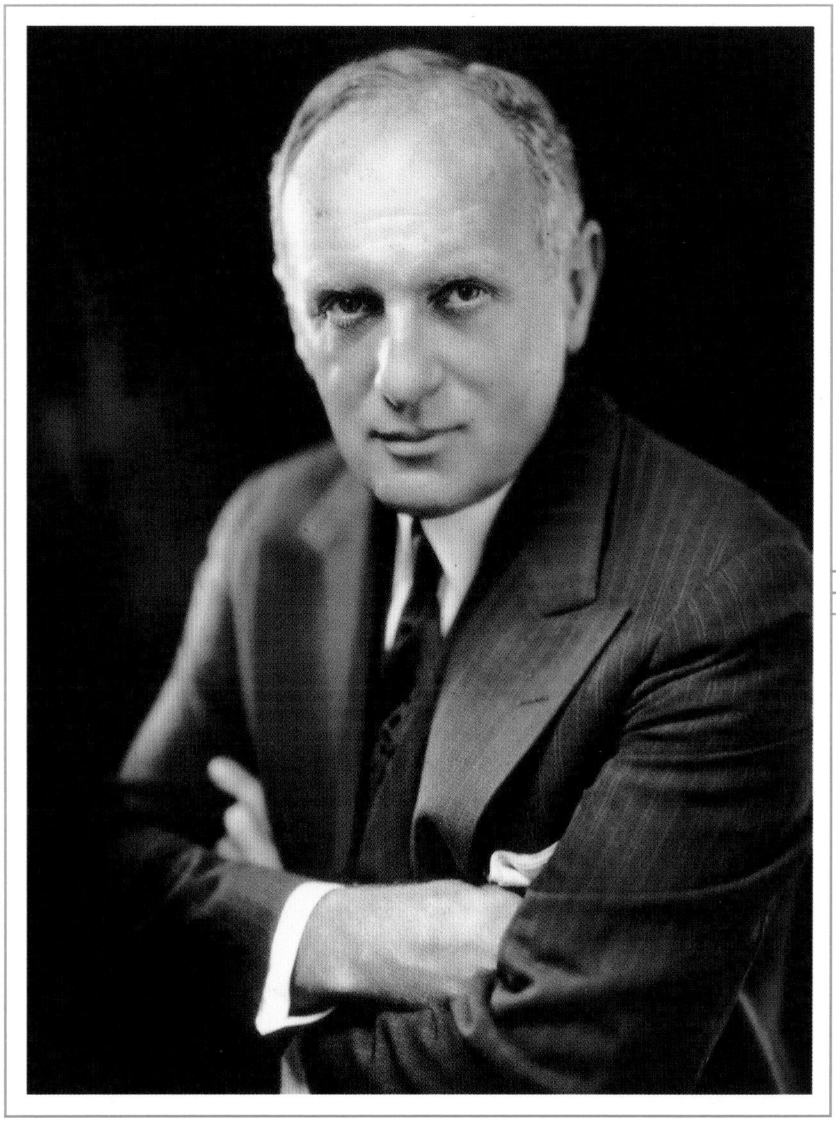

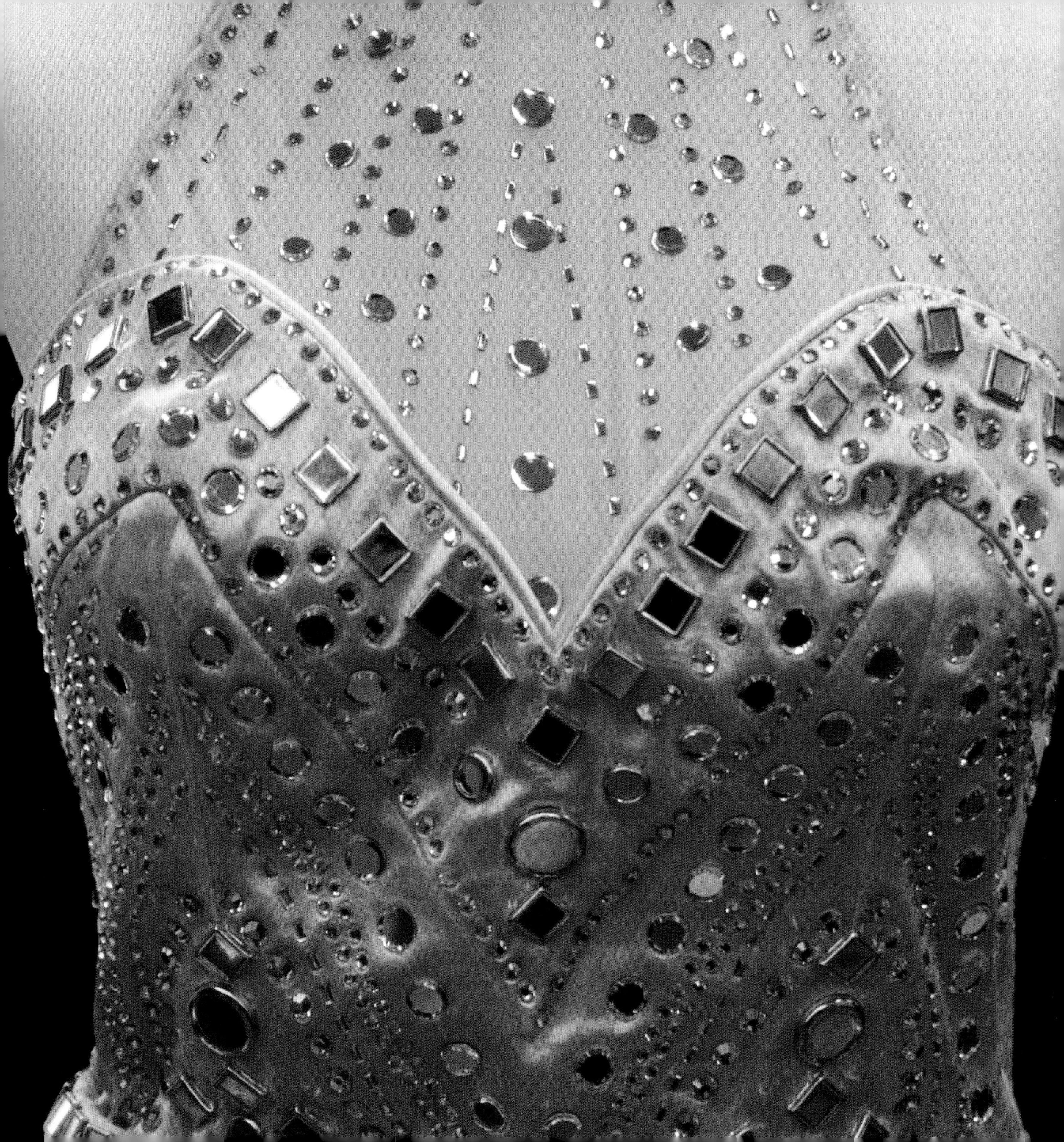

COSTUME DESIGN

The Rockettes' costumes have dazzled audiences through the years. Some of the greatest designers of the day have created costumes for the legendary dance troupe, including Bob Mackie, Erté, and Vincente Minnelli.

Vincente Minnelli was one of the first costume and set designers. He became one of Hollywood's finest directors, husband of Judy Garland and father of Liza Minnelli.

The Father of the Art Deco style, Erté, designed elaborate costumes for the Rockettes that seem to be an extension of the Music Hall itself.

Bob Mackie, "the sultan of sequins and rajah of rhinestones," not only designs clothes for Barbie and Cher, but also costumes for the Rockettes.

Famed Broadway designers James Morcom, John William Keck, Marco Montedoro, and Frank Spencer were at one time designers for the dance troupe.

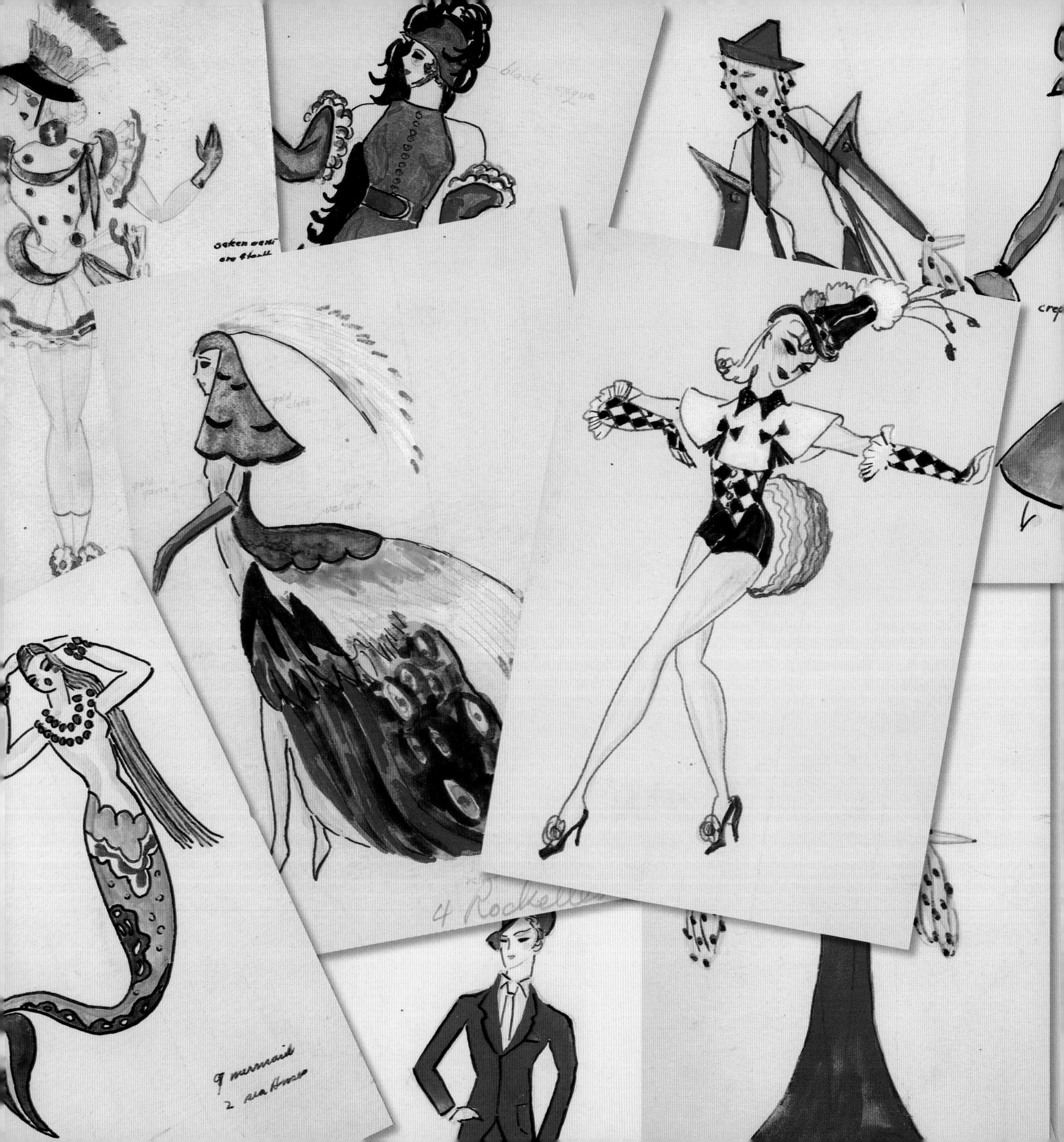
black
velvet
9 mermaid

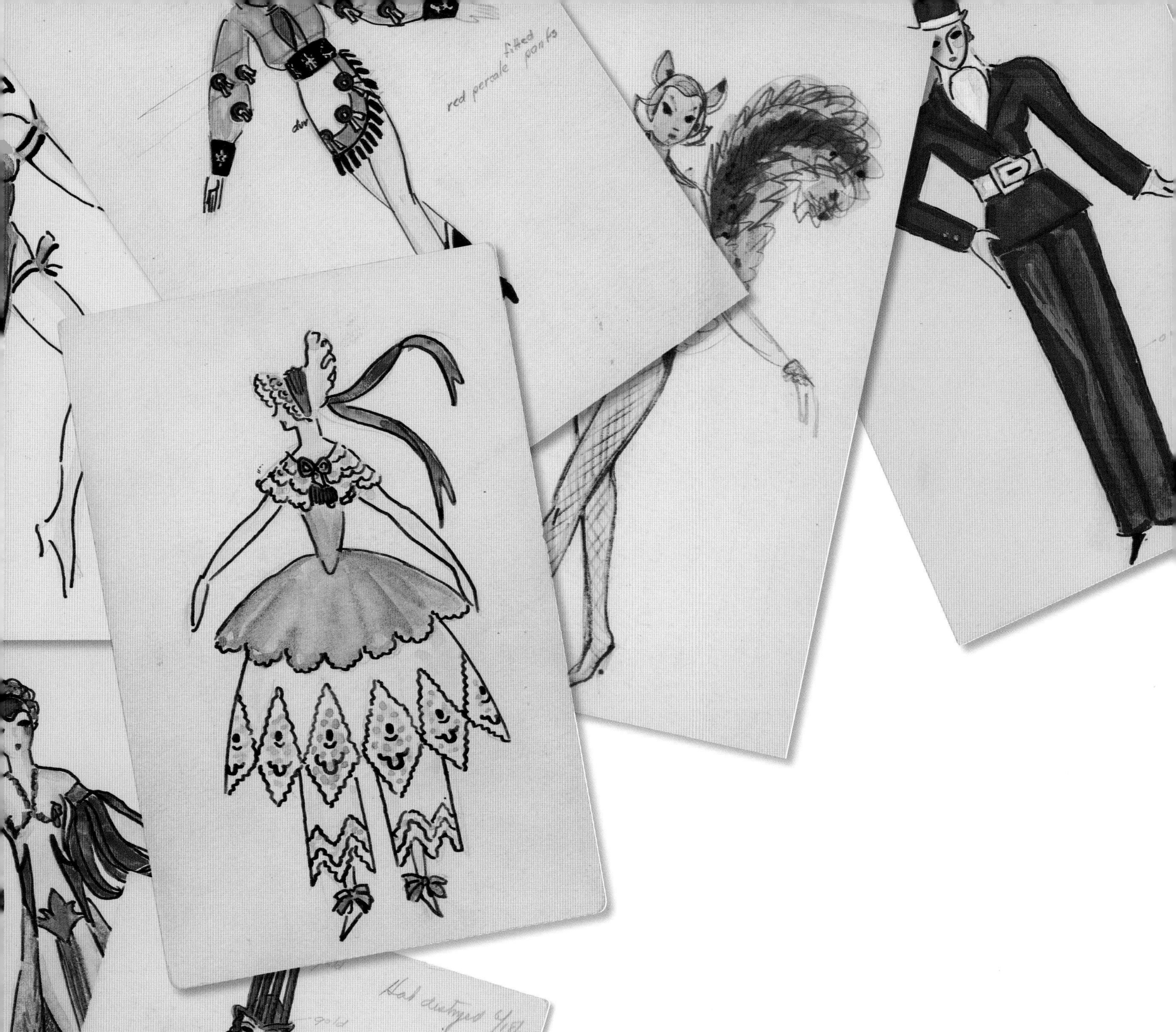

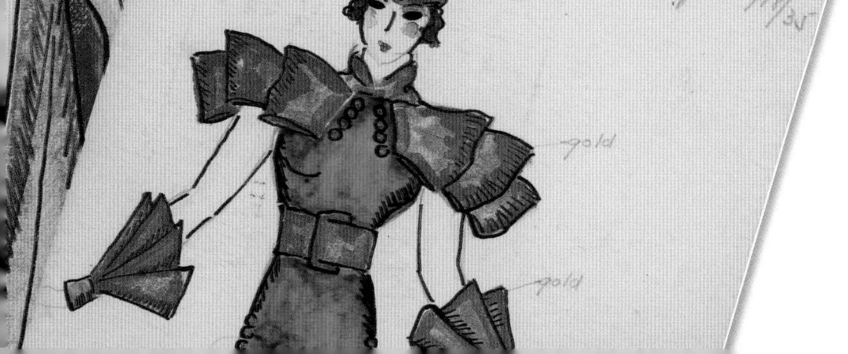

Original sketches of the Rockettes' early costumes are still used today for design inspiration and ideas.

In the early days, designers created hand-painted costume cards that seamstresses used to make the costumes.

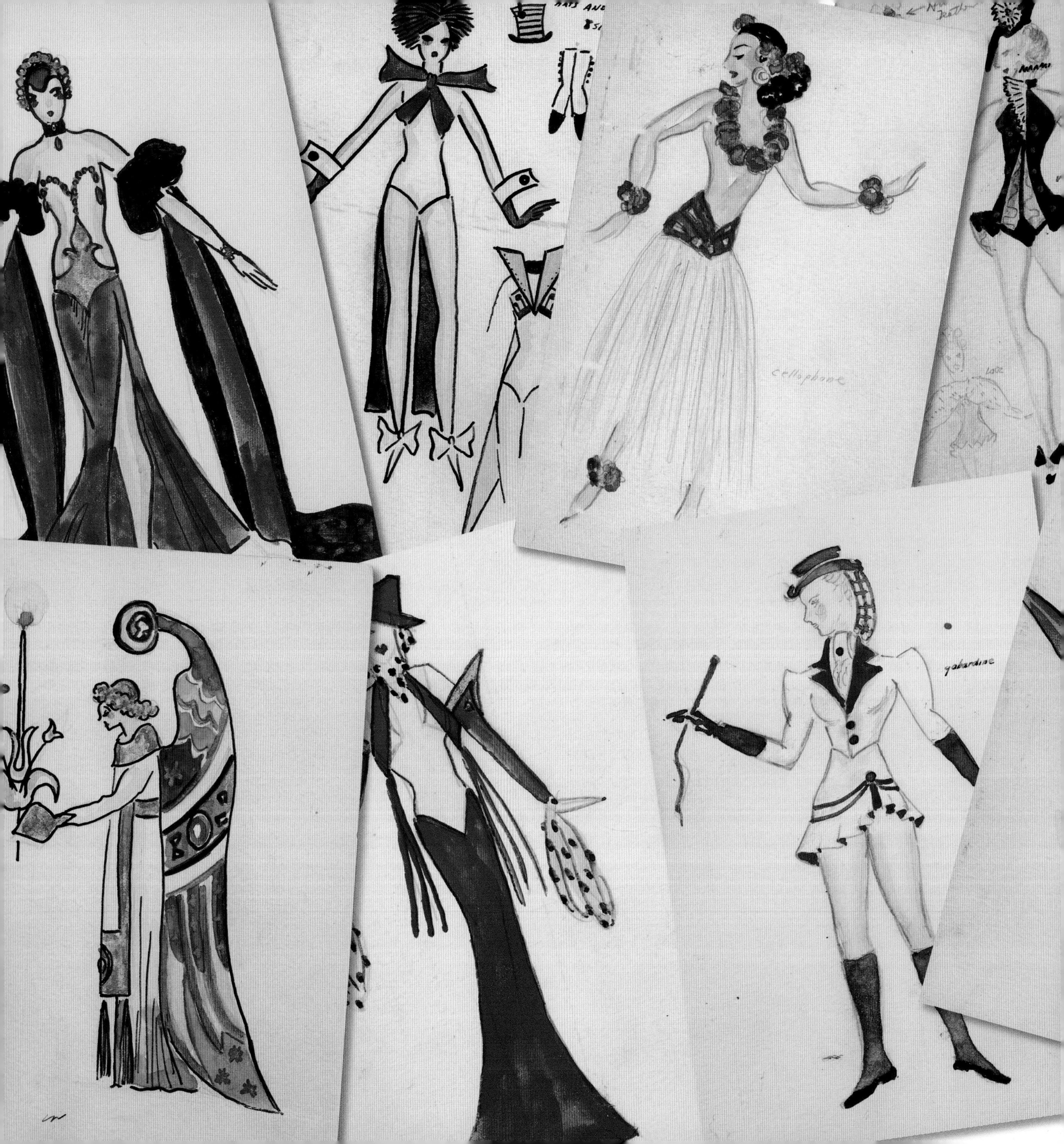
cellophane
gabardine

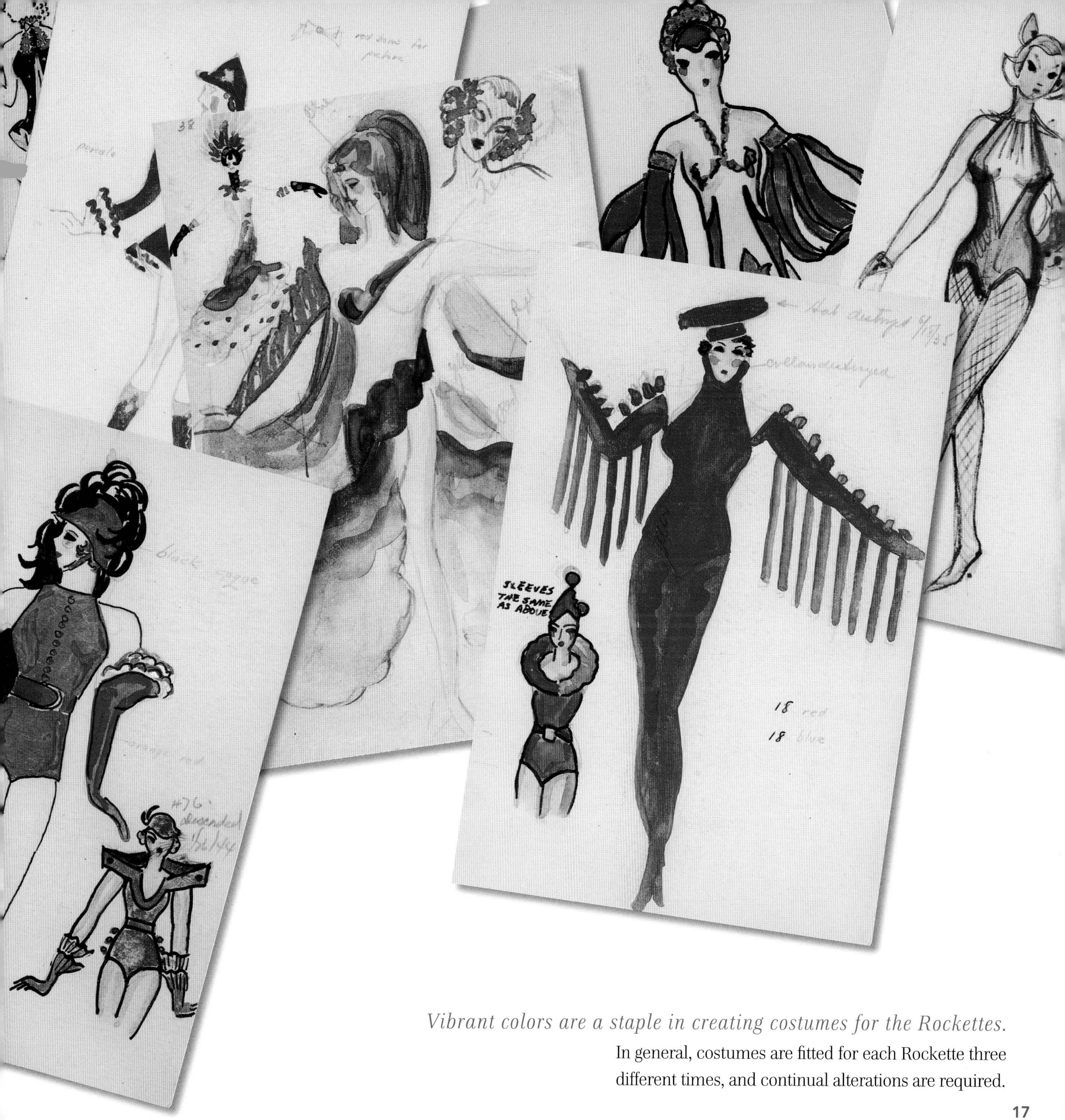

Vibrant colors are a staple in creating costumes for the Rockettes.
In general, costumes are fitted for each Rockette three different times, and continual alterations are required.

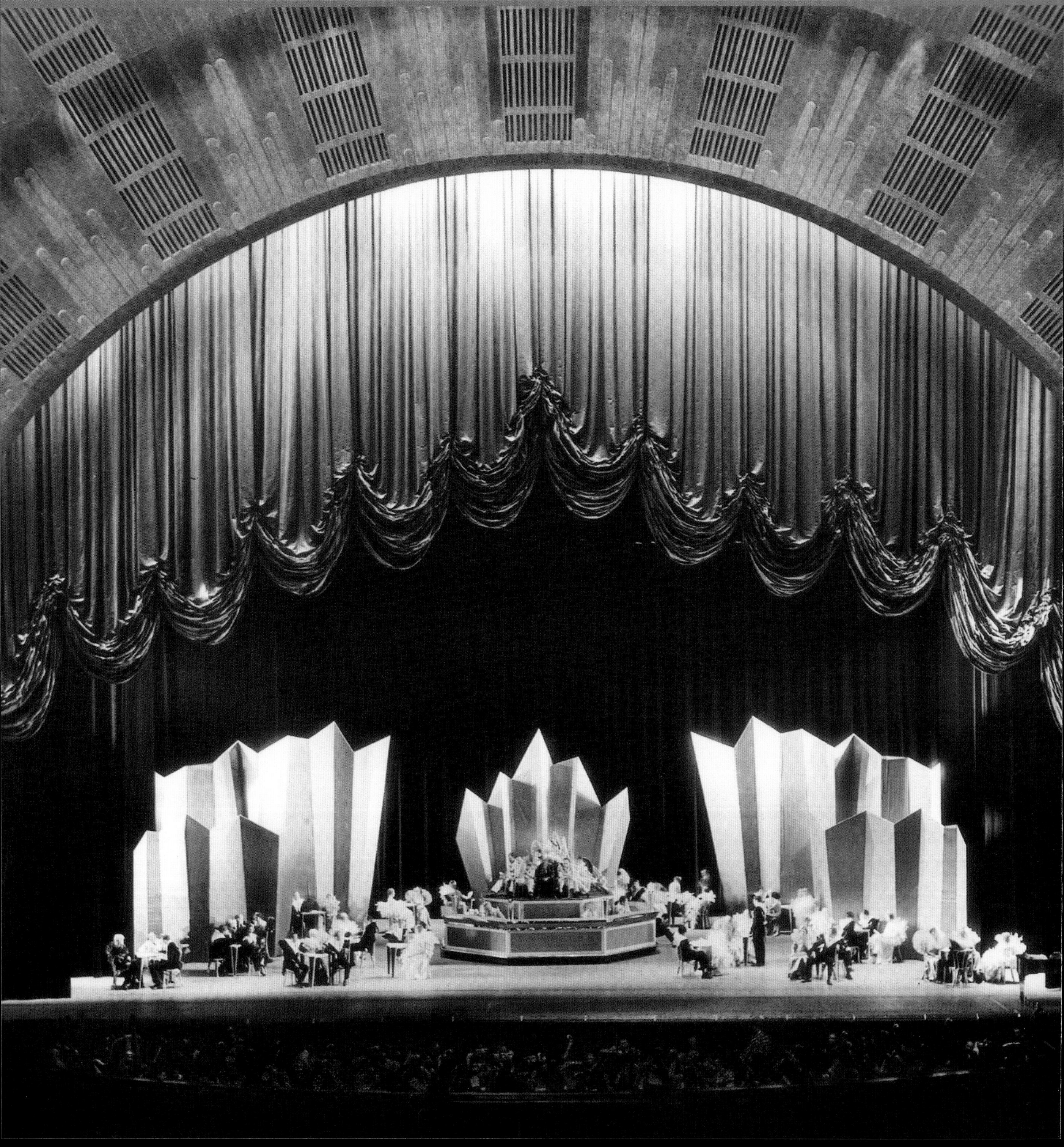

HISTORY OF THE ROCKETTES

Under the supervision of their founder, Russell Markert, the Radio City Rockettes began kicking up their heels in 1925, dazzling audiences with their exactness, precision, and uniformity. They were first known as the "Missouri Rockets" and made their show debut in St. Louis.

Radio City Music Hall officially opened its doors on December 27th, 1932, just two days after Christmas in one of our Nation's darkest periods, the Great Depression. Opening night was described as "the hottest ticket in town. More than 100,000 people had requested admission, but only 6,200 could be obliged. The fortunate few would not only see a spectacular new show, but also be the first to inspect a new theatre."[2]

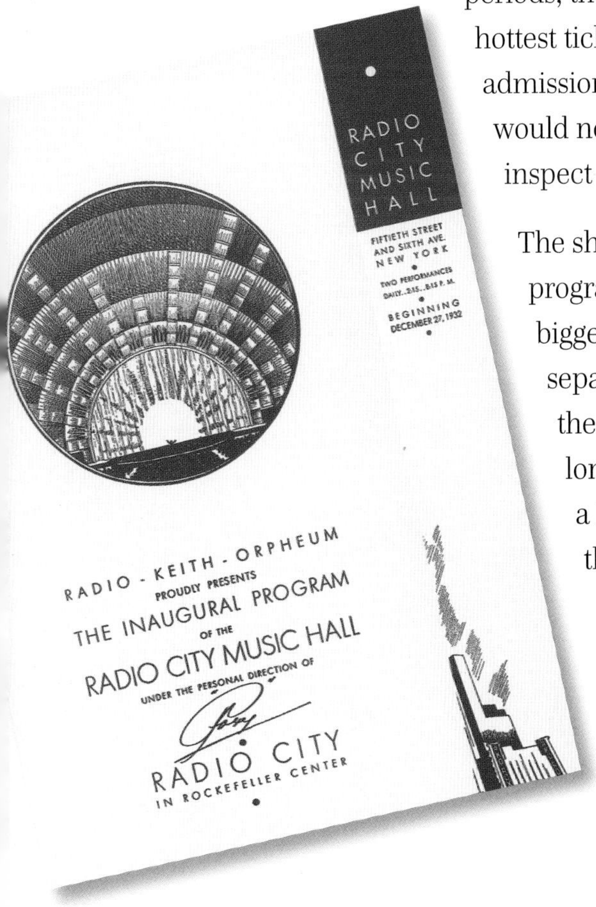

The show was scheduled to start at 9 P.M. "The opening night program documents the size of what must have been the biggest variety or vaudeville show in history. Nineteen separate acts were scheduled. Nobody involved remembers the precise running time, but all agree that it was painfully long."[3] The Roxyettes' dance number was to the song "With a Feather in Your Cap." Their perfect precision won over the opening night crowd.

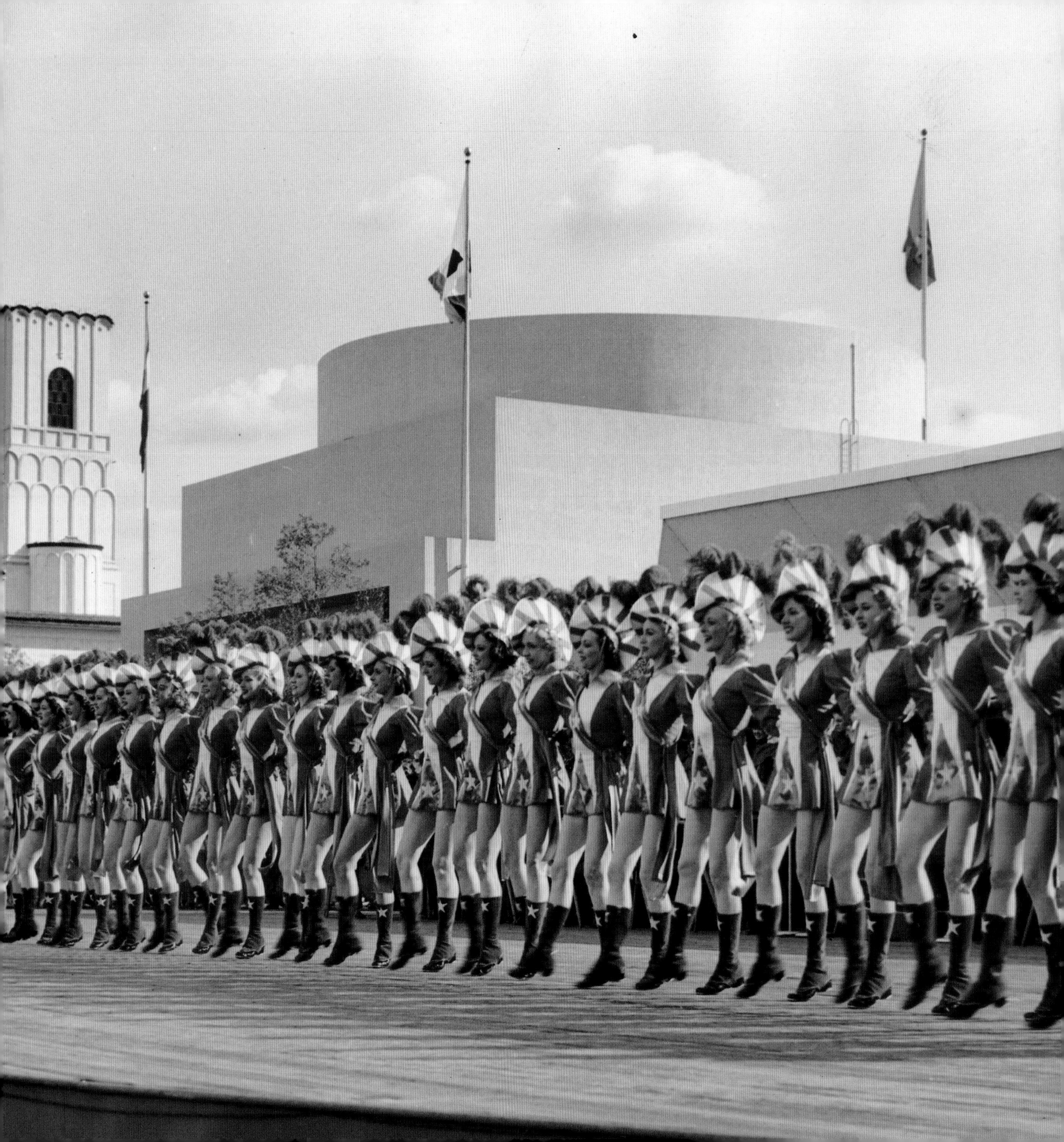

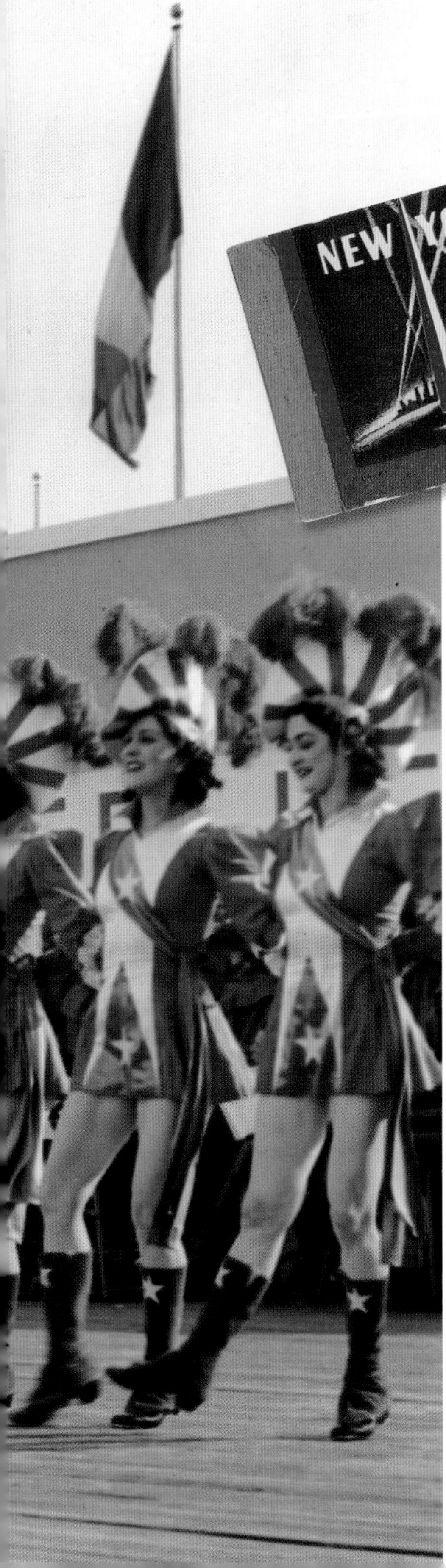

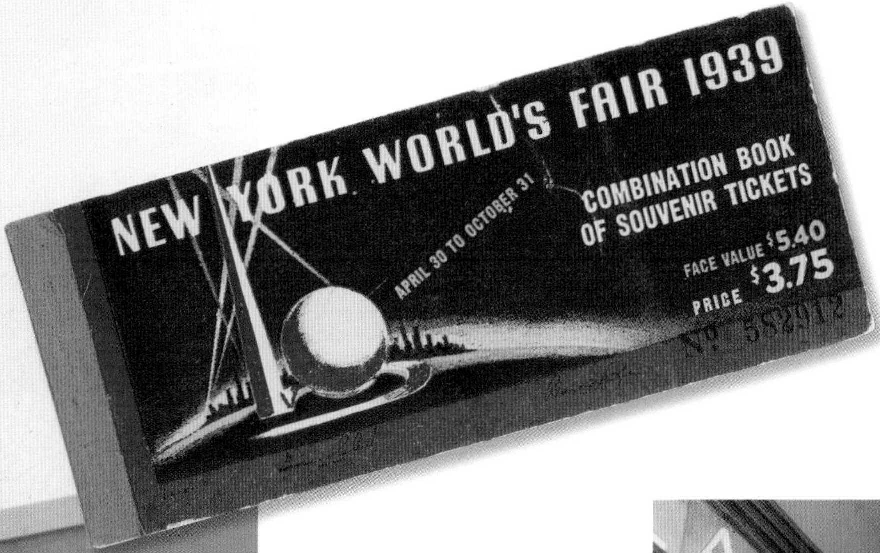

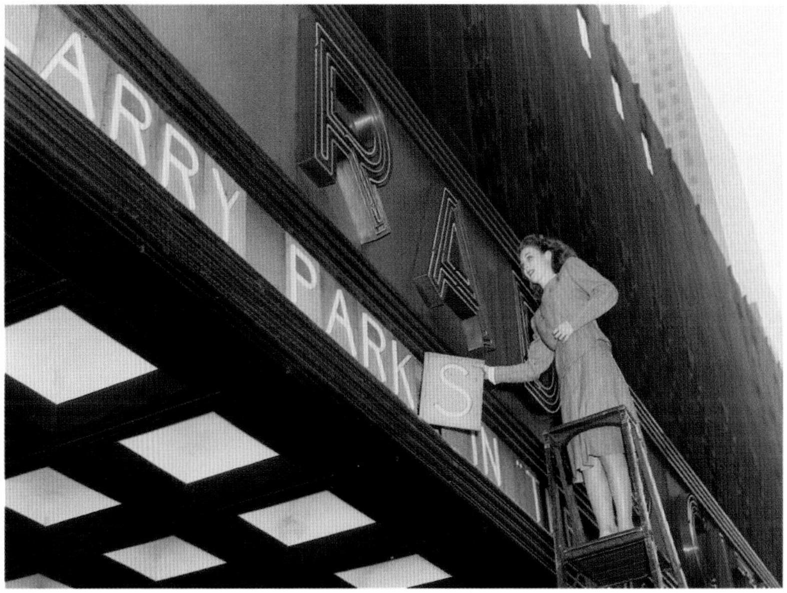

Since 1933 more than seven hundred movies have opened at the Music Hall. They include Larry Parks starring in The Jolson Story.

A movie showing at the Music Hall virtually guaranteed a successful run in theatres around the country. *A Christmas Carol* premiered at the Music Hall in the 1938 Christmas season…and in keeping with the spirit of that film, our special guests of this show were none other than the Vienna Choir Boys, making their Music Hall debut. Movies that have opened at the Music Hall include the original *King Kong, National Velvet, White Christmas, Mame, Breakfast at Tiffany's, To Kill a Mockingbird, Mary Poppins, 101 Dalmatians,* and *The Lion King.* Radio City Music Hall featured a new movie every week accompanied by a lavish and unique stage production starring the Rockettes.

At left, the Rockettes perform at the New York World's Fair in 1939.

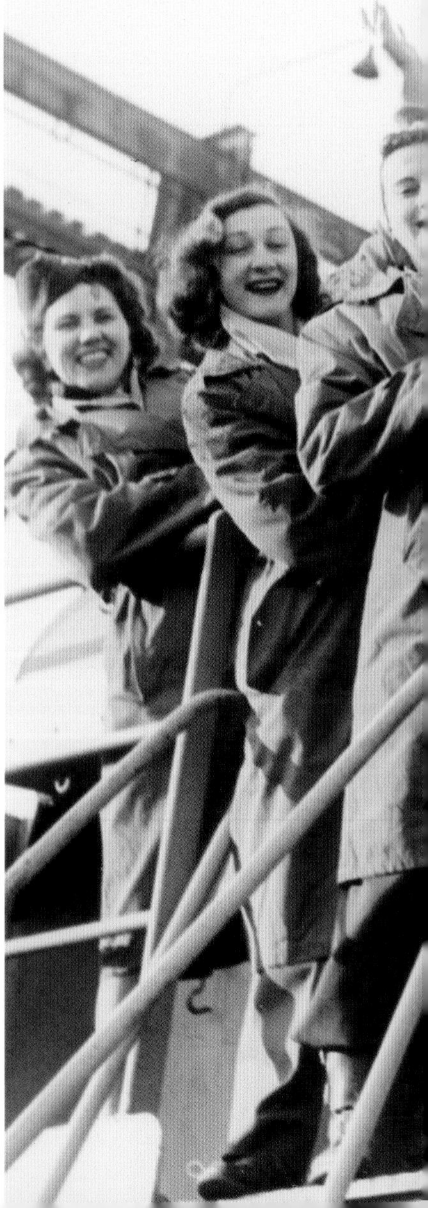

After the attack on Pearl Harbor, the United States entered World War II. The Rockettes joined the USO and traveled abroad to entertain the troops.

The Rockettes supported the wartime effort by traveling across the United States as well. They were involved in wartime shows at the Copacabana, the Army Air Corps base in Pawling, New York, and at the Stage Door Canteen. The Rockettes and Eleanor Roosevelt even hosted a War Bond Rally at Madison Square Garden.

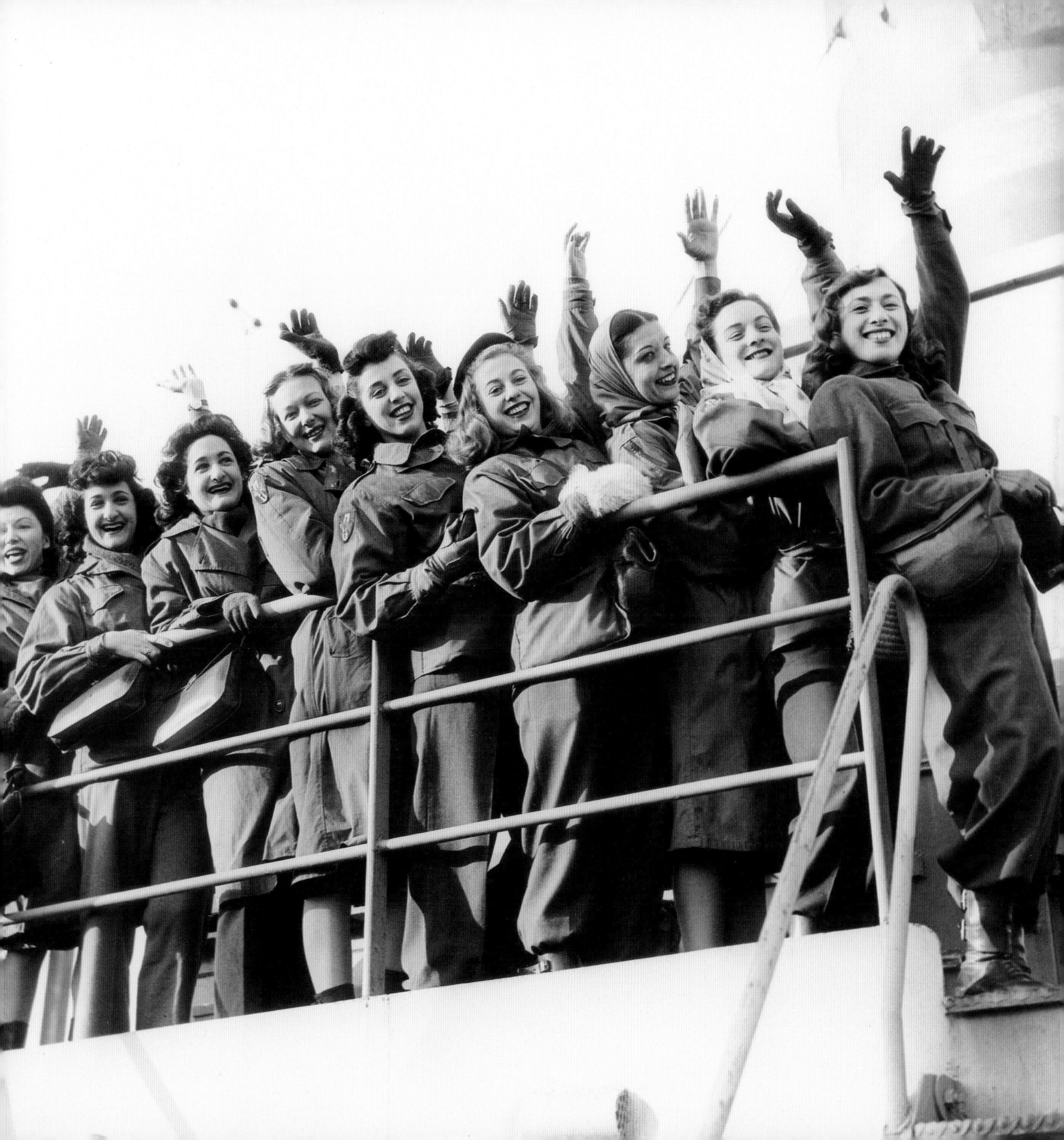

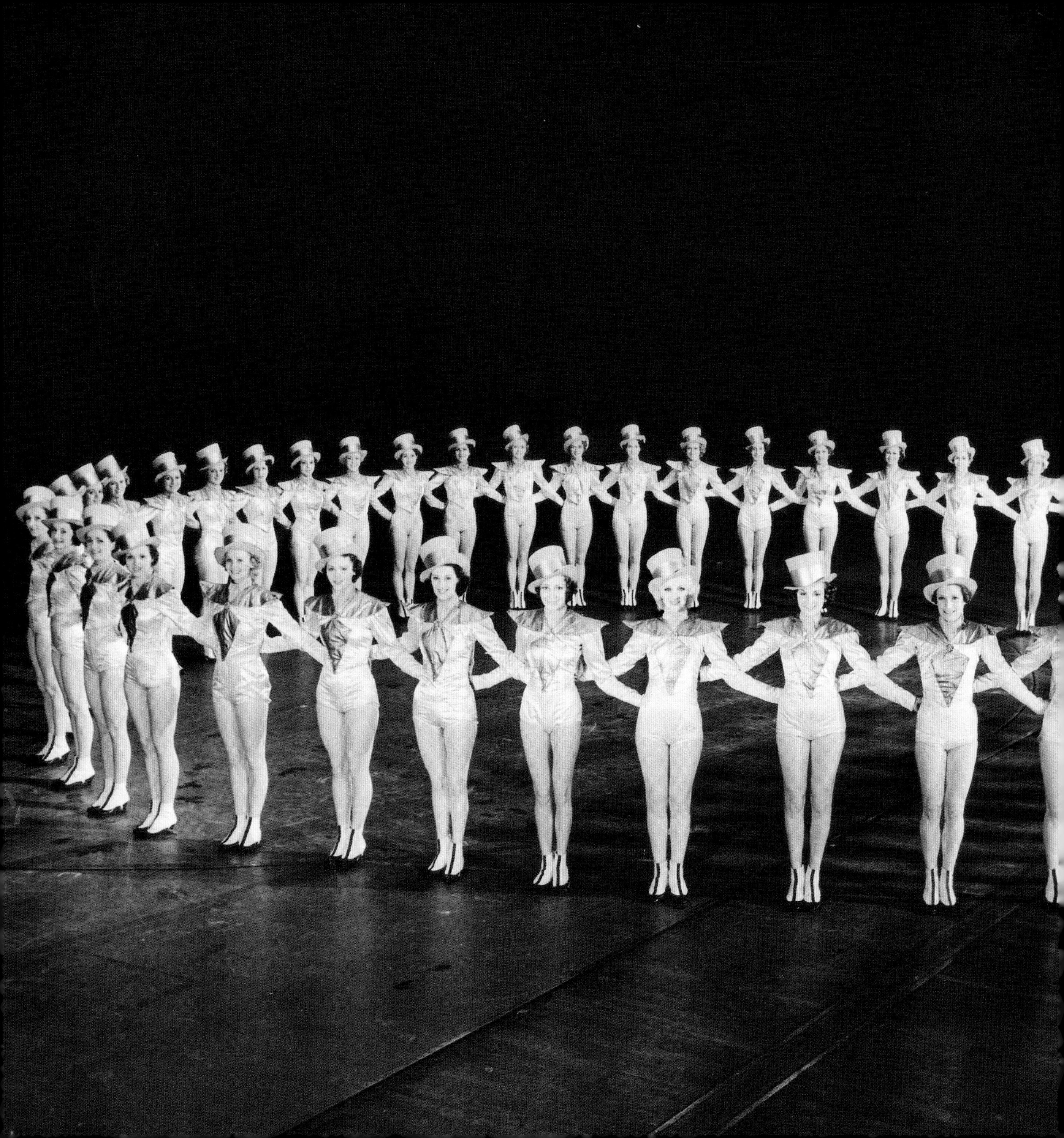

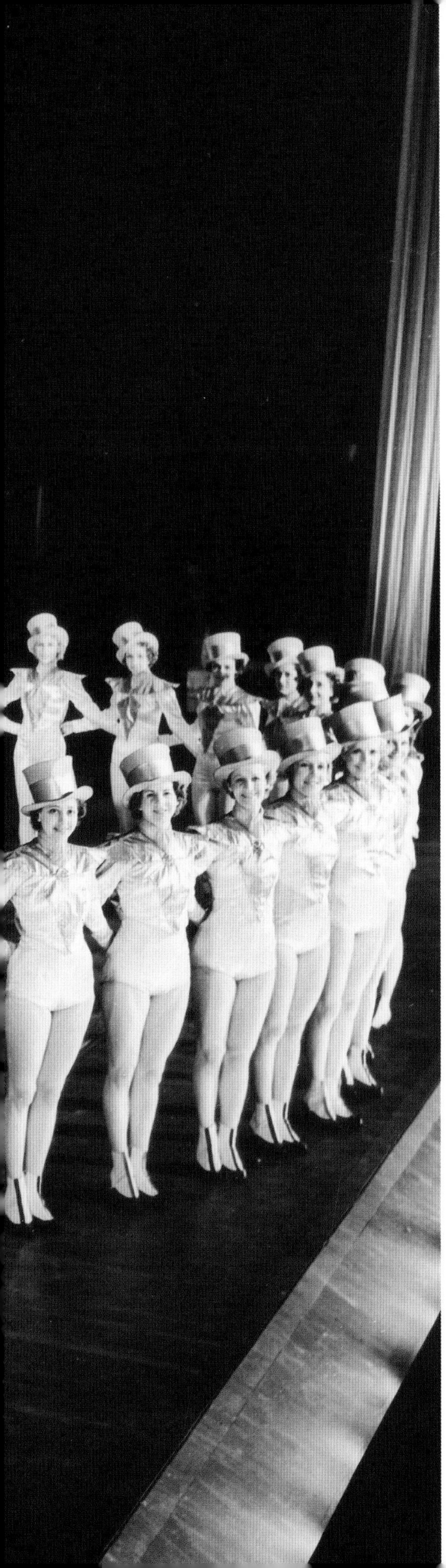

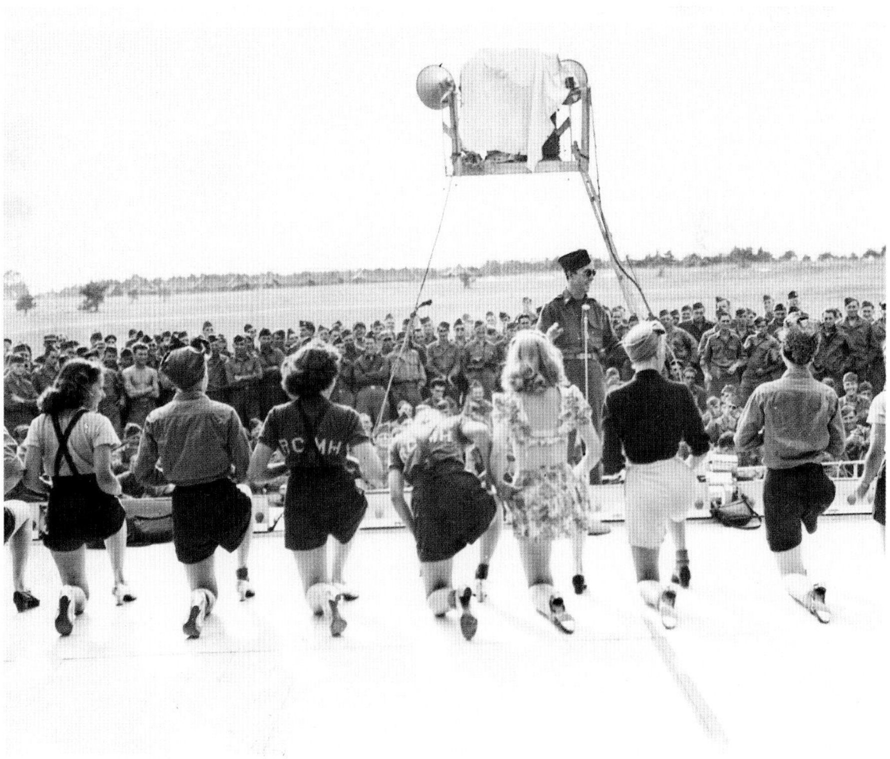

The Rockettes perform for the U.S. troops.

At left, the Rockettes continued to do regular shows at the Music Hall, but a troupe of eight dancers ventured out to perform for Army Air Corps, and made other special appearances in New York.

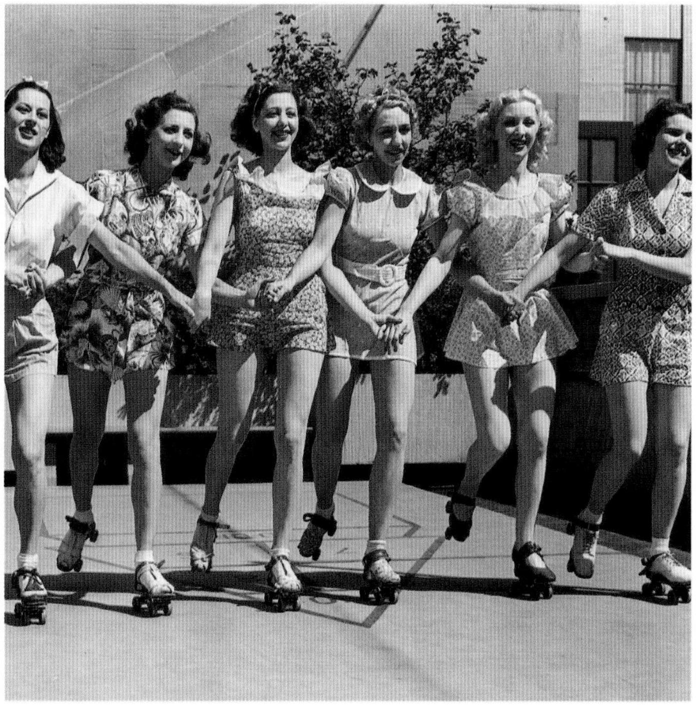

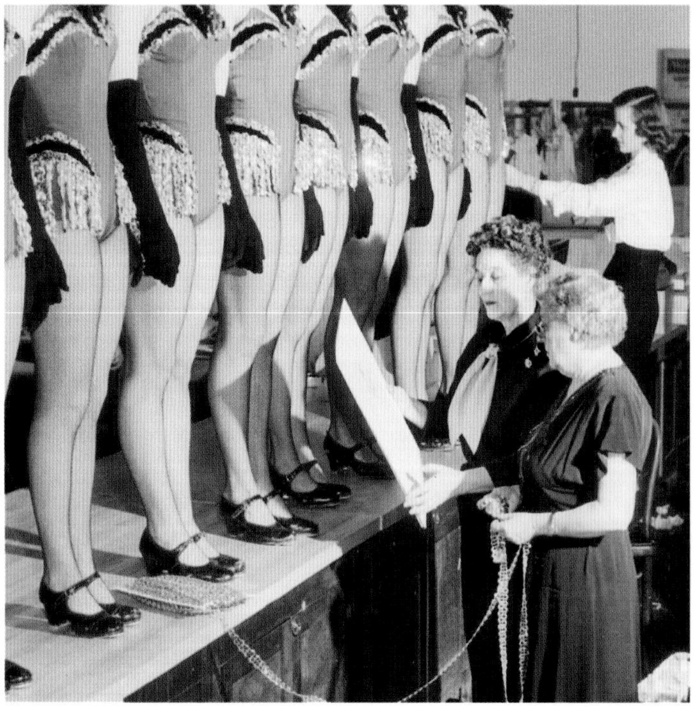

The Rockettes practically lived at Radio City Music Hall. There were often three shows to learn: the current performance and rehearsals for the next two shows, as well as costume fittings.

On right, the troupe performed in the Macy's Thanksgiving Day Parade in 1958. This event is still viewed by millions of Americans each year.

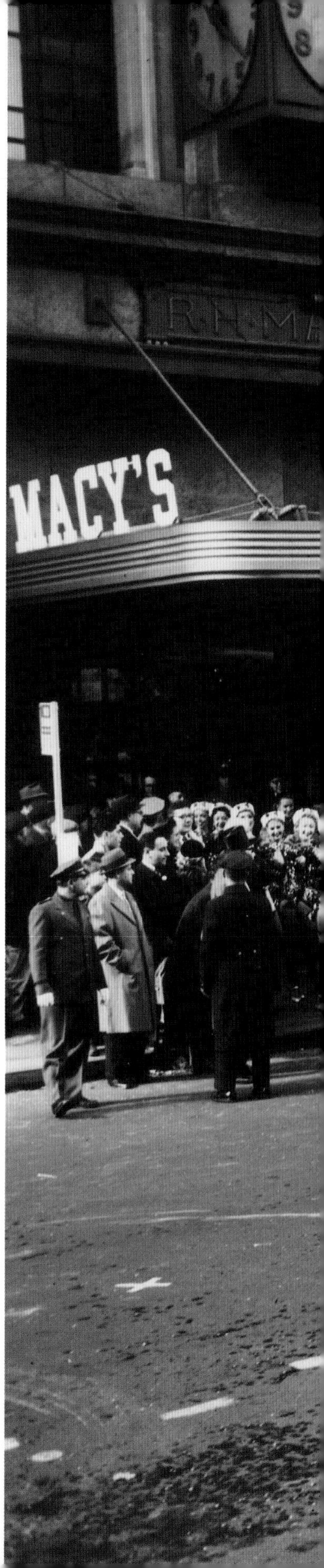

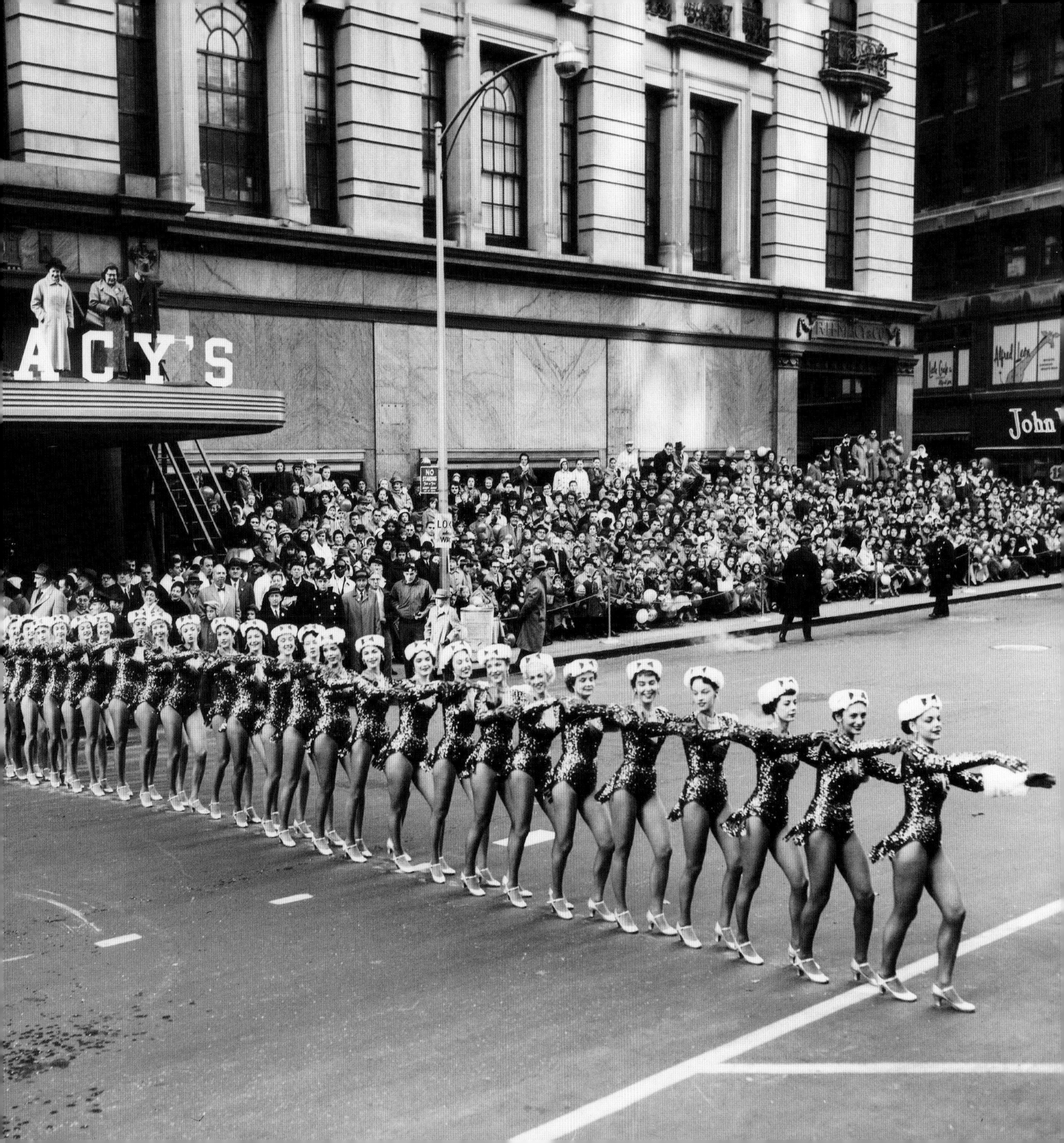
ACY'S
John

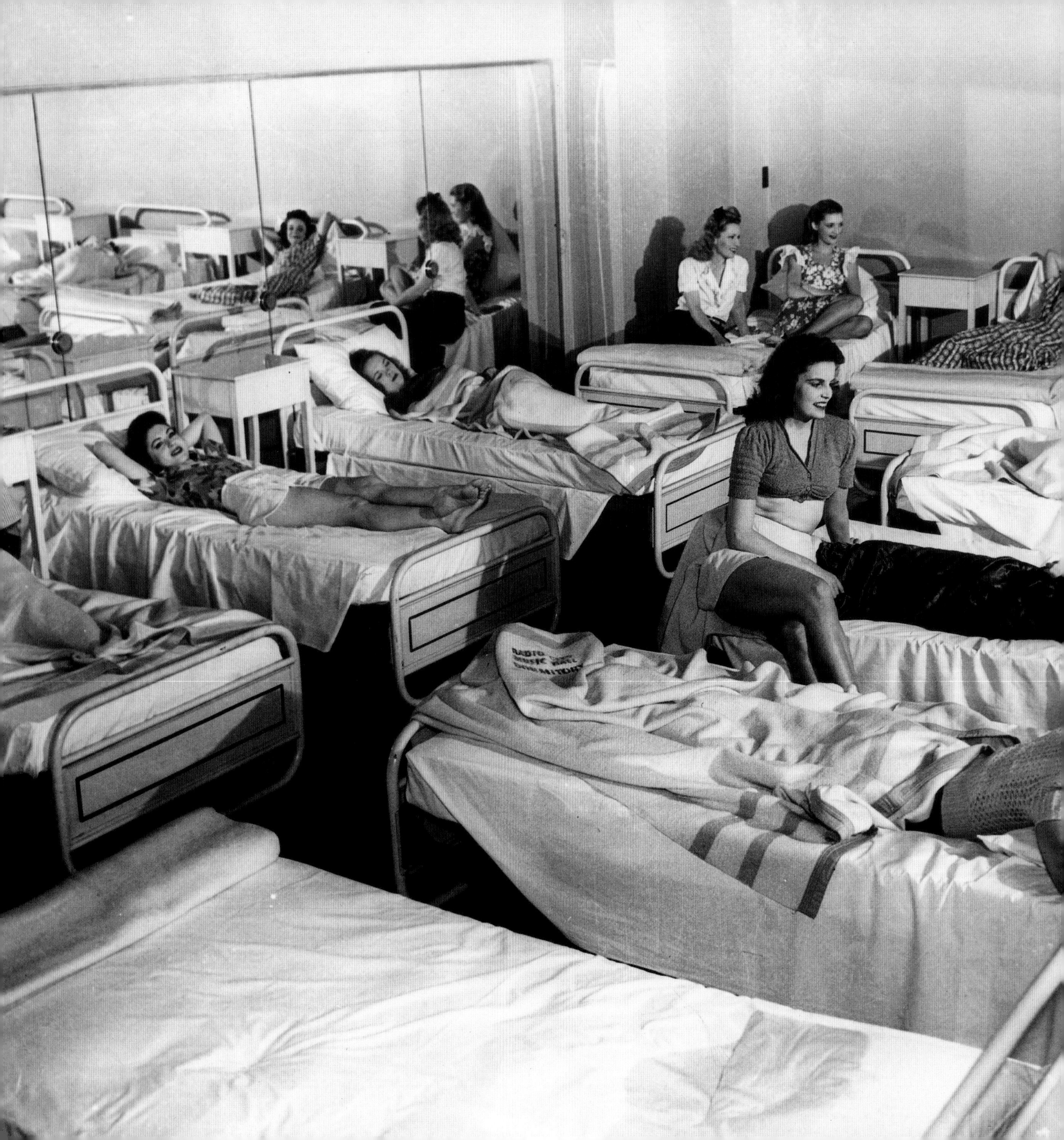
RADIO

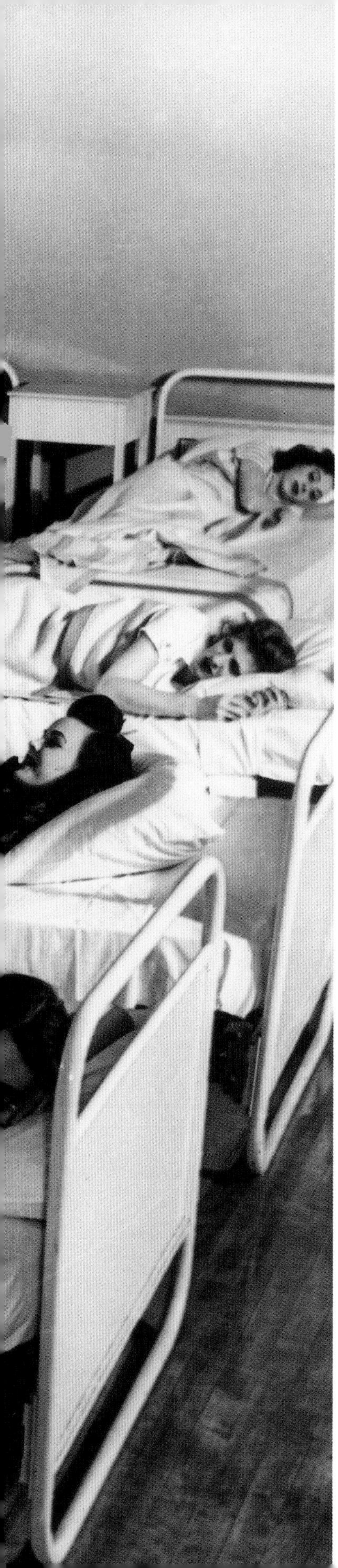

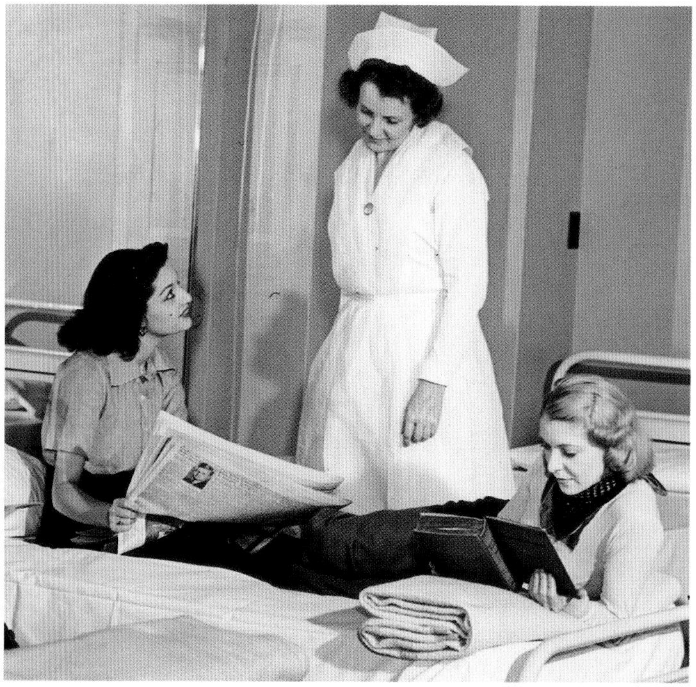

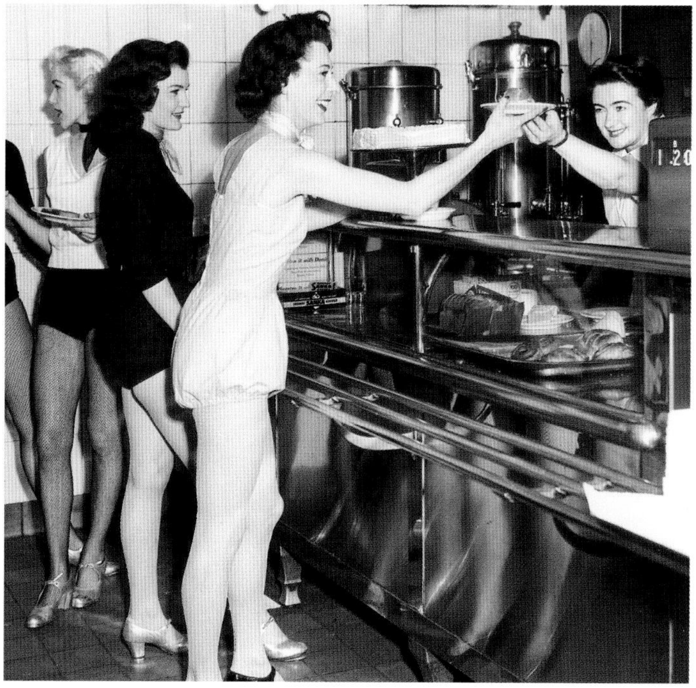

The Rockettes were required to stay after the late movie to practice the next show on the Great Stage. The schedule didn't leave much time to return home to sleep or eat.

"When the Music Hall was built, Roxy insisted it should be a livable city unto itself. Incorporated into the backstage area was a twenty-six bed dormitory, a hospital staffed by a trained nurse, a cafeteria, a tailor shop, and numerous other amenities."[4]

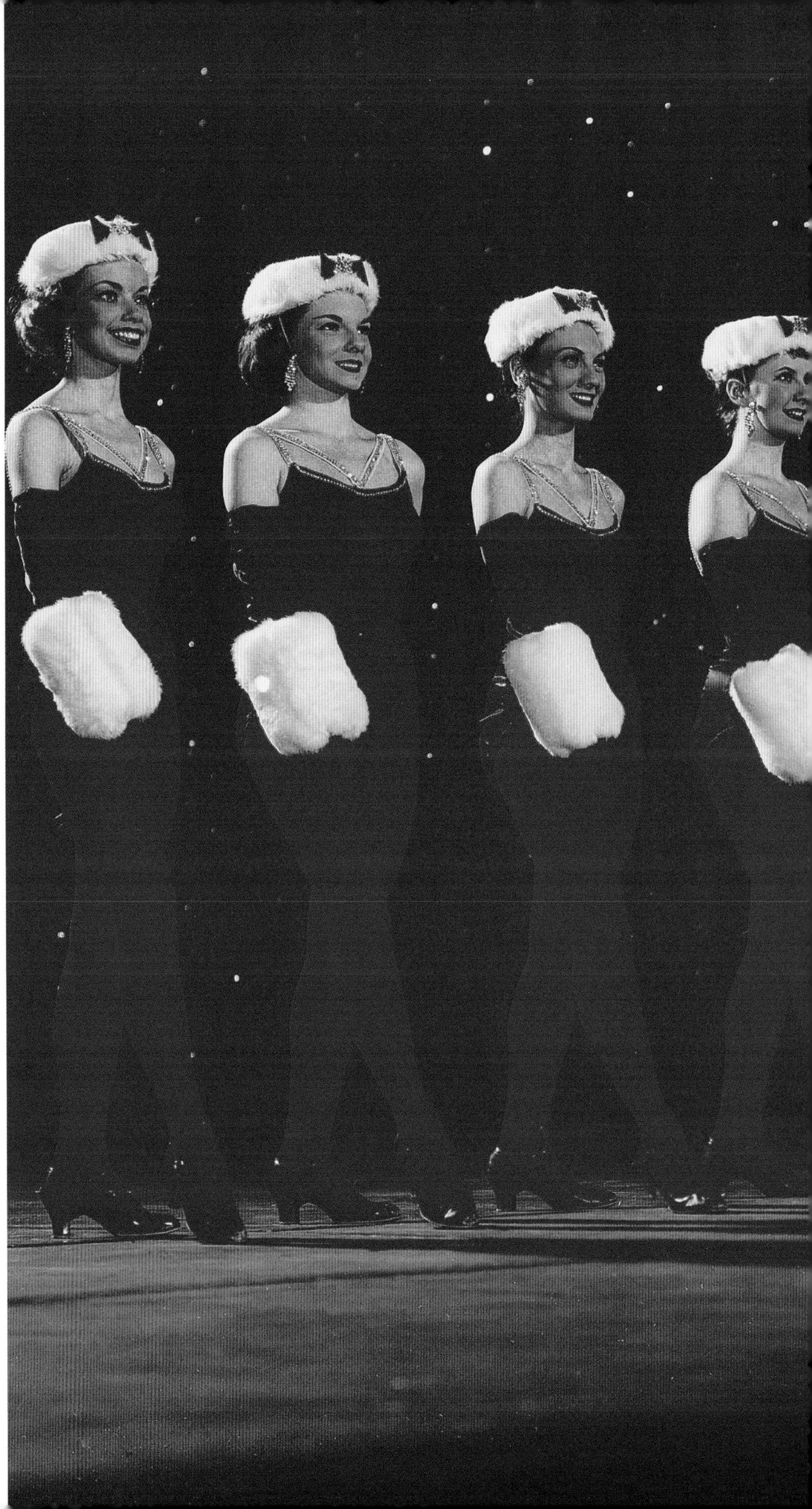

Eastman Kodak created a color photomural featuring the Rockettes. It was the largest mural of its kind ever made, and was hung in New York City's Grand Central Terminal.

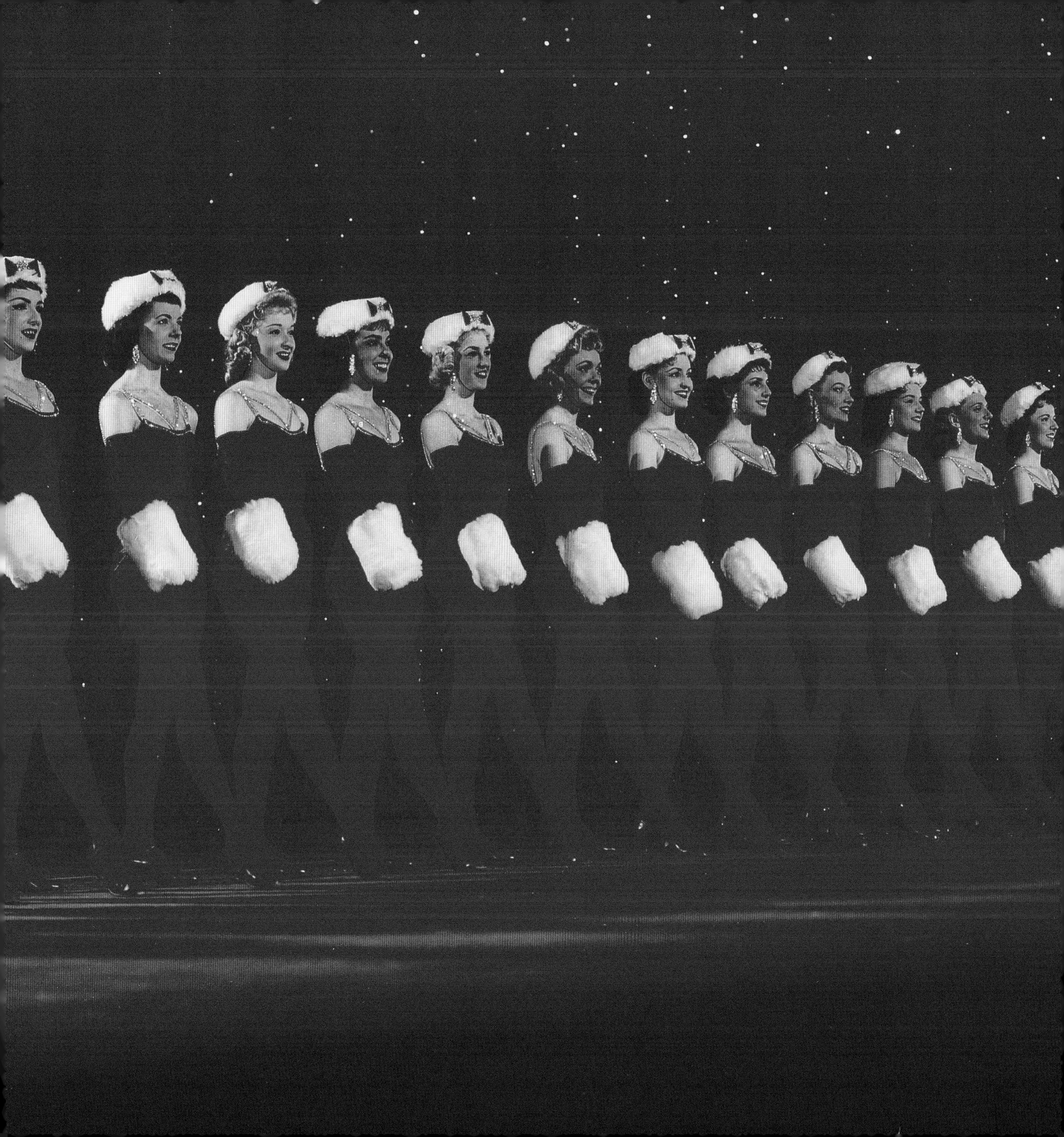

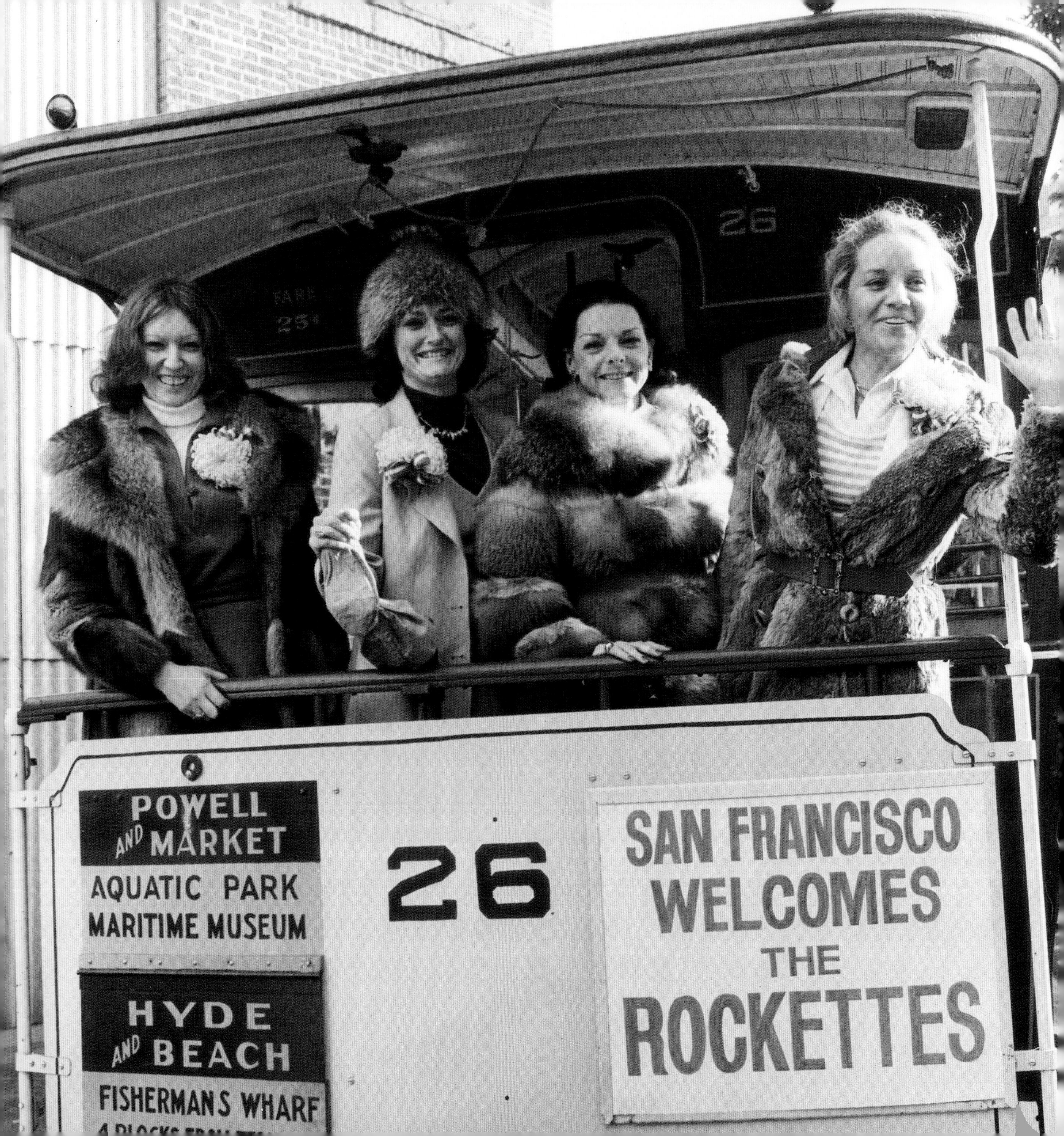
26
FARE
25¢
POWELL AND MARKET
AQUATIC PARK
MARITIME MUSEUM
HYDE AND BEACH
FISHERMANS WHARF
26
SAN FRANCISCO
WELCOMES
THE
ROCKETTES

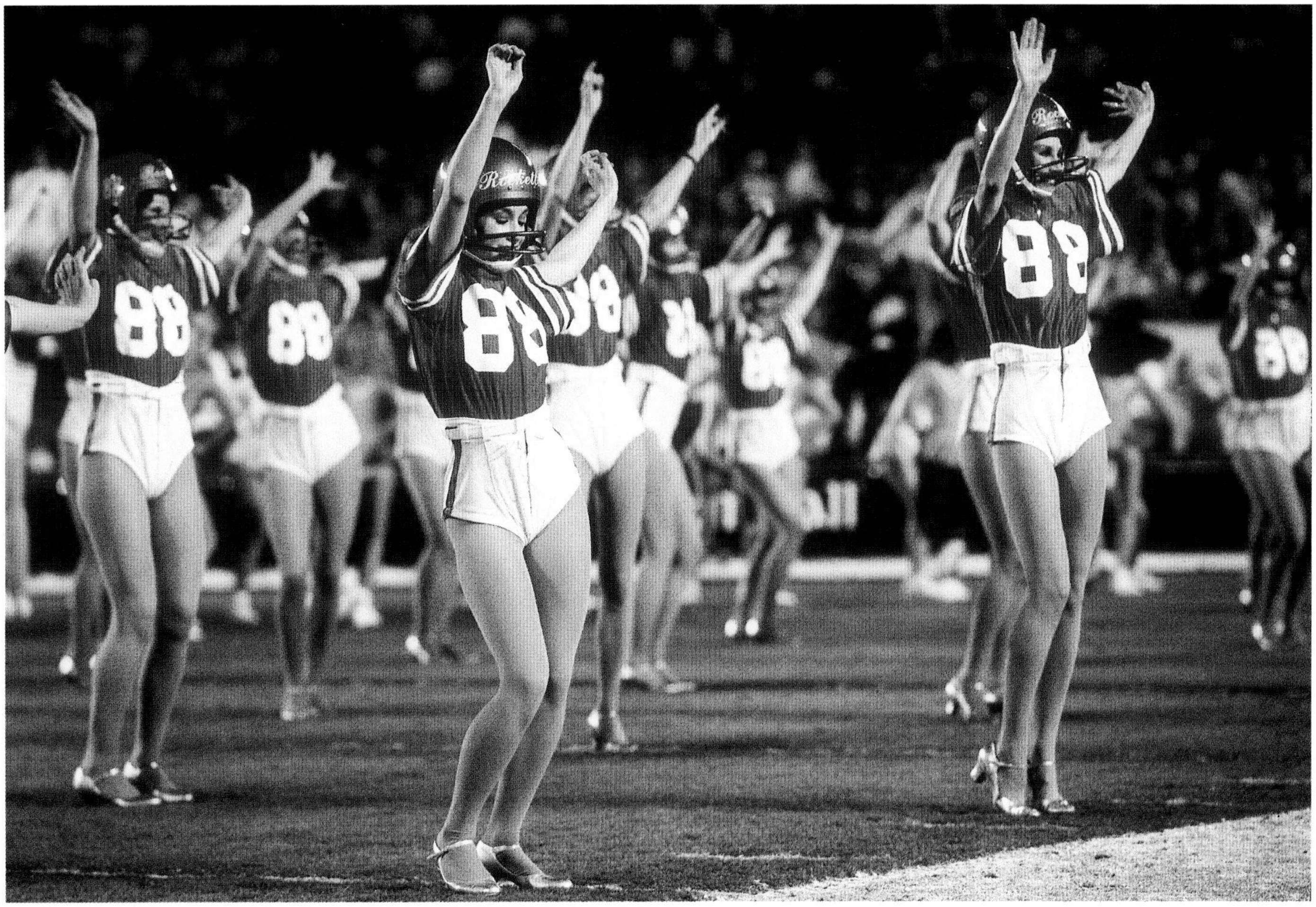

In 1988, the Rockettes starred in the Super Bowl Halftime Show in San Diego, a spectacle seen by almost one billion people around the world.

In the 1970's, Radio City management began closing the theatre for weeks at a stretch, leaving the once busy Rockettes with time on their hands. The troupe petitioned for the right to take the show on the road when the Music Hall was dark. In 1977, the Rockettes made a West Coast swing, appearing at Harrah's in Lake Tahoe, Nevada, Las Vegas, and San Francisco, California.

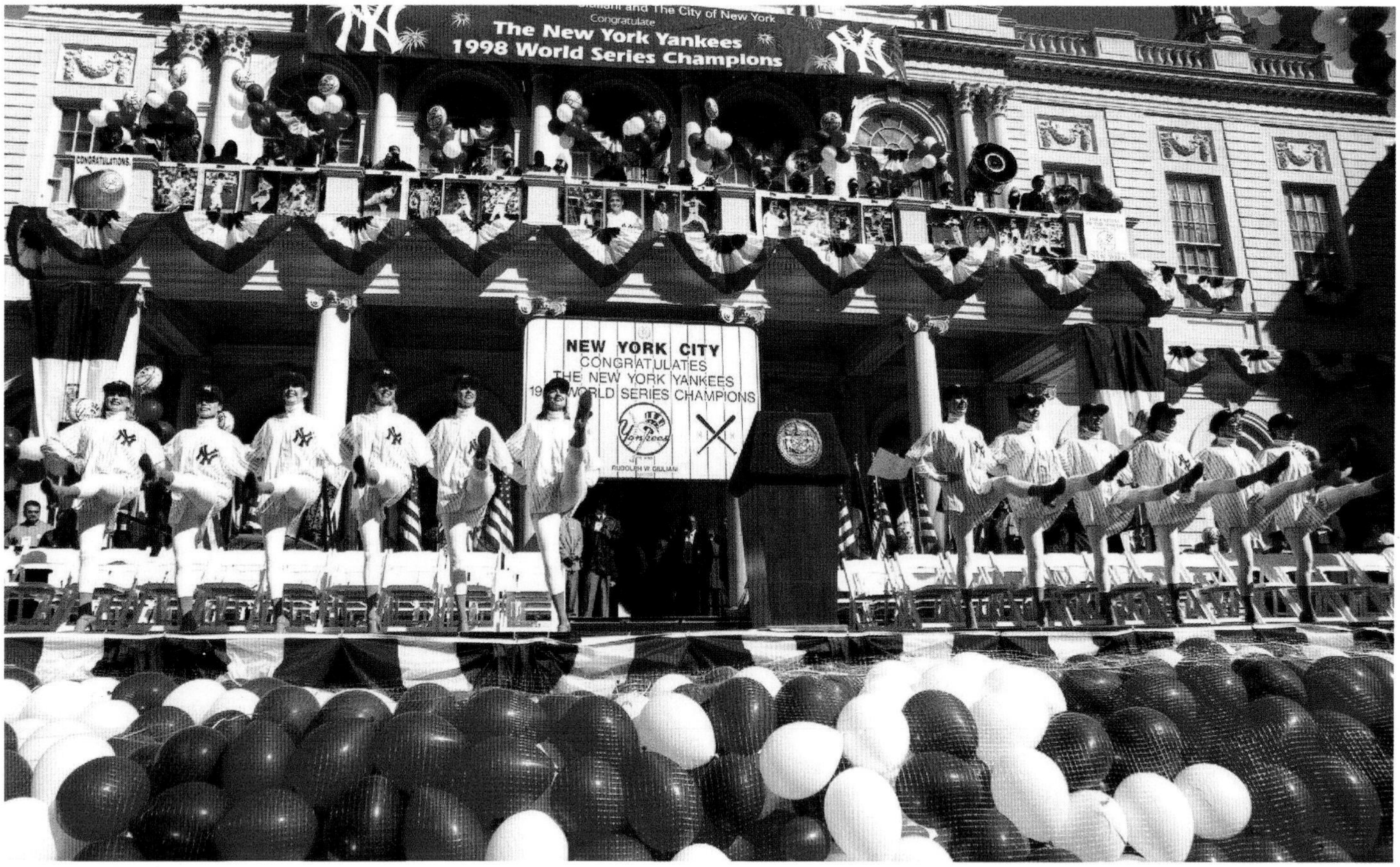

The Rockettes performed at the celebration of the New York Yankees, 1998 World Series Champions.

In the 1990's, the Rockettes appeared at many New York sporting events. Right, the dance troupe entertains the New York Liberty basketball fans during half-time.

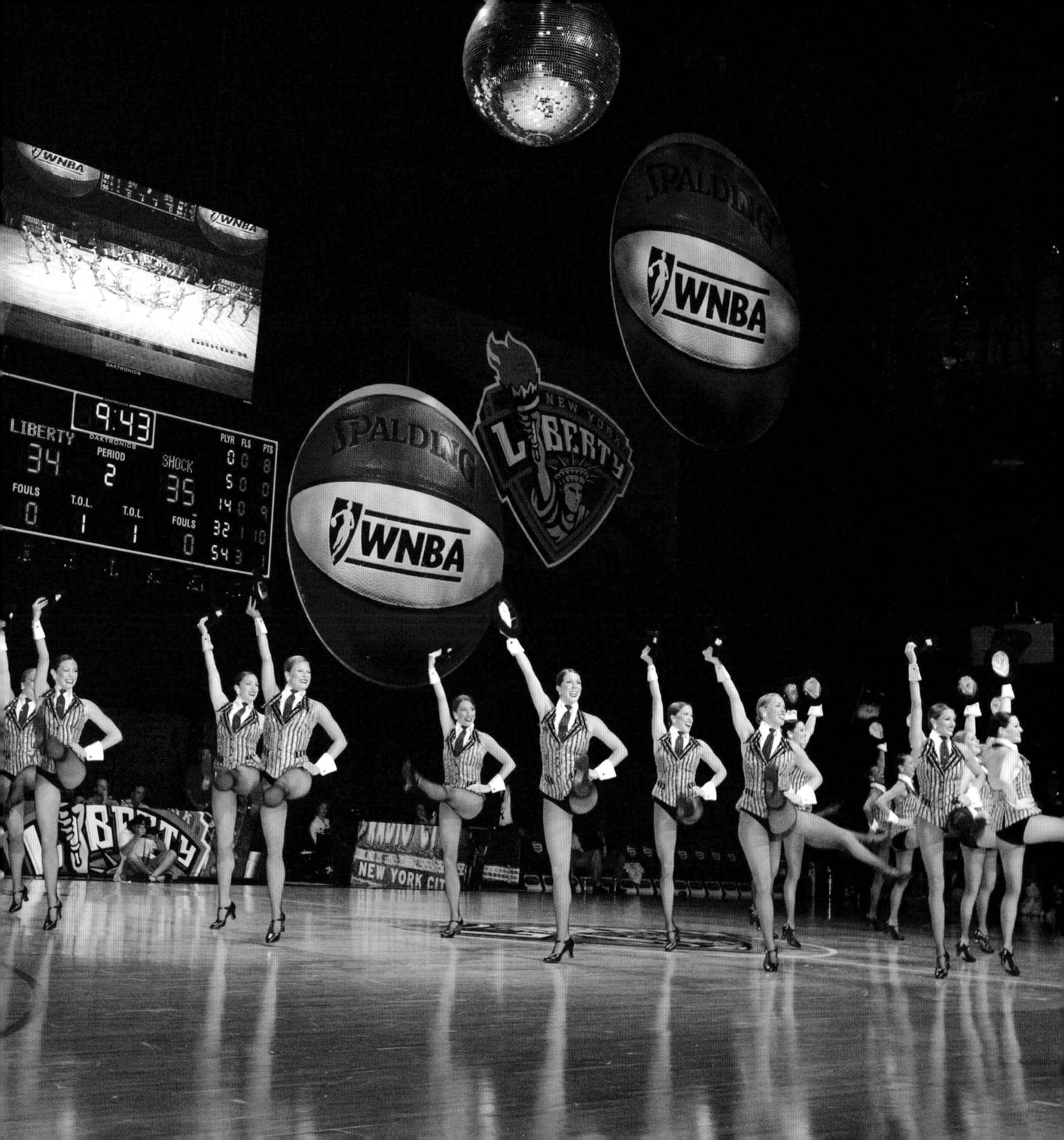
WNBA
SPALDING
WNBA
SPALDING
WNBA
NEW YORK
LIBERTY
9:43
LIBERTY
34
PERIOD
2
SHOCK
35
FOULS
0
T.O.L.
1
T.O.L.
1
FOULS
0
PLYR FLS PTS

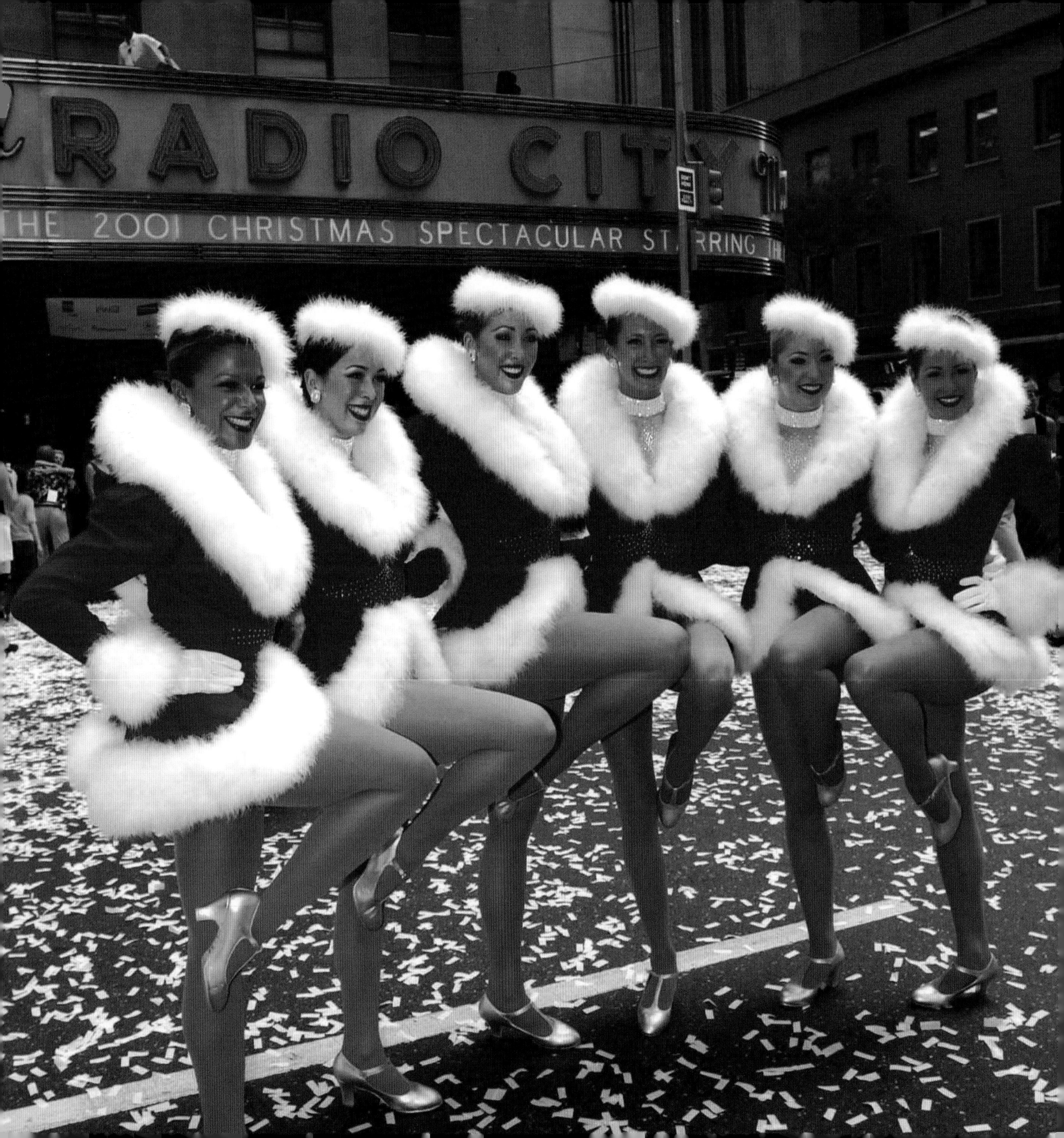
RADIO CITY
THE 2001 CHRISTMAS SPECTACULAR STARRING

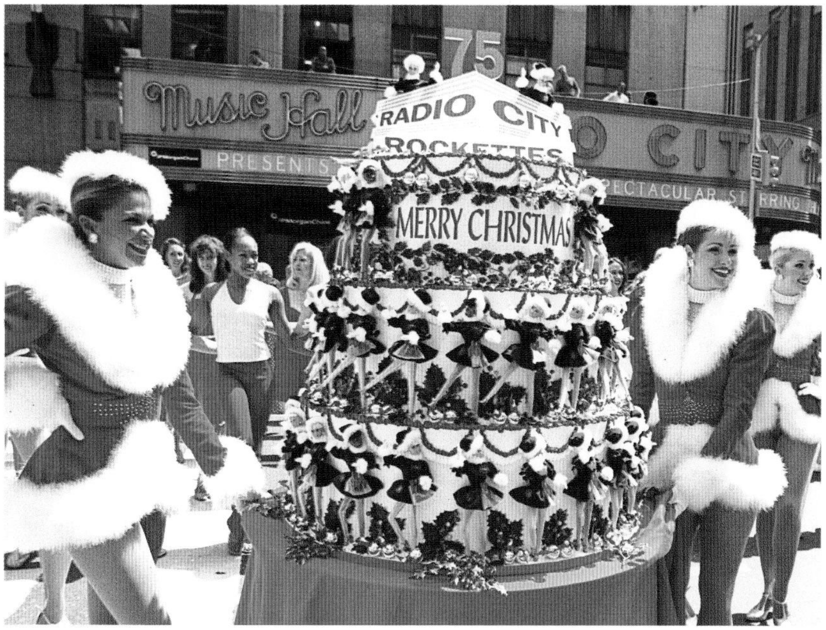

For the Rockettes, 2000 was a year of celebrations. Radio City Music Hall marked the seventy-fifth anniversary of the Rockettes, with more than 3,000 women having shared in the legacy by performing as a Radio City Rockette. The Rockettes also helped the New York Yankees celebrate their World Series victory.

In 2001, the Rockettes were invited to perform at President Bush's presidential inauguration in Washington, D.C., where they danced their way down the steps of the Lincoln Memorial.

In 2005, the Rockettes performed at their second presidential inauguration.

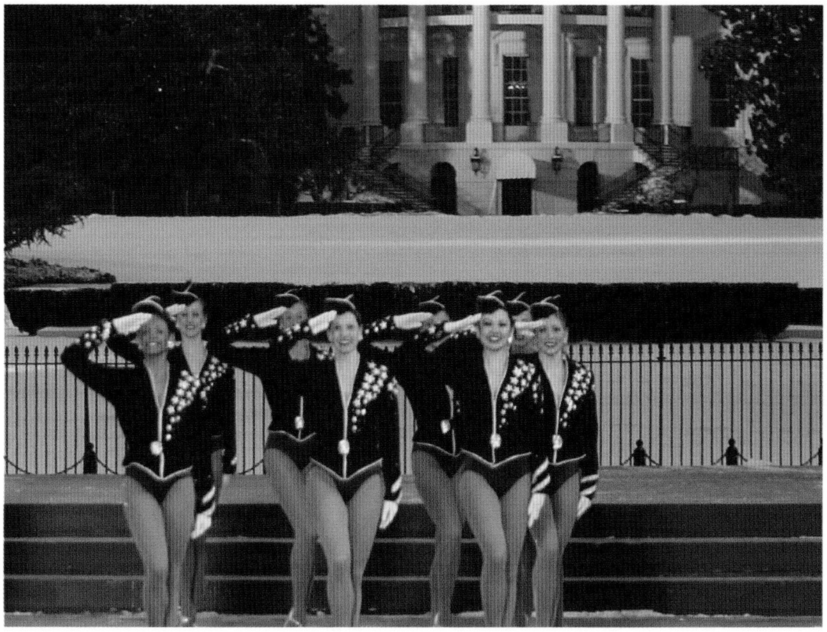

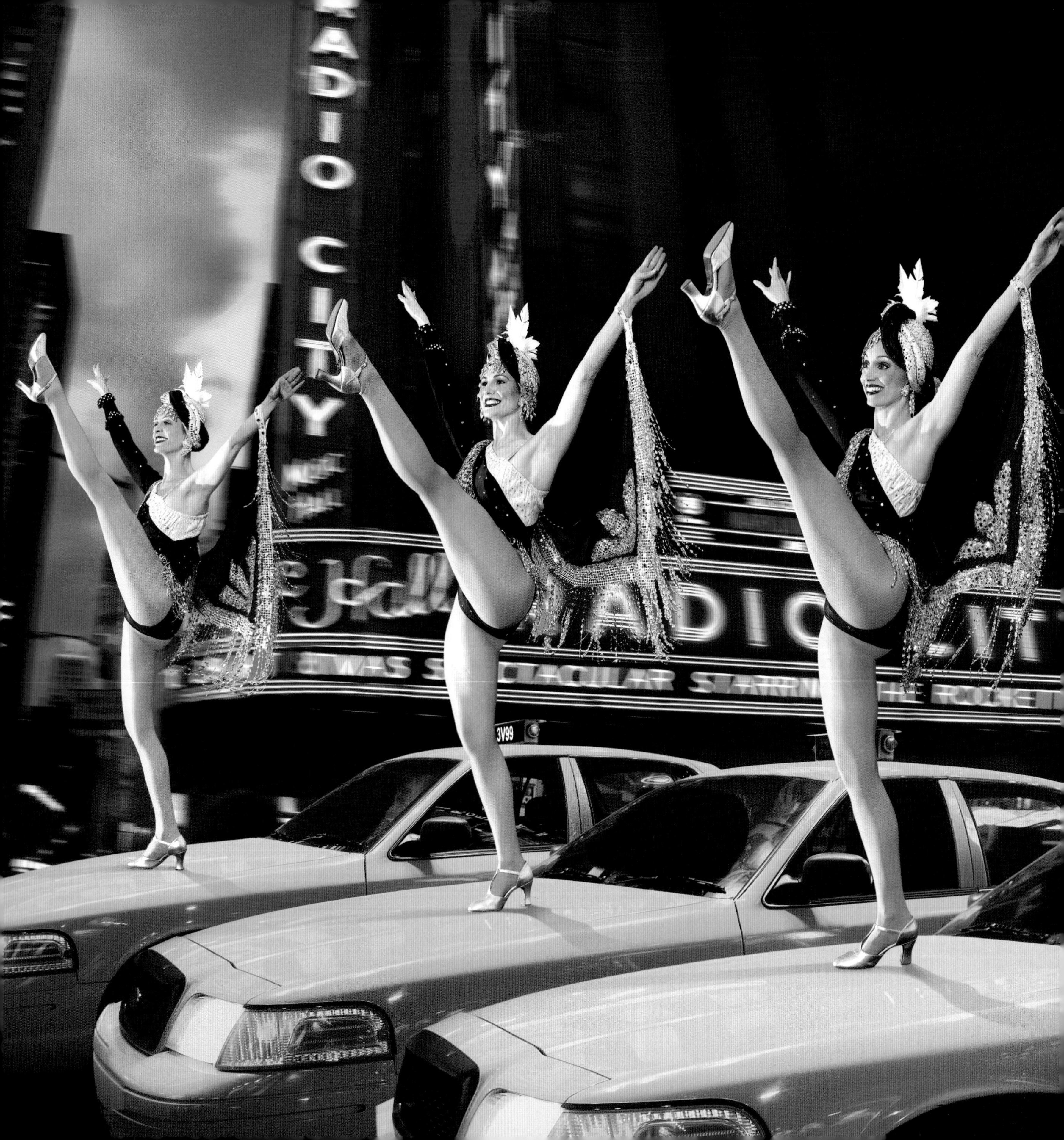
RADIO CITY
3V99

THE ROCKETTES TODAY

The 2007 Rockettes play an integral role in many MSG Entertainment productions and special events. They've tapped their way through the dreams of thousands of young girls, many of whom hope to one day add their legs to that world-famous kick line.

So you want to be a Rockette? Open auditions are held annually and hundreds of women answer the call. Rockettes must be between 5'6" and 5'10½" and must demonstrate proficiency in tap, jazz, ballet, and modern dance. They need to display a radiant energy that will shine across the footlights to their audience. Rockettes must also be able to sing and, of course, perform those eye-high kicks.

The Rockettes and their performance style has always been both entirely glamorous and deceivingly complex. As the stars of the legendary *Christmas Spectacular*, the Radio City Rockettes have been showcasing their signature precision dance style within unforgettable production numbers such as the "Parade of the Wooden Soldiers."

Today's Rockettes pay tribute to their history, modeling archival costumes from performances through the decades.

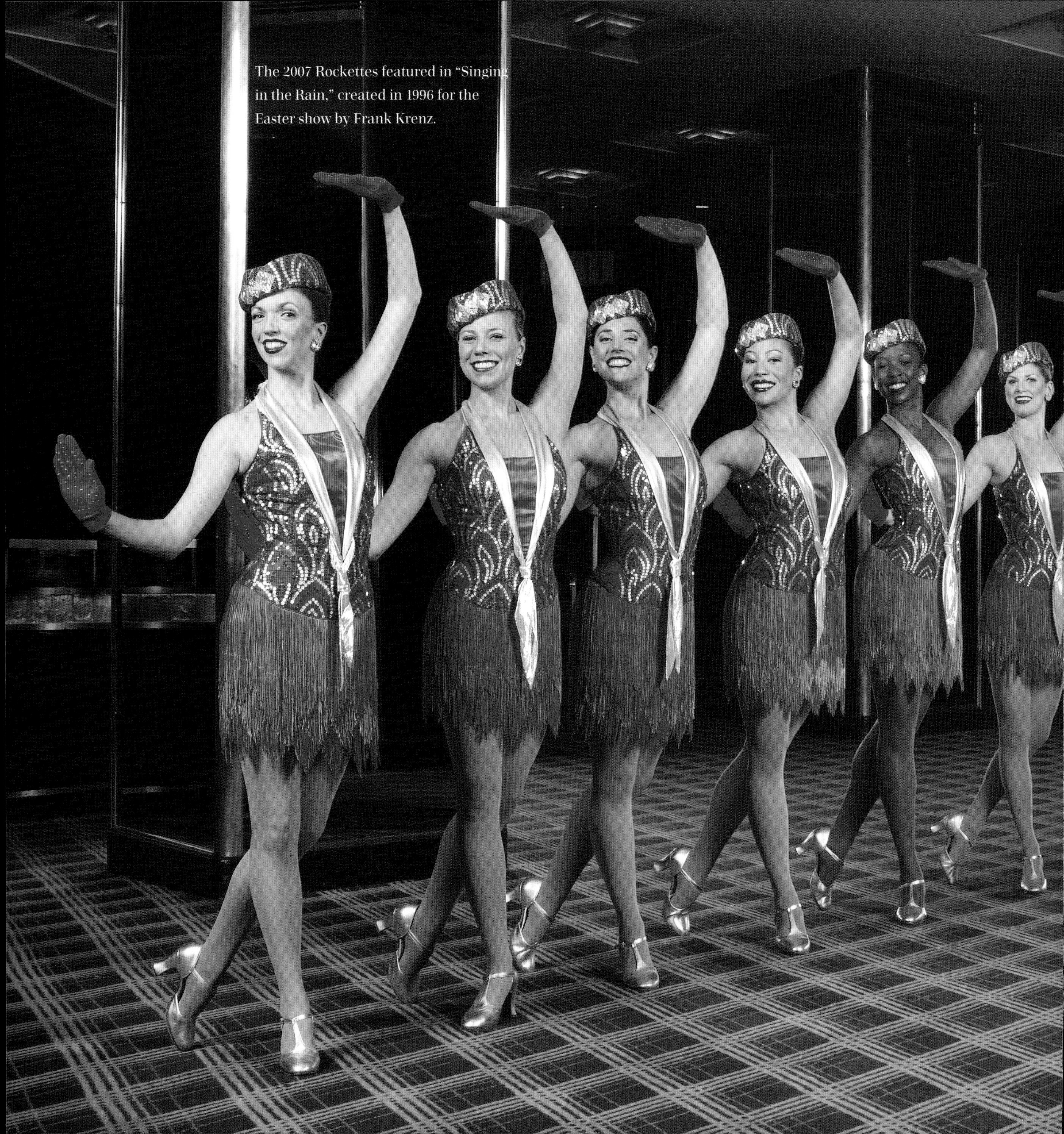

The 2007 Rockettes featured in "Singing in the Rain," created in 1996 for the Easter show by Frank Krenz.

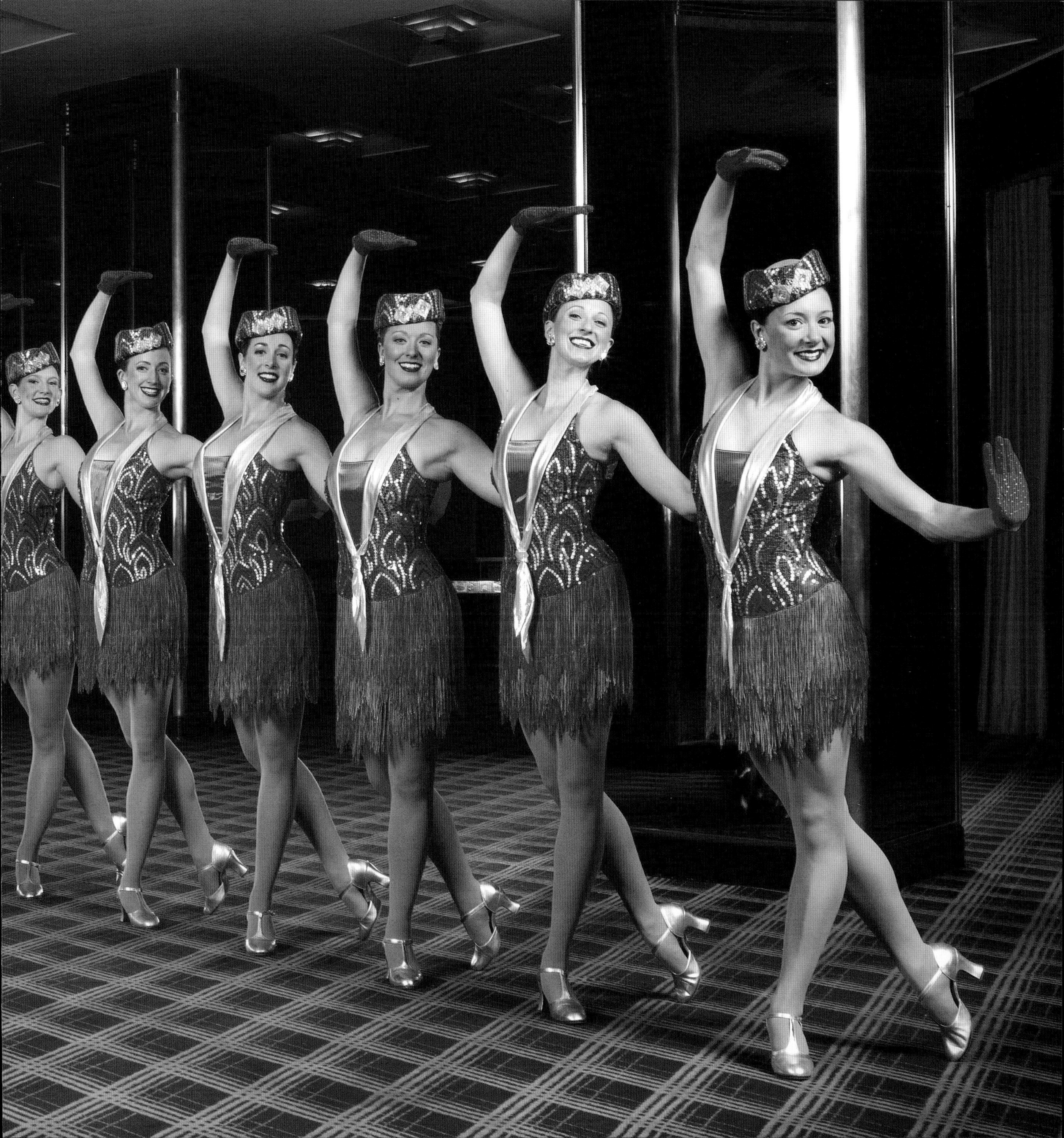

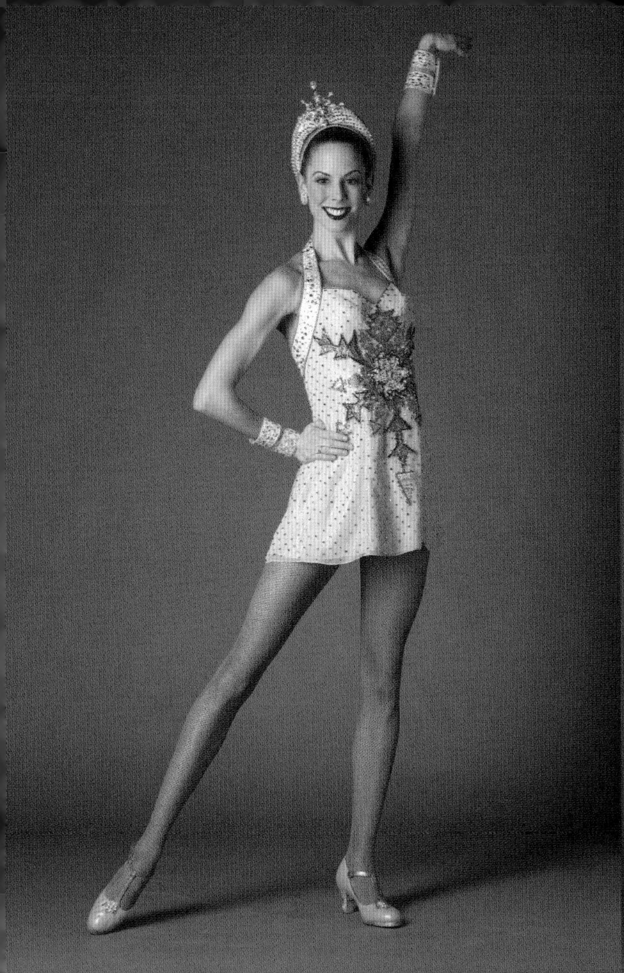
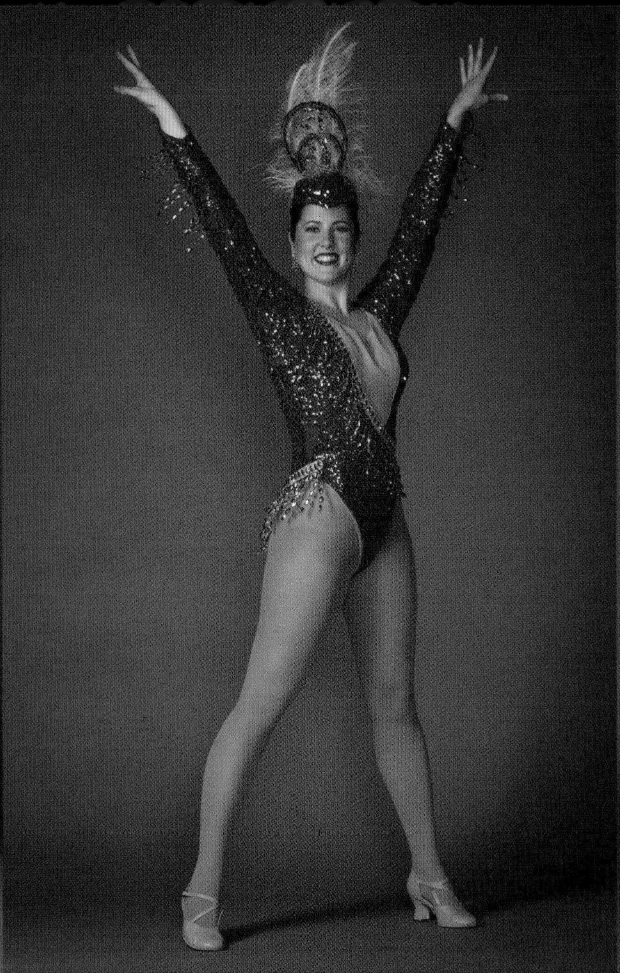
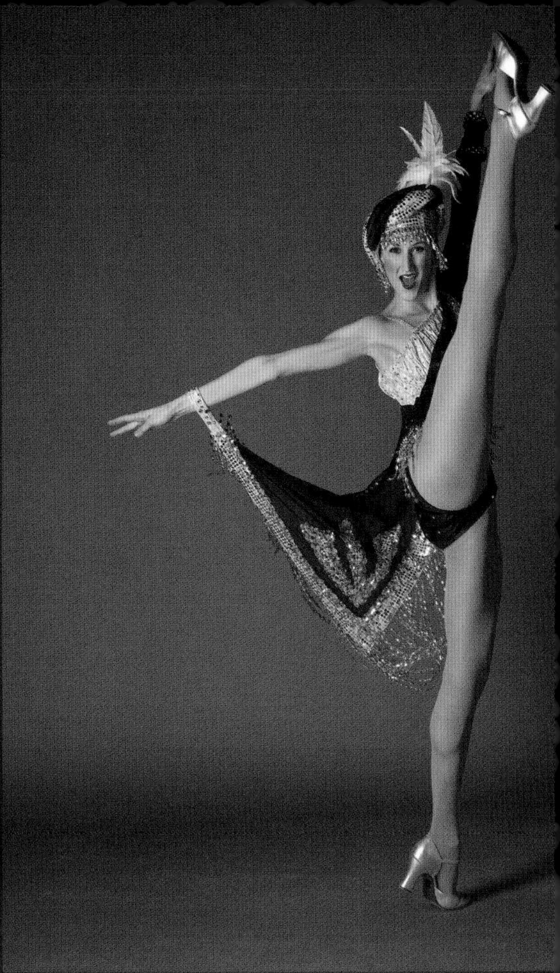
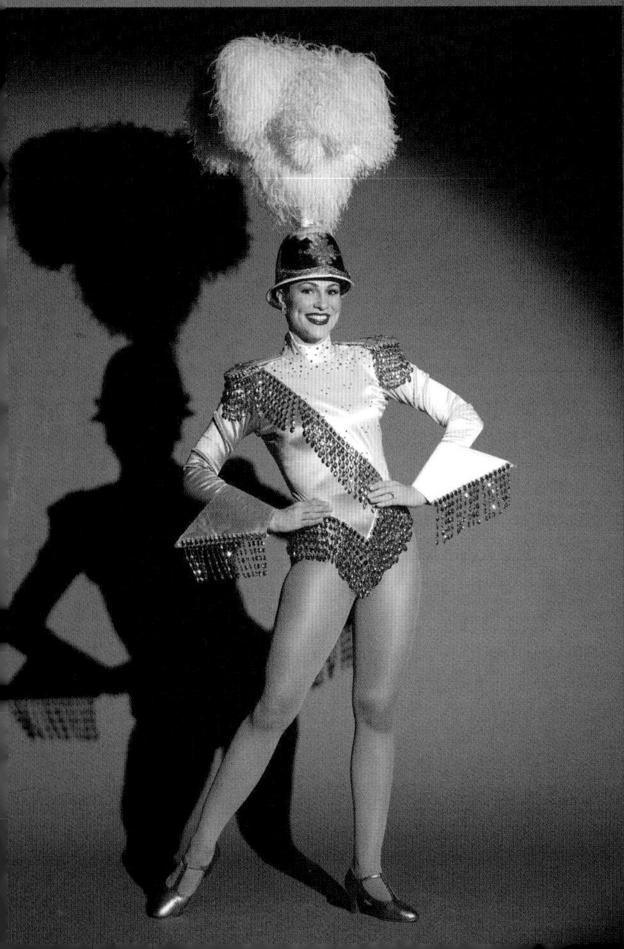
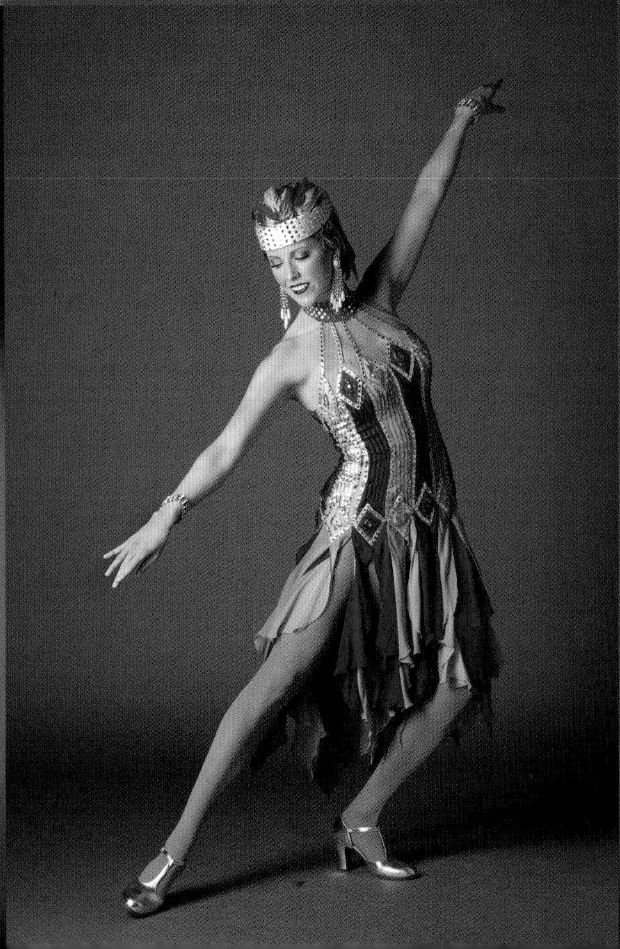
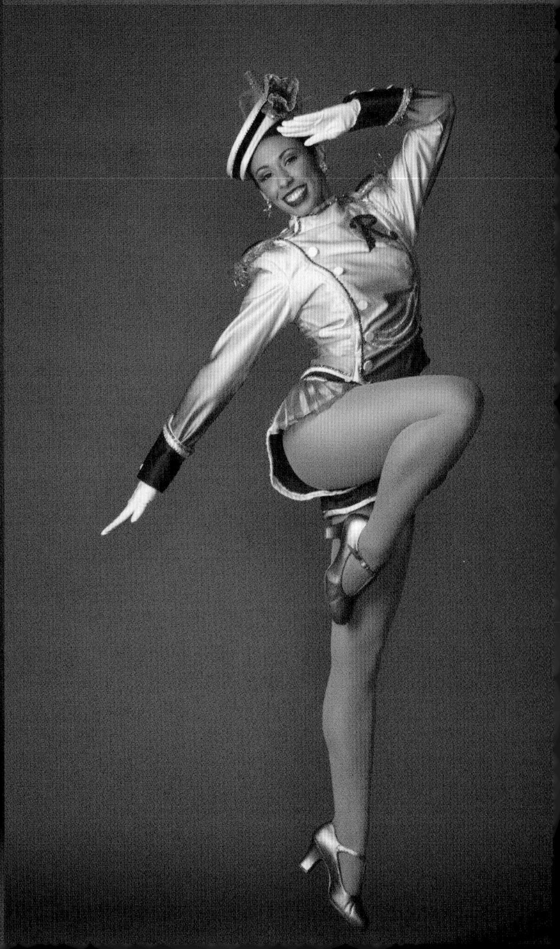

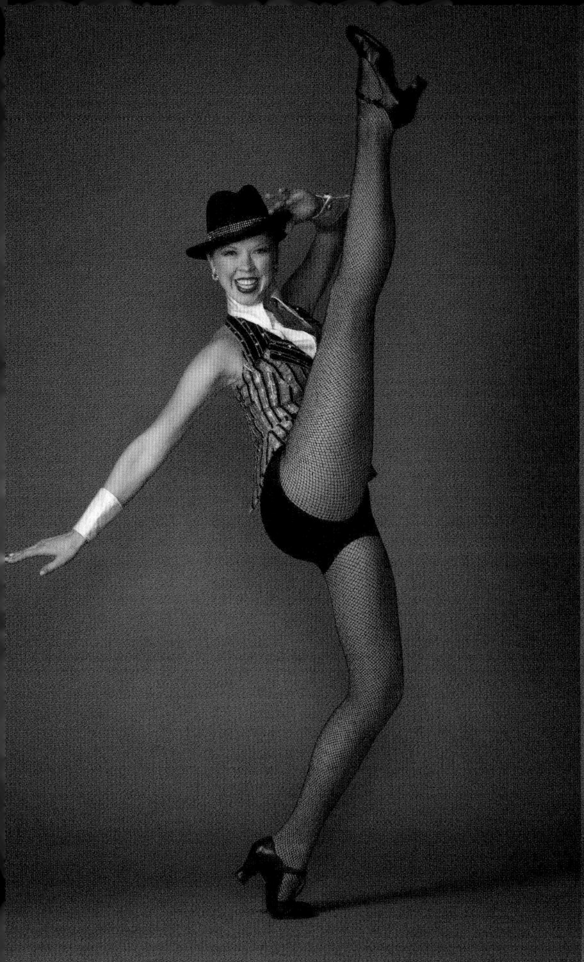
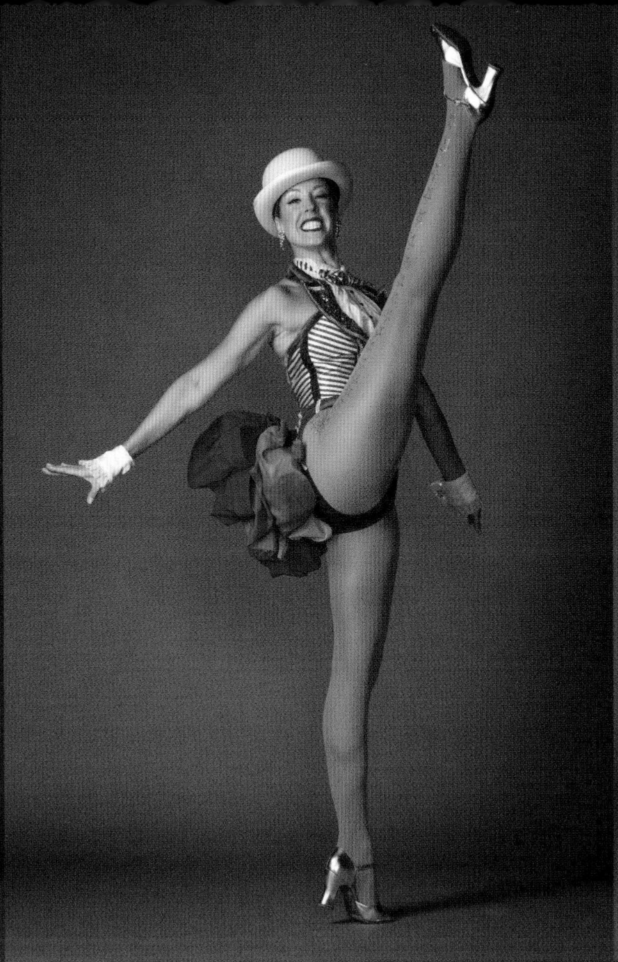
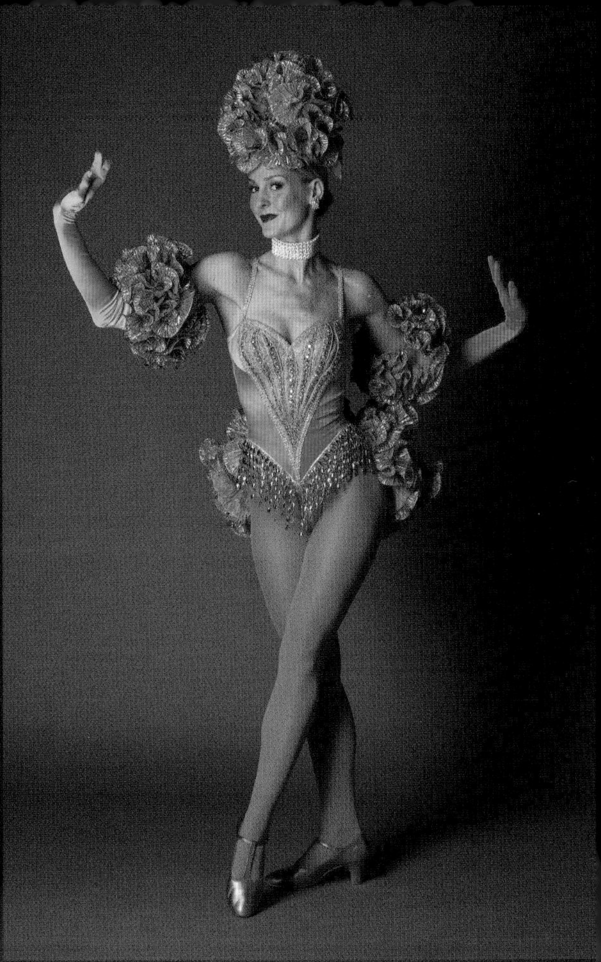
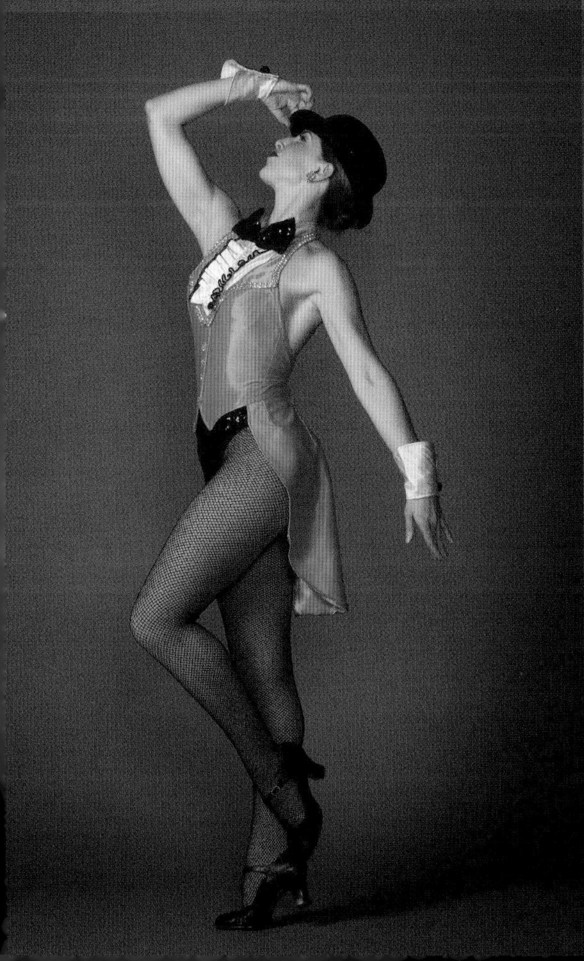
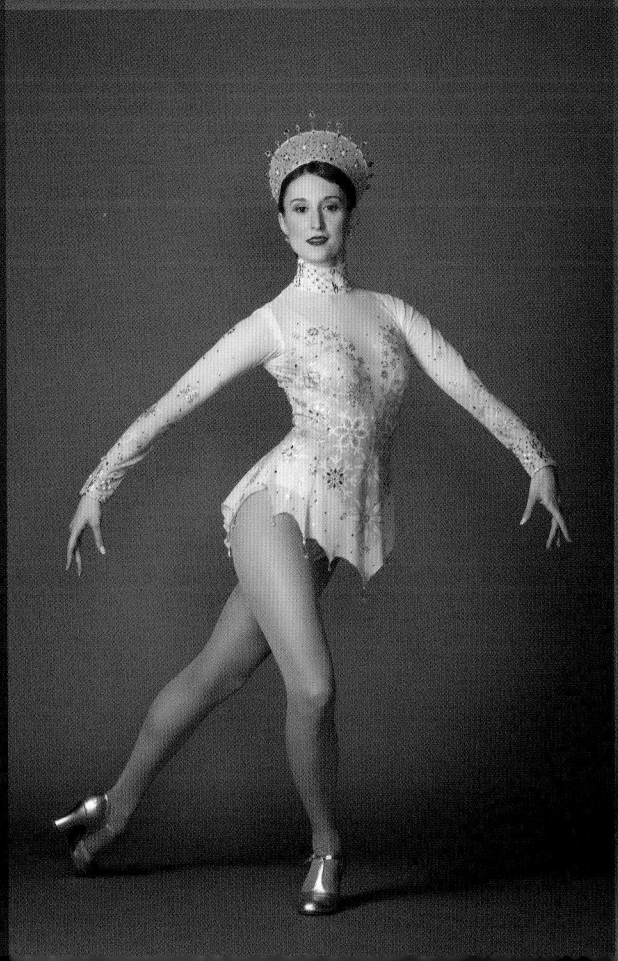
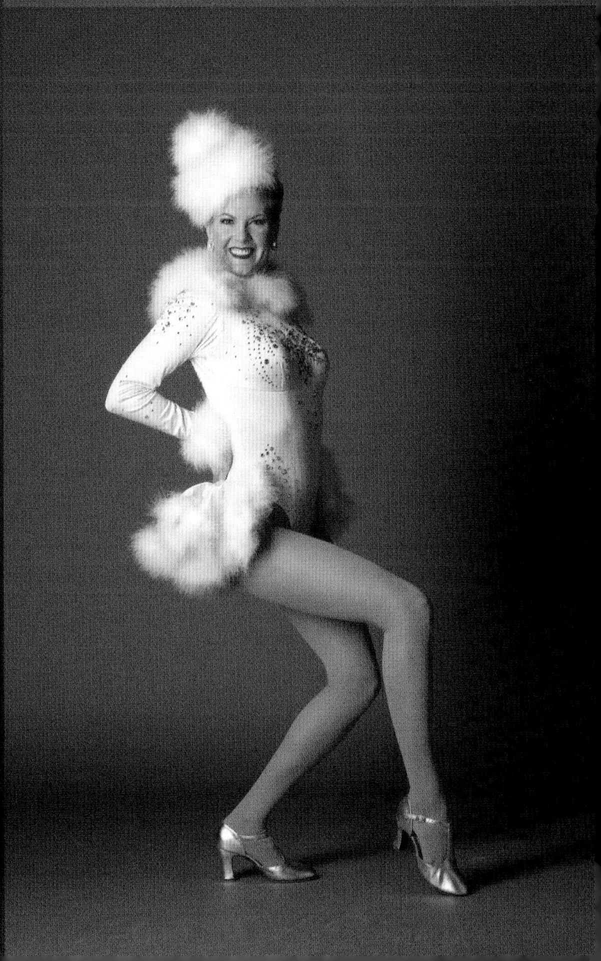

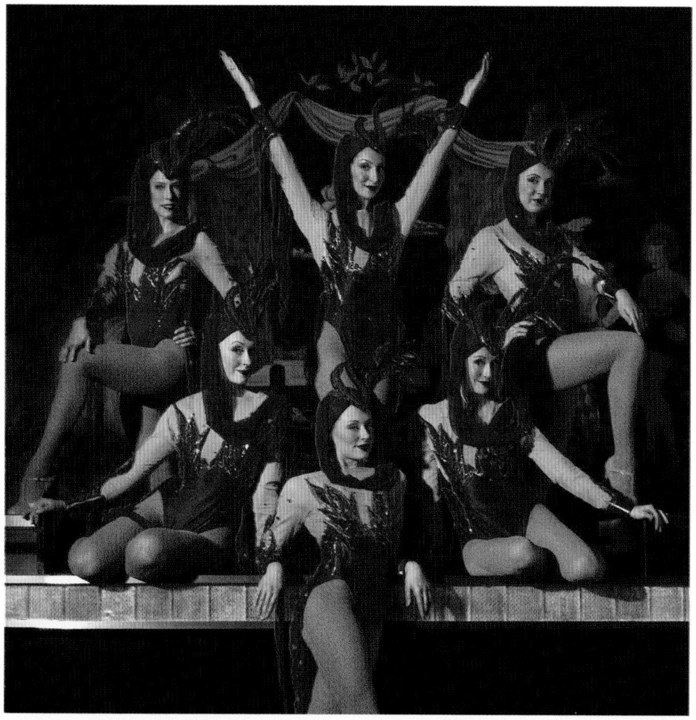
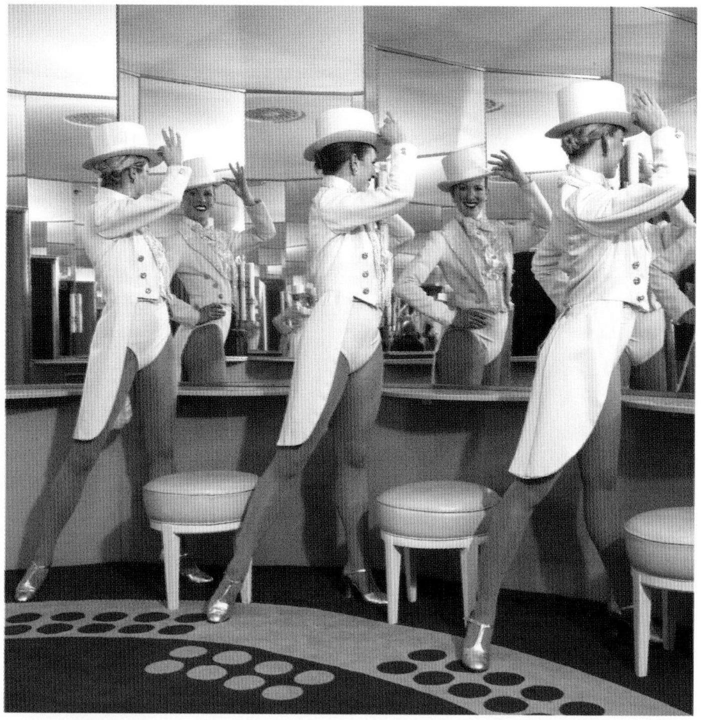
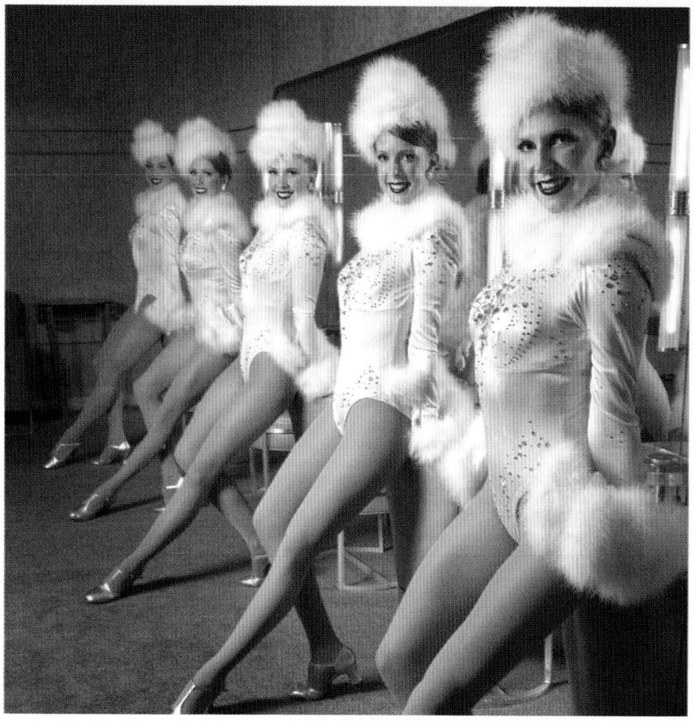
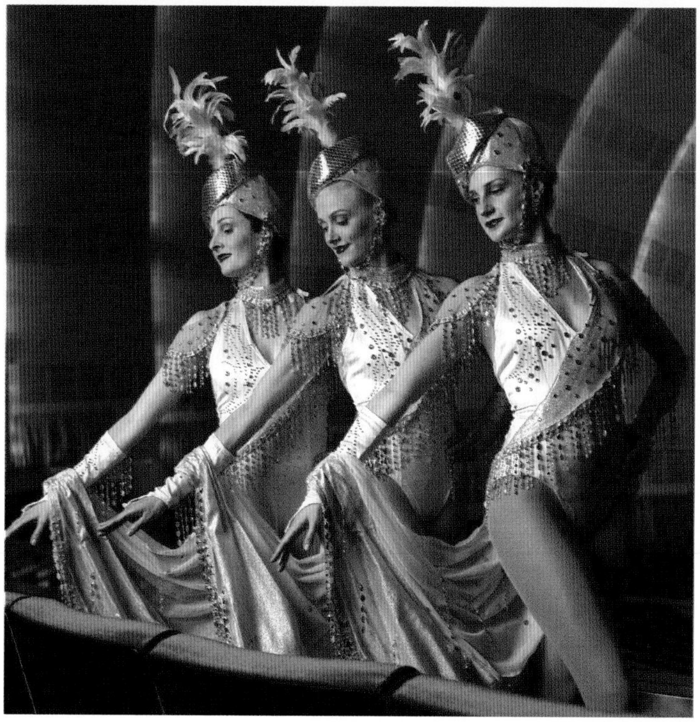

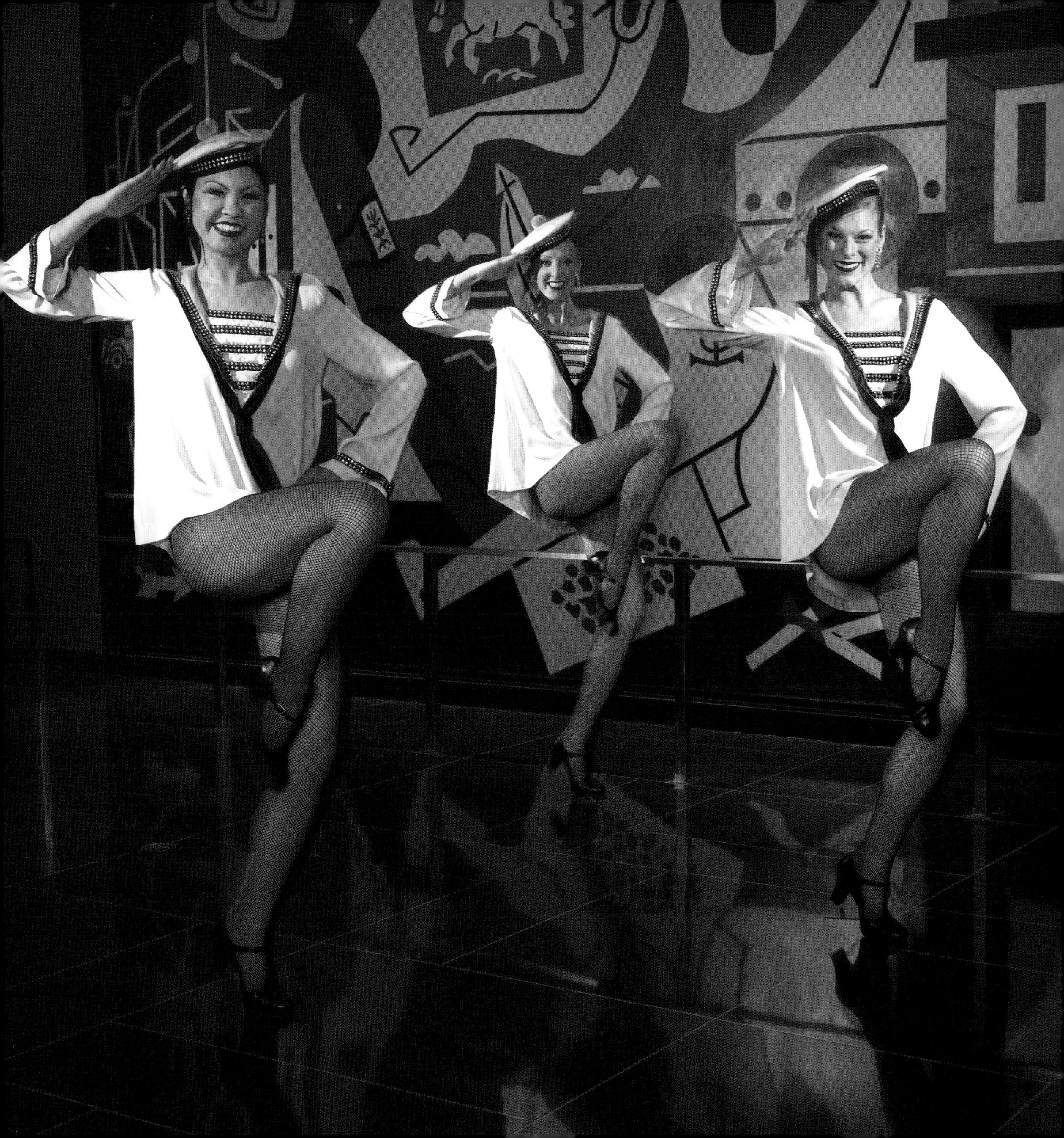

The "Model" costume debuted in the Christmas Spectacular in 2000.
Worn by today's Rockettes, it was created by Gregg Barnes.

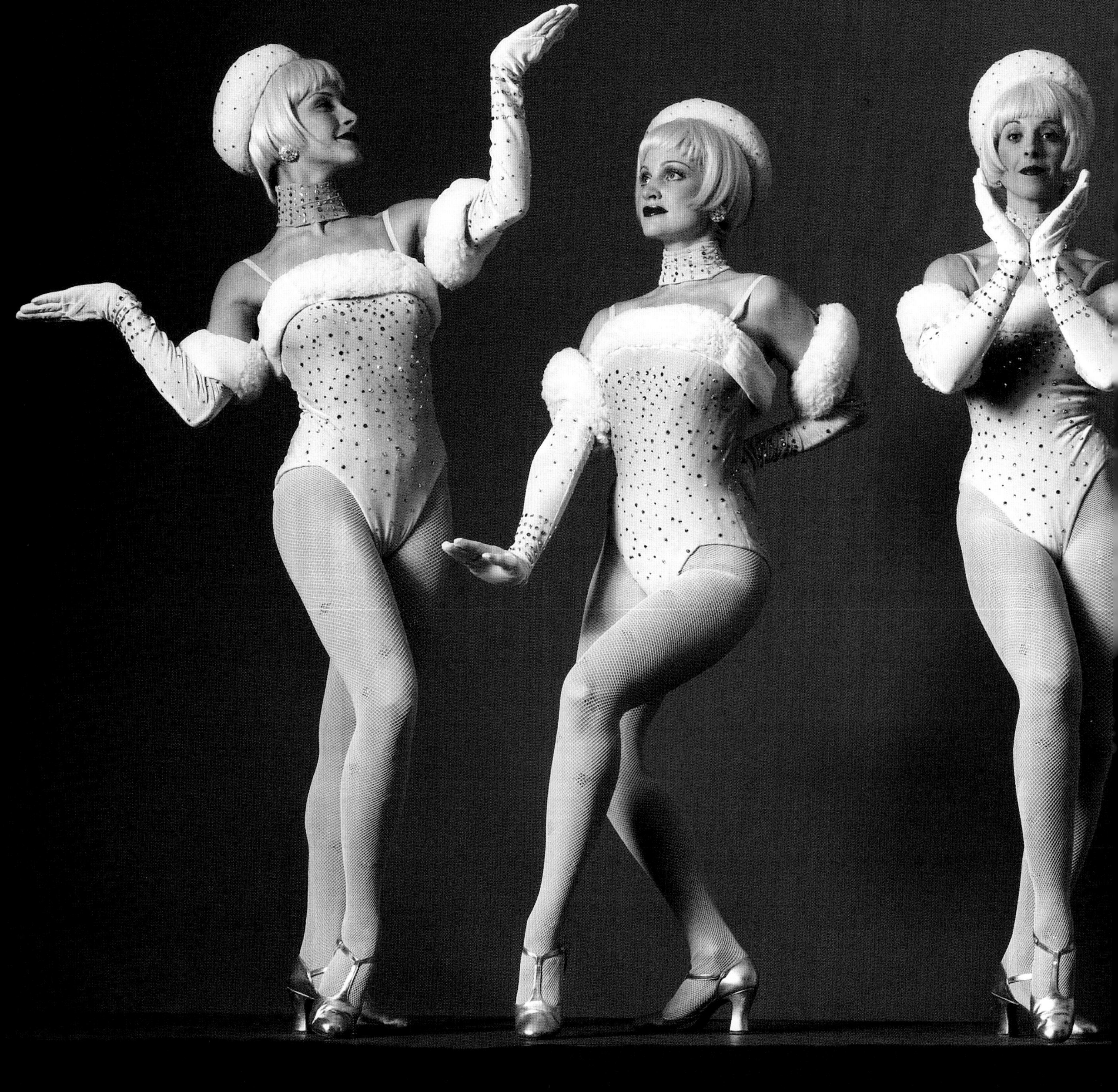

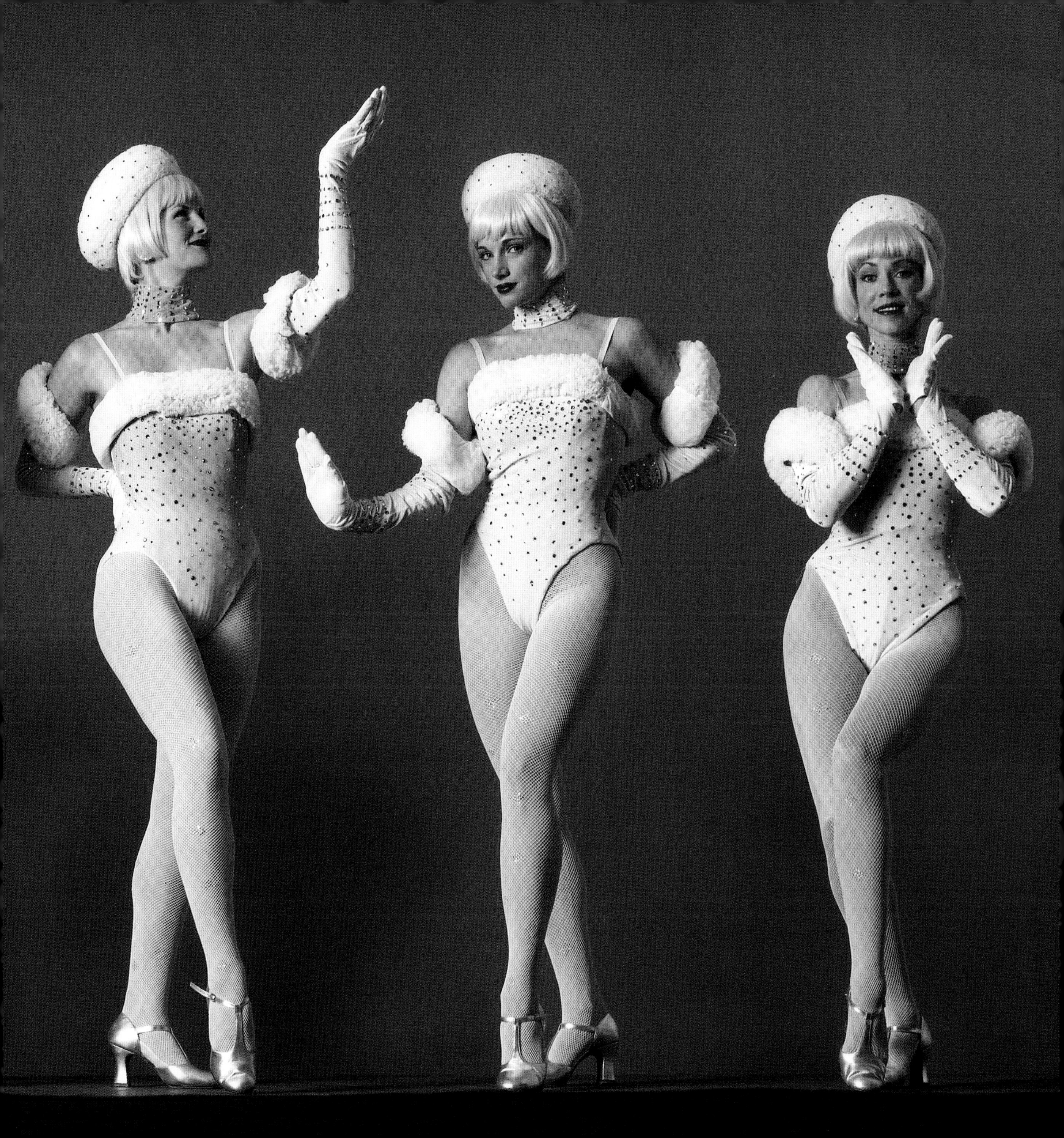

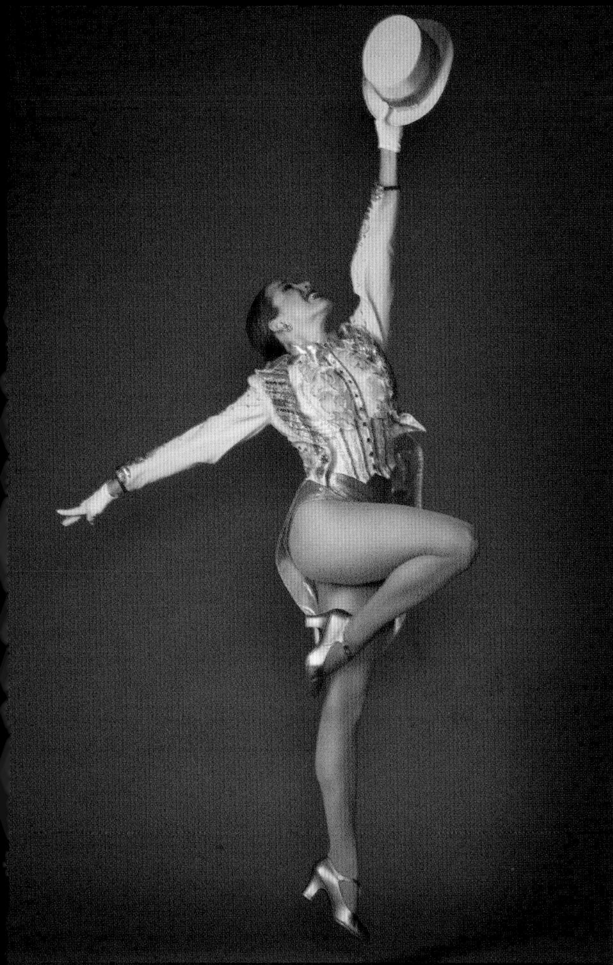
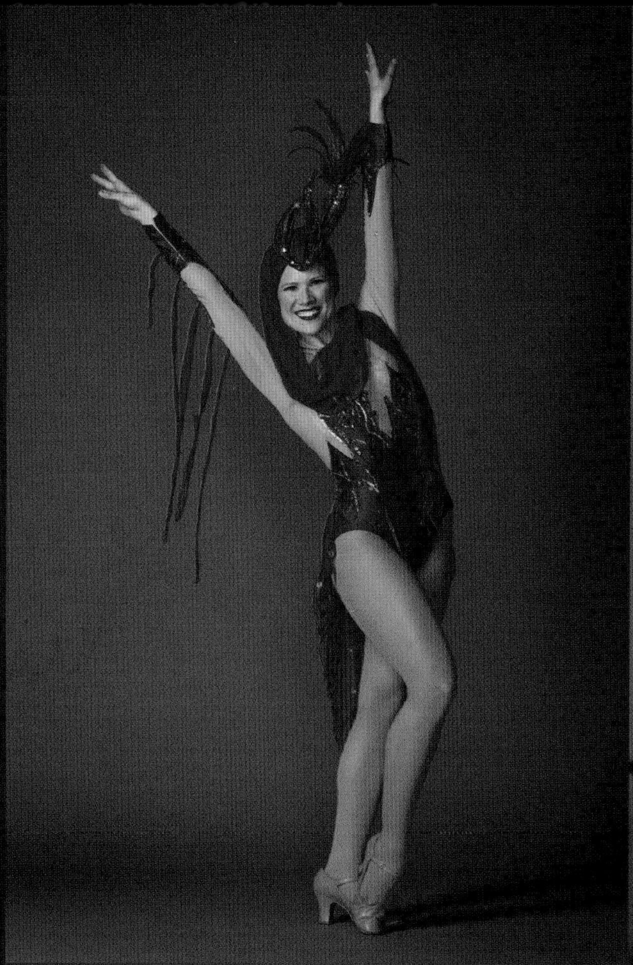
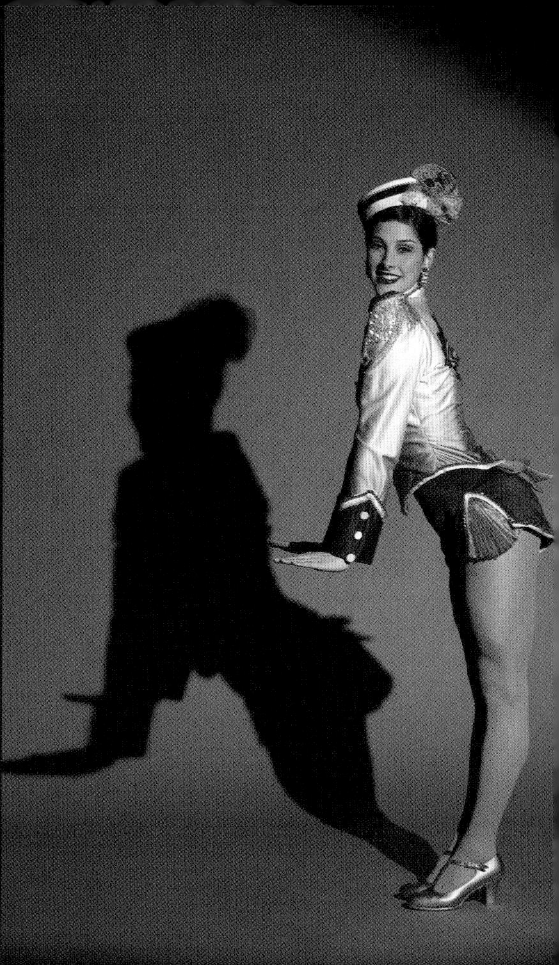
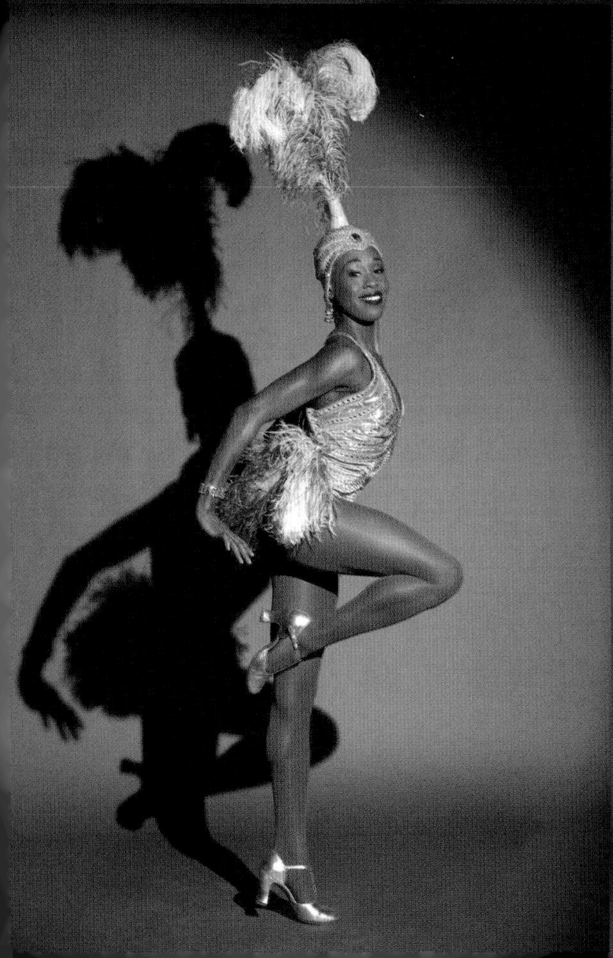
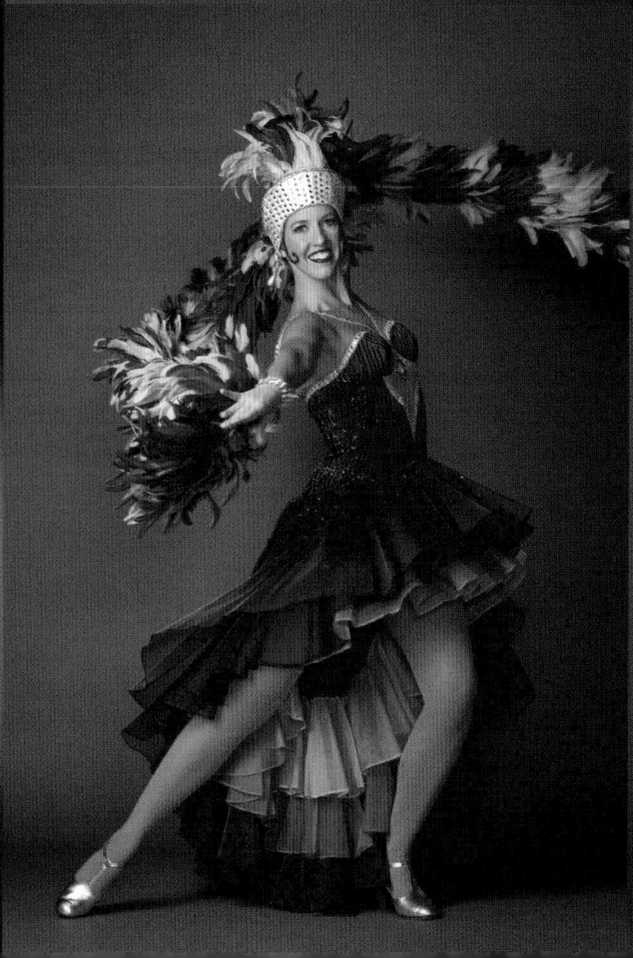
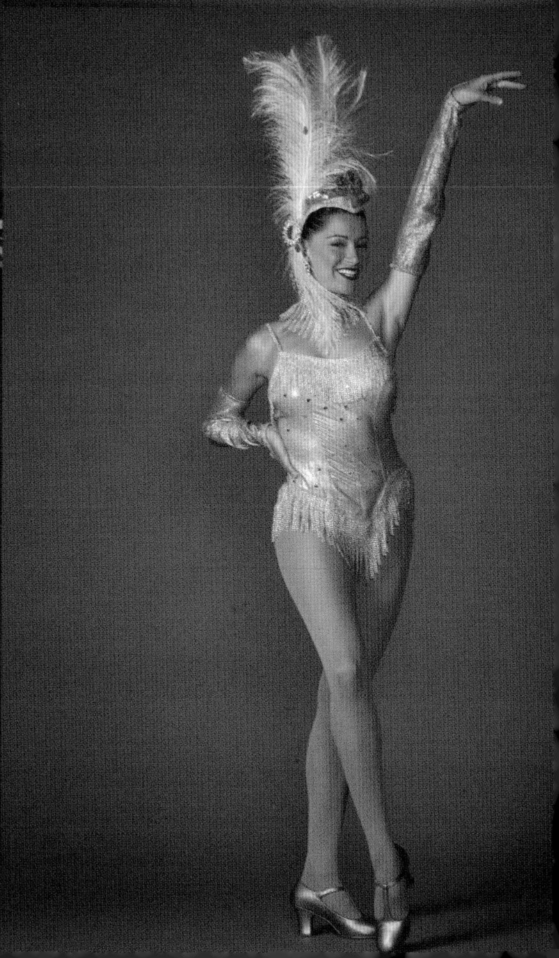

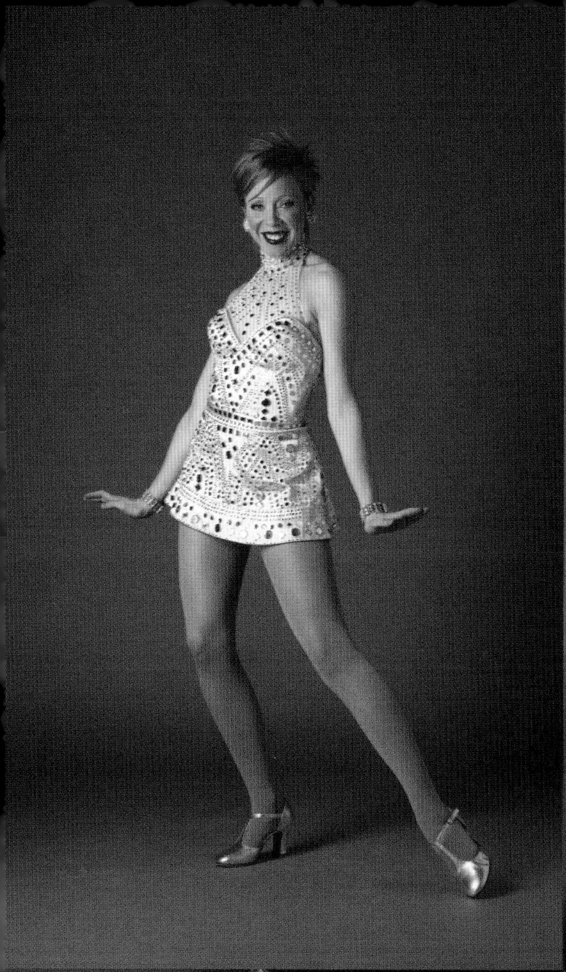
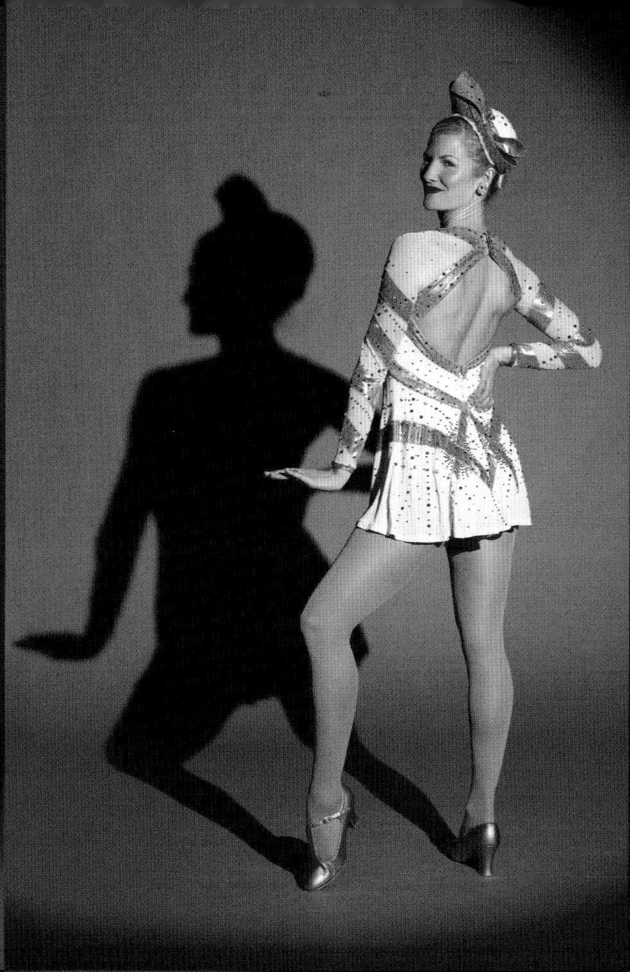
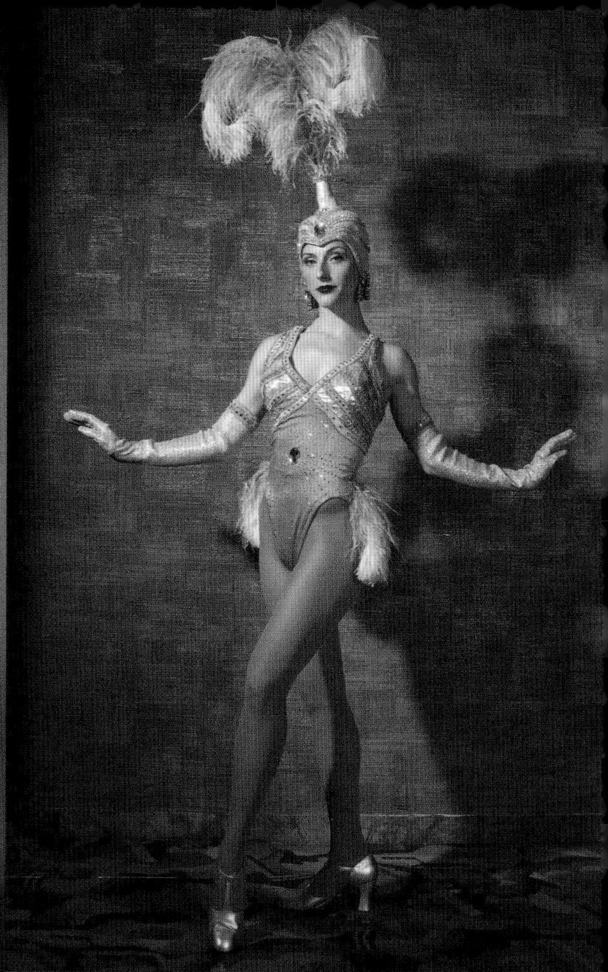
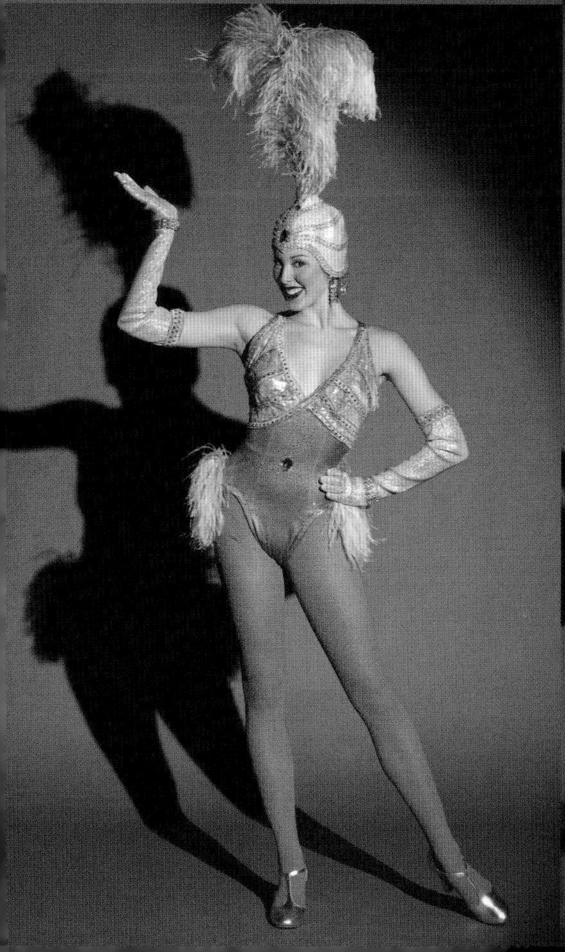
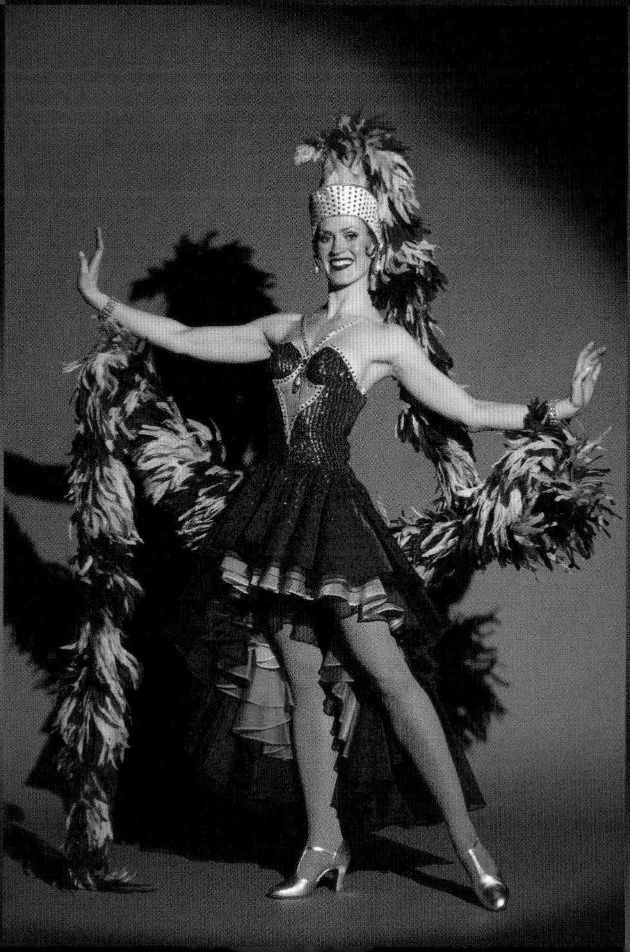
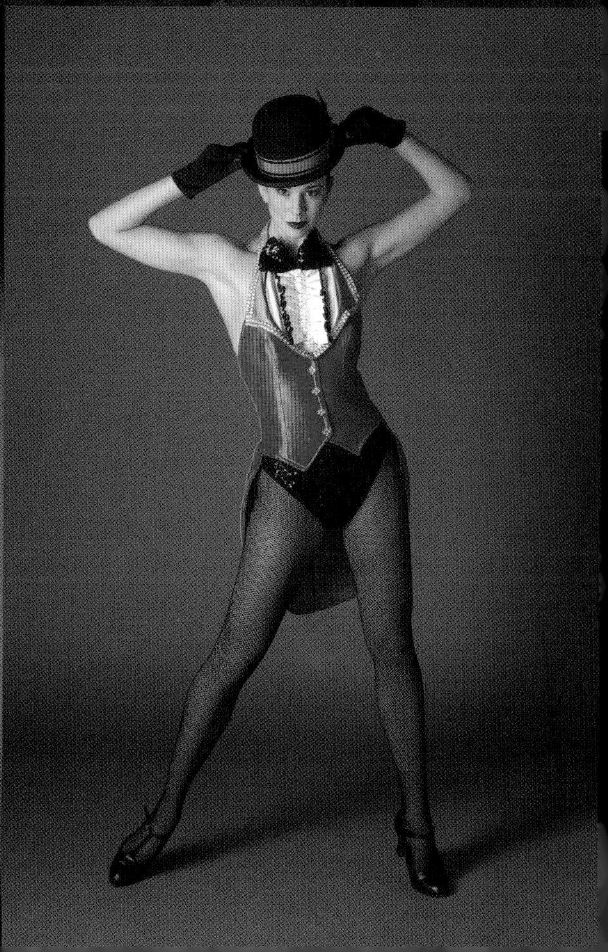

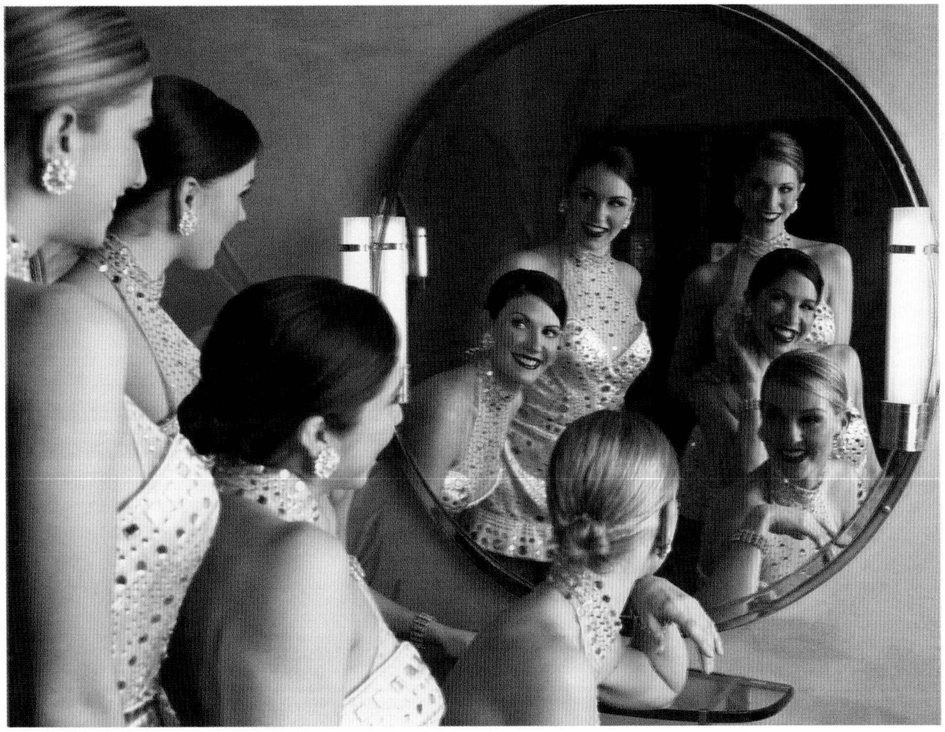

This Ladies' Lounge is the work of Witold Gordon. Done on parchment paper, the fourteen scenes represent the application of cosmetics through history. Beginning with Eve, it wraps around traveling through ancient Egypt, Medieval England, 18th Century France, Persia and China, amongst other eras to the "modern day" flapper girl.

The lounges of Radio City Music Hall are plush, elegant, and serve as mini-galleries that house some very significant works of art. Erté designed this costume for the Easter Show Finale in 1990.

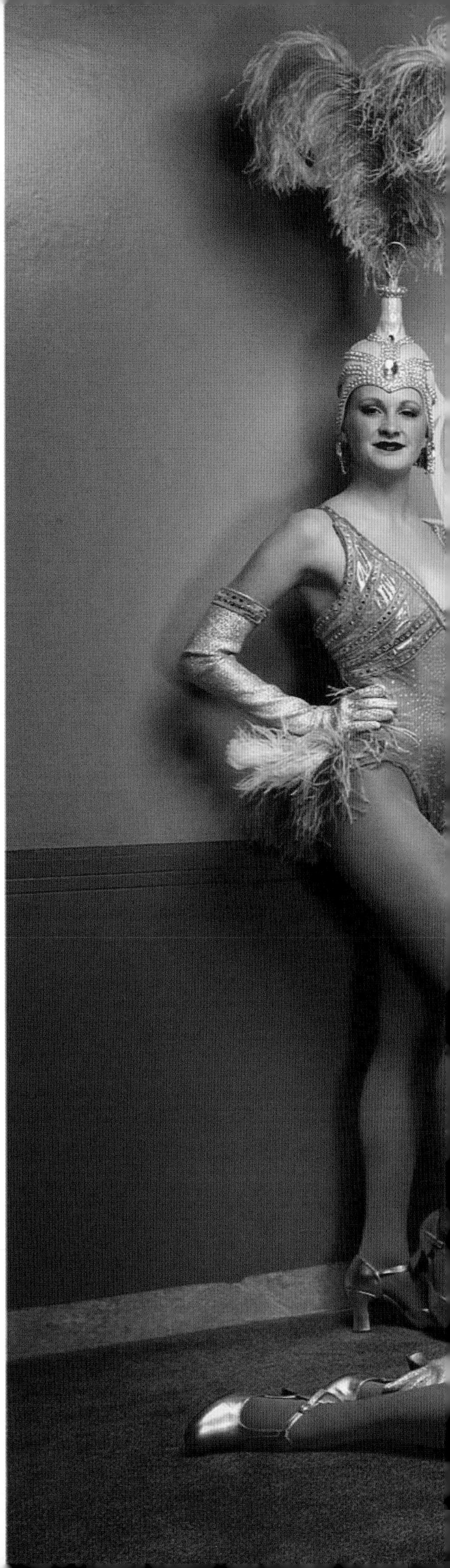

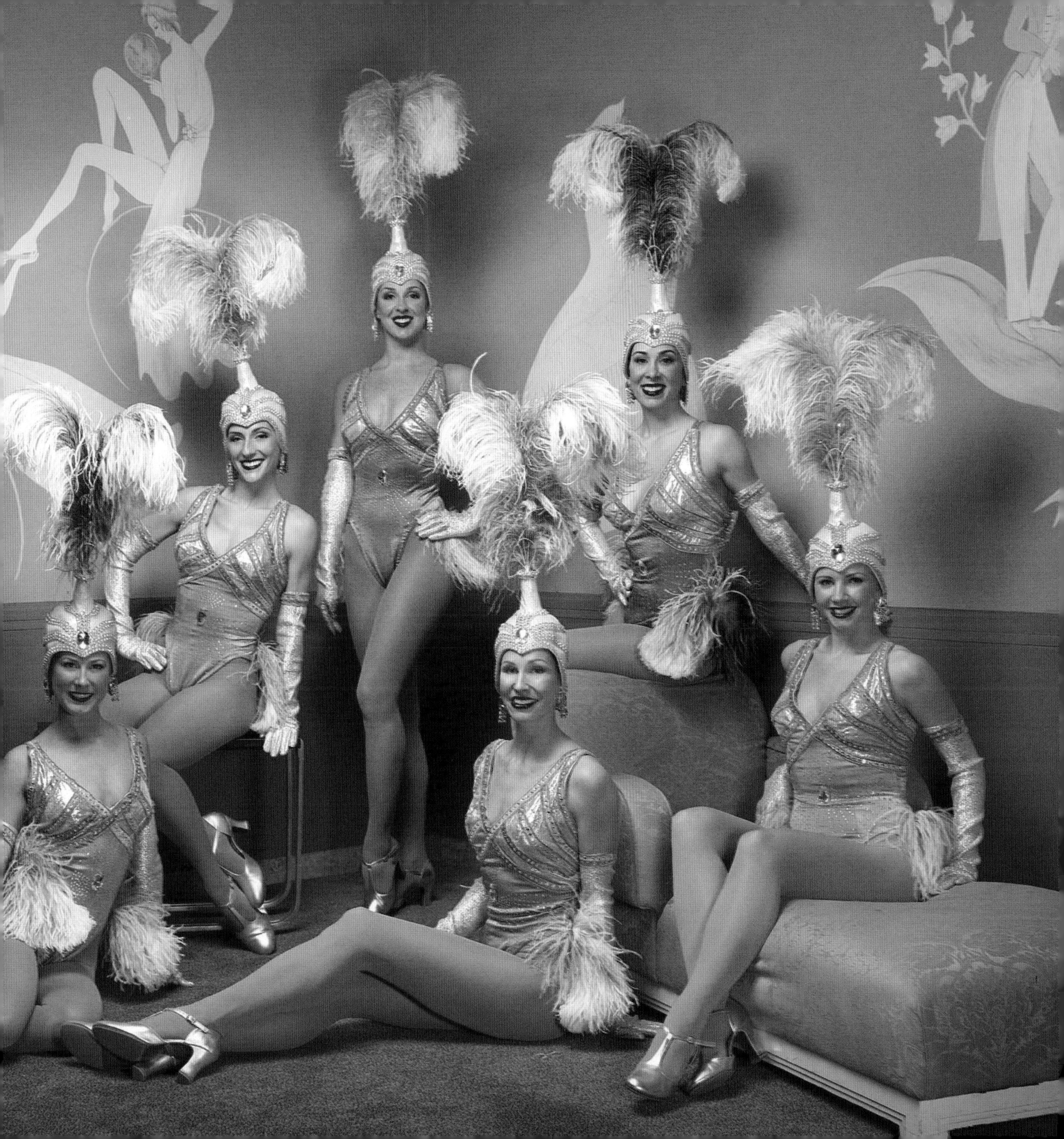

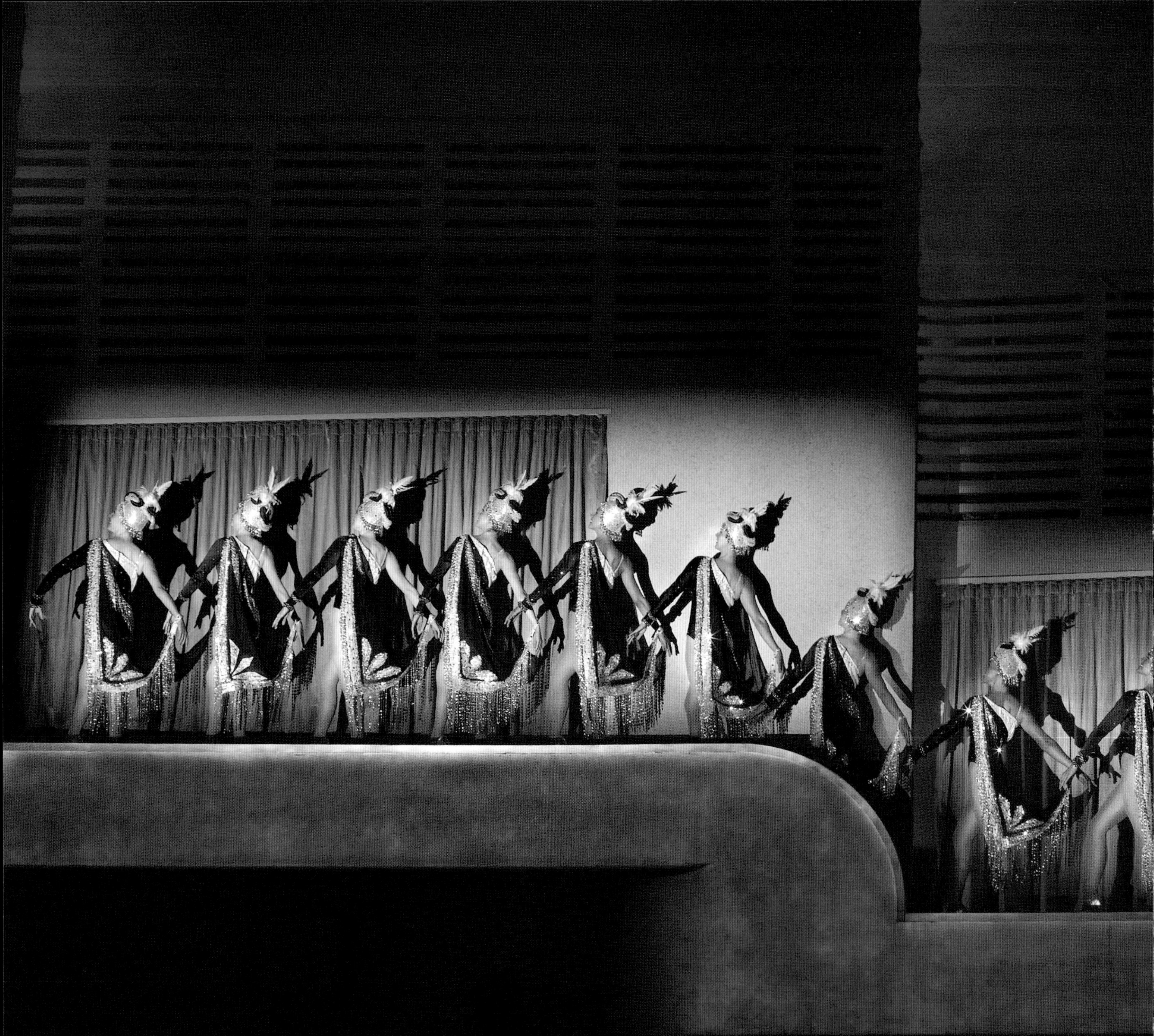

The Choral Staircases were designed to bring performers closer to the audience. Concealed doors behind the curtains enable performers to move on and off the platforms and surround the audience with entertainment.

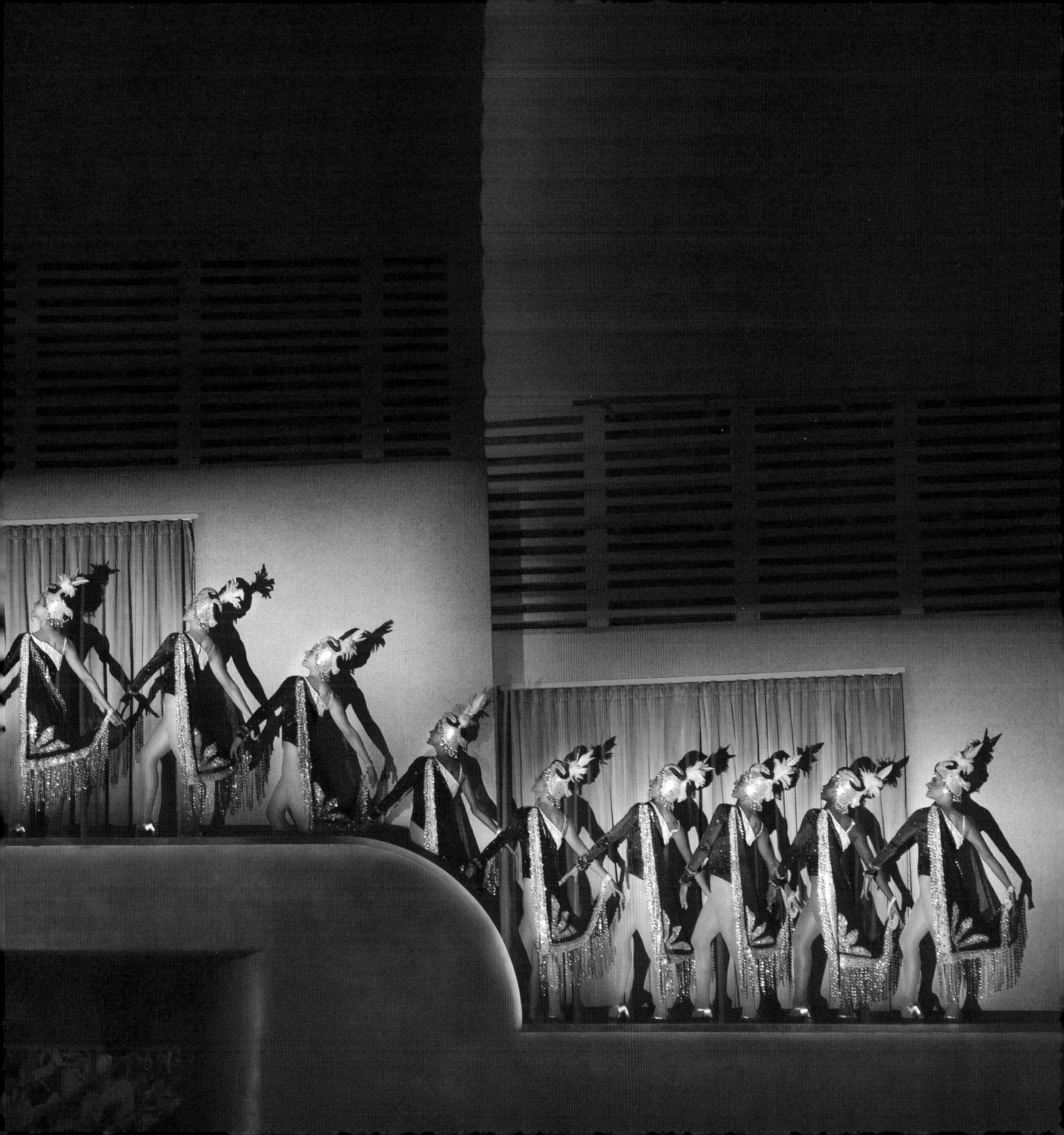

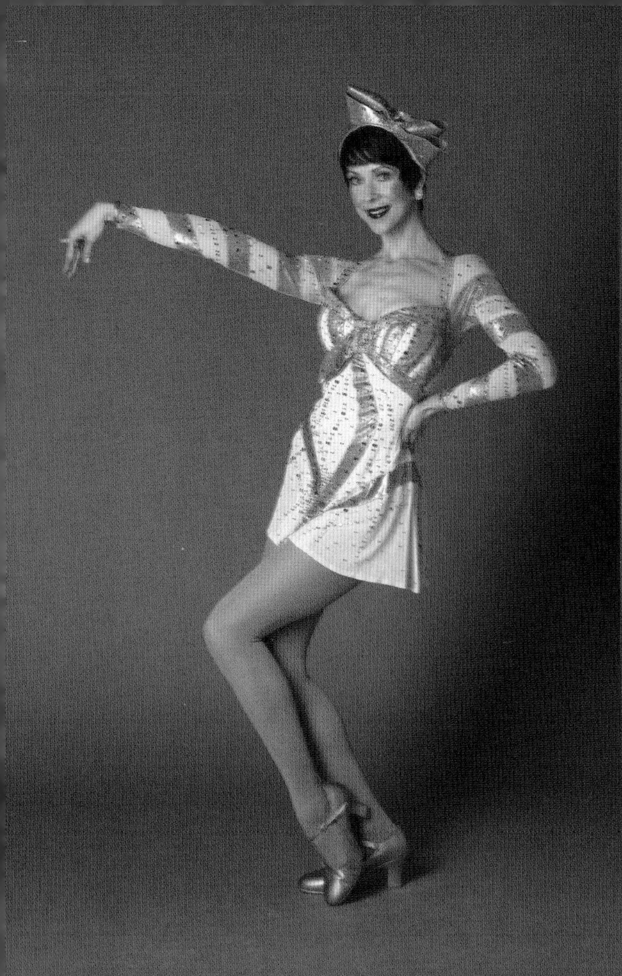
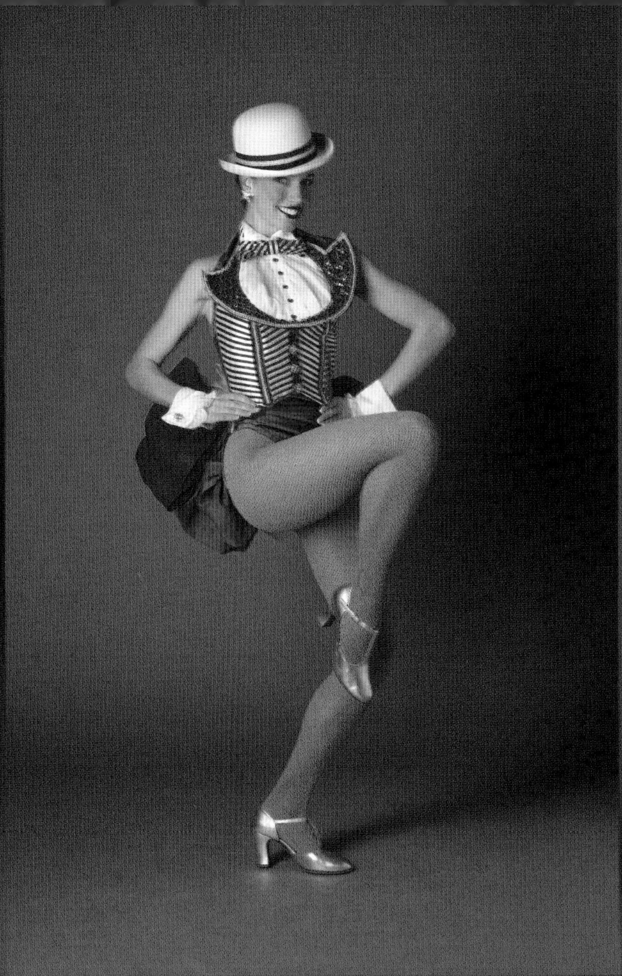
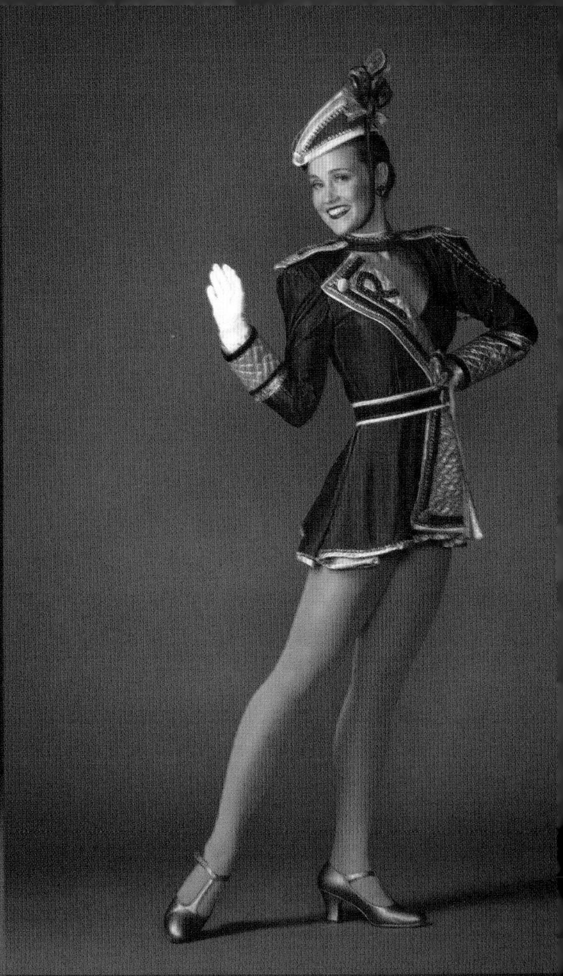
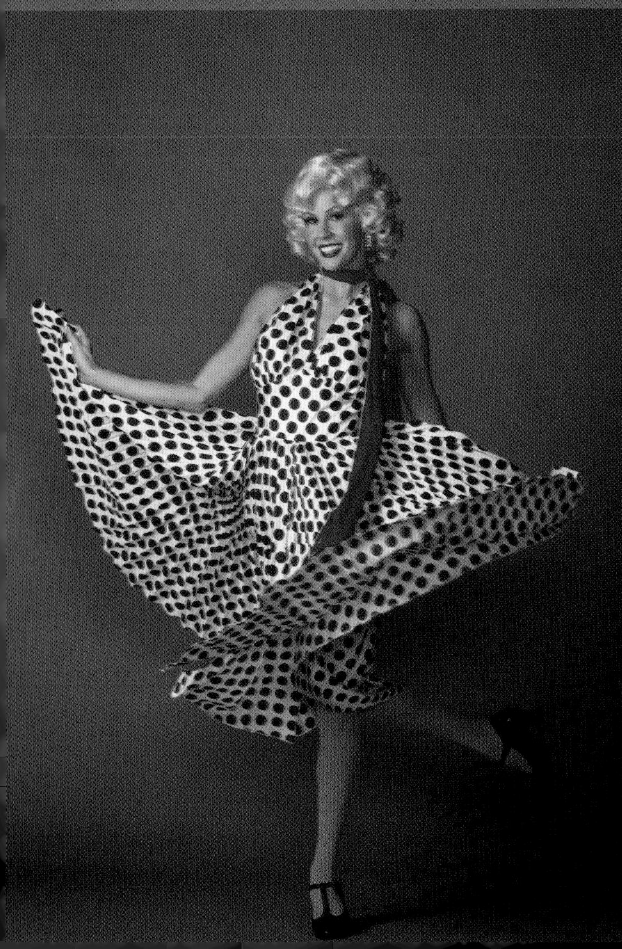
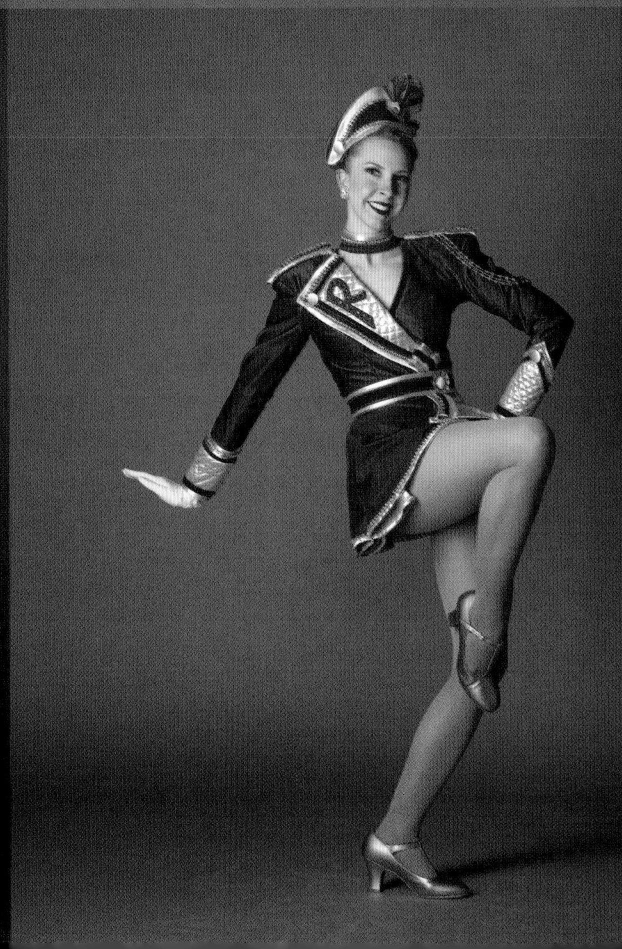
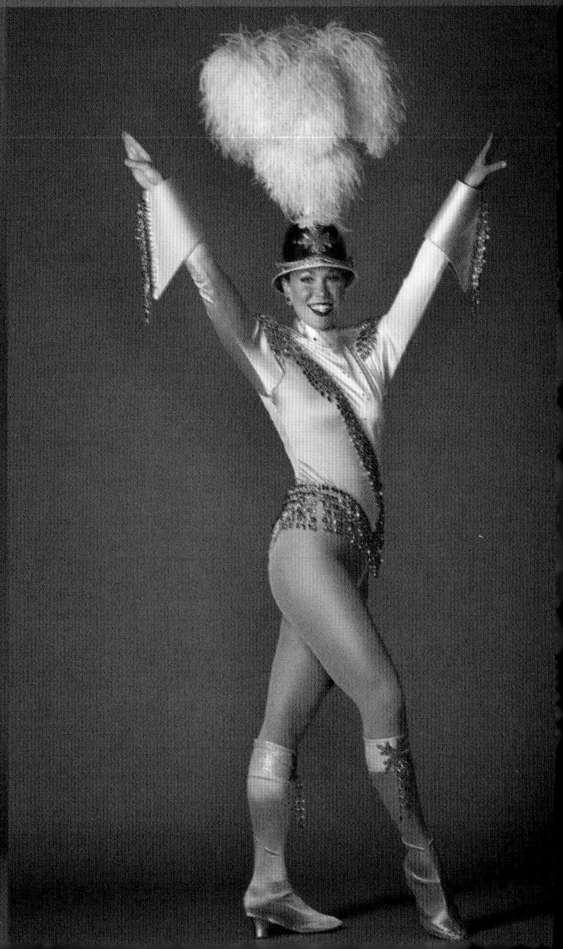

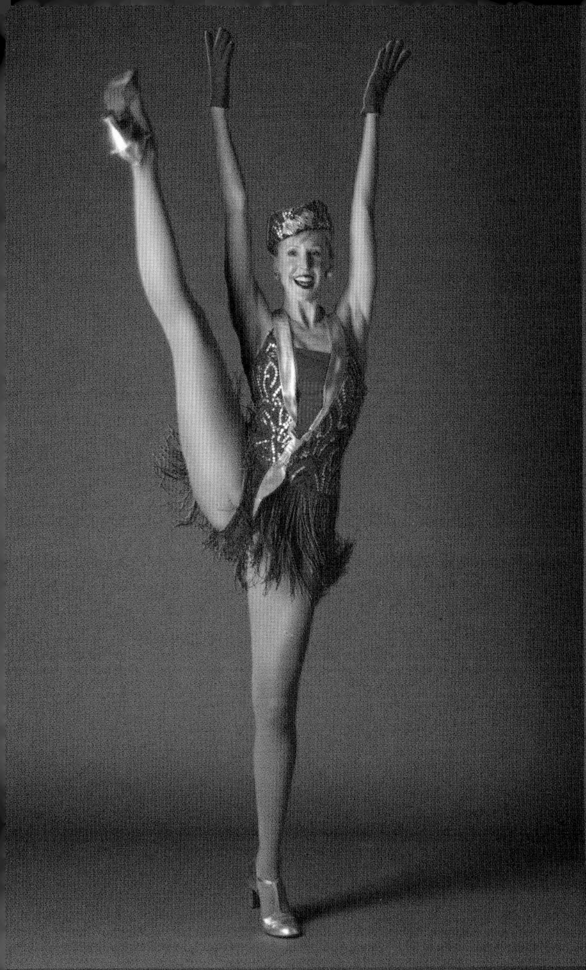
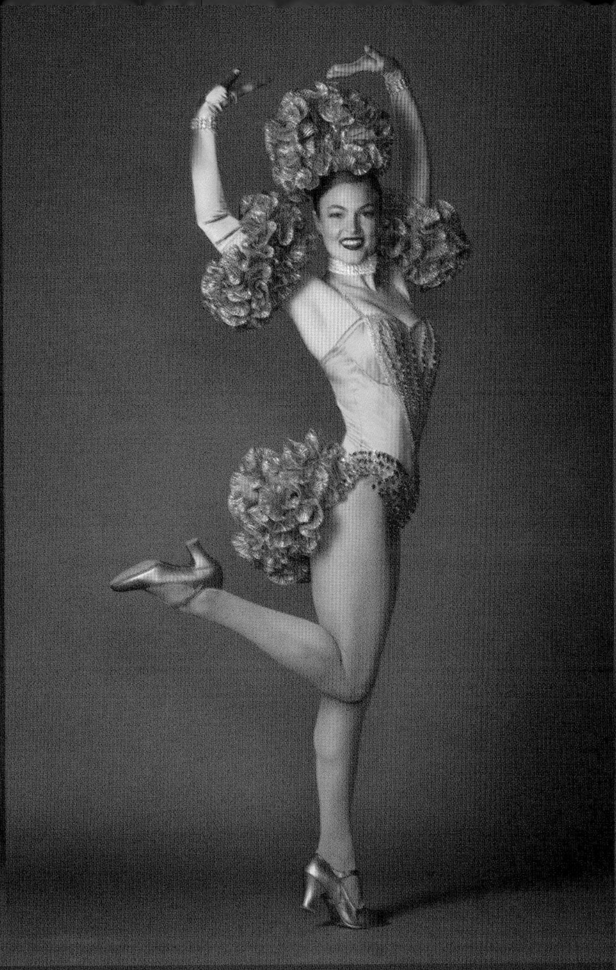
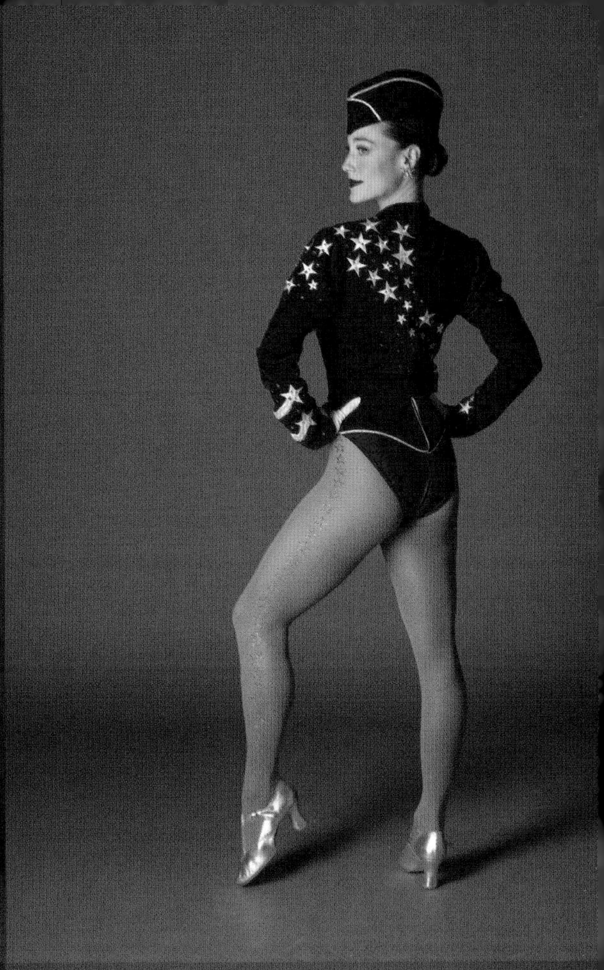
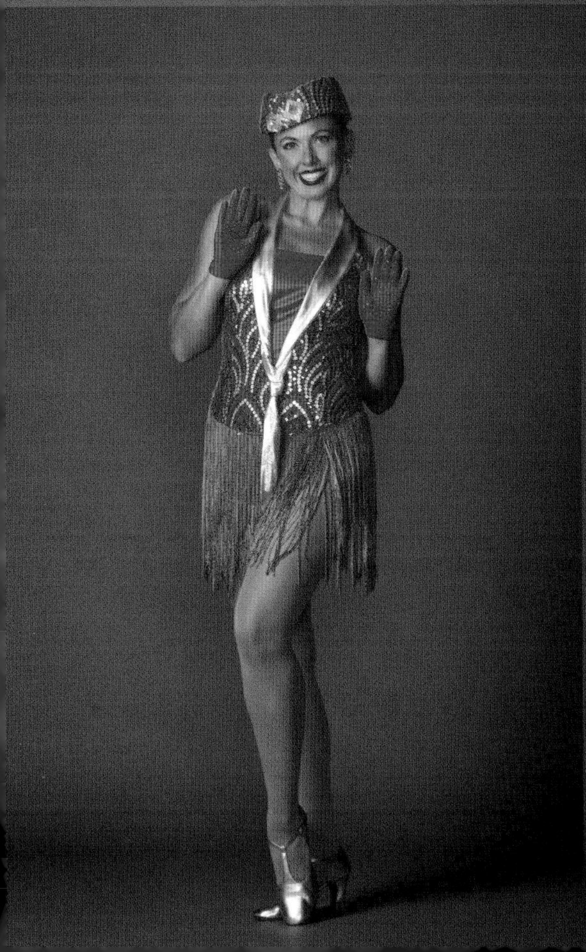
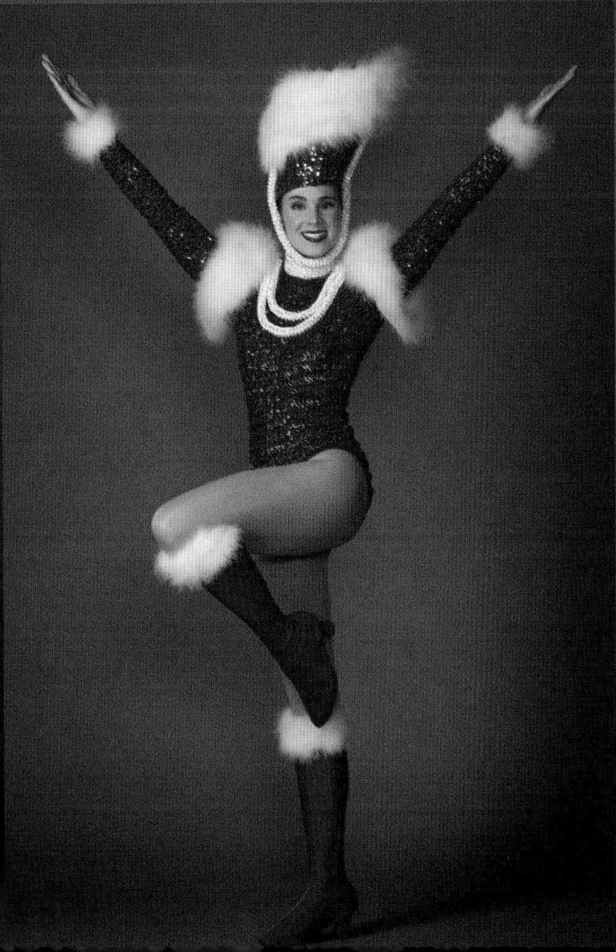
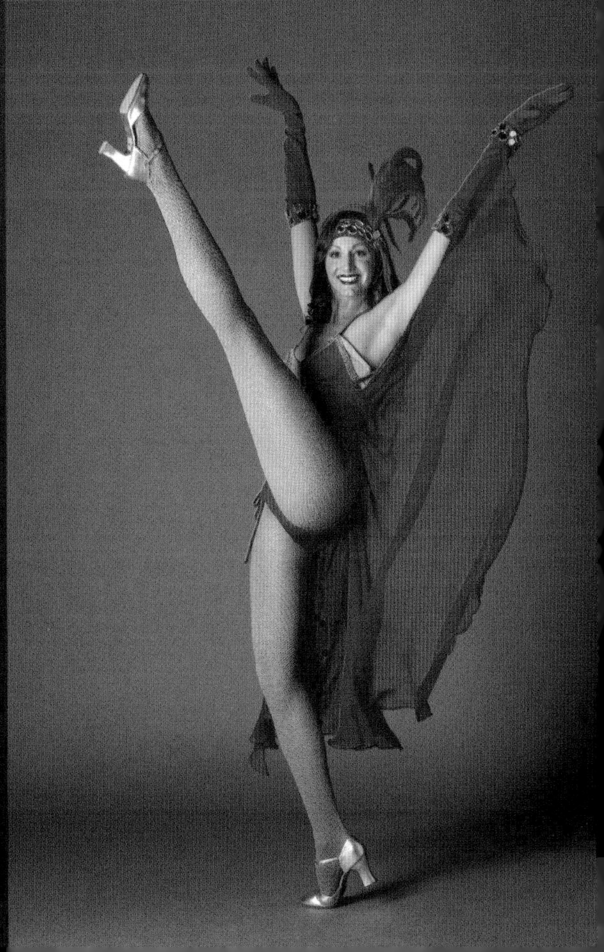

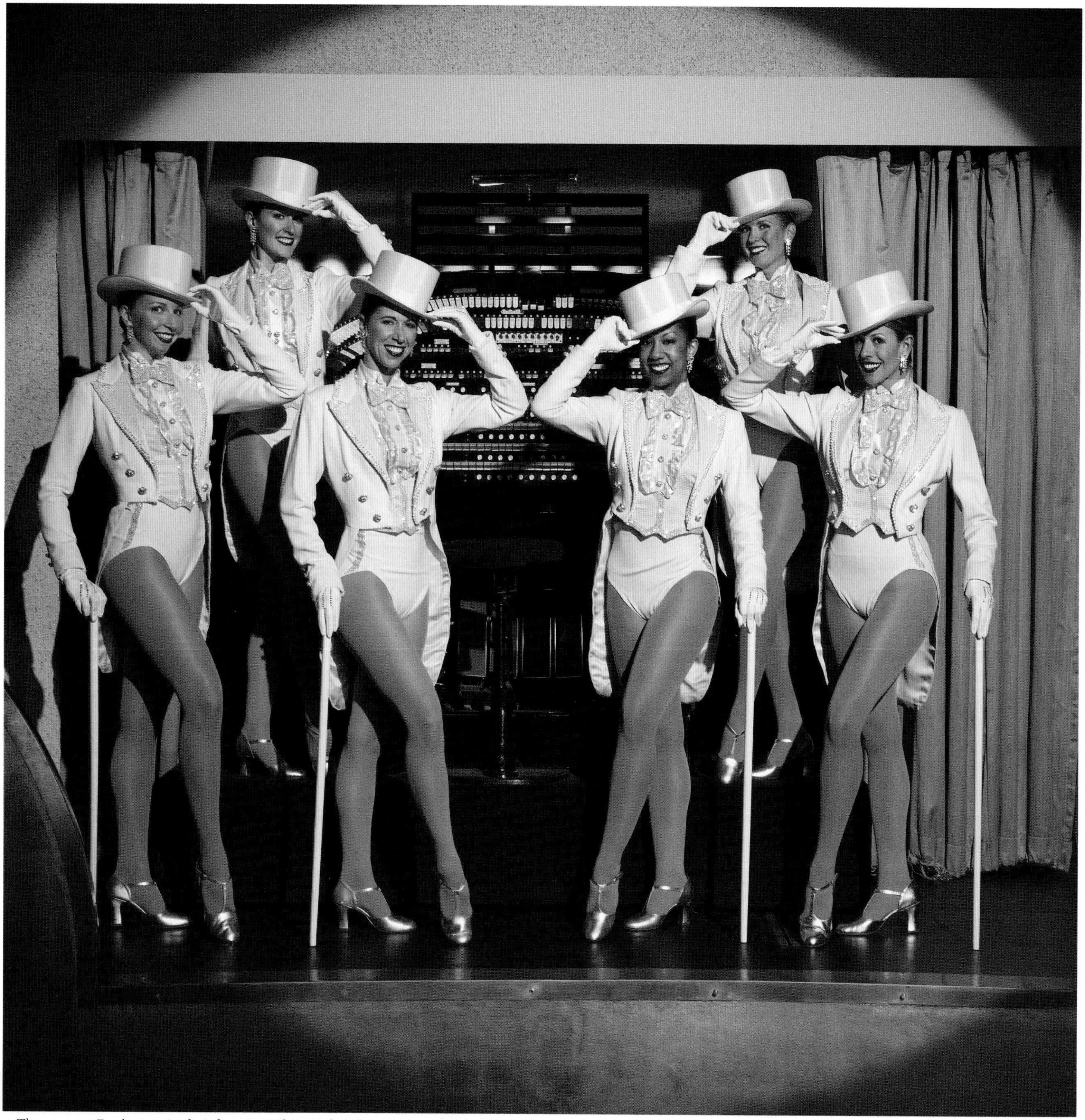

The current Rockettes tip their hats in "White Tails," the 1979 creation by Frank Spencer for *New York Summer.*

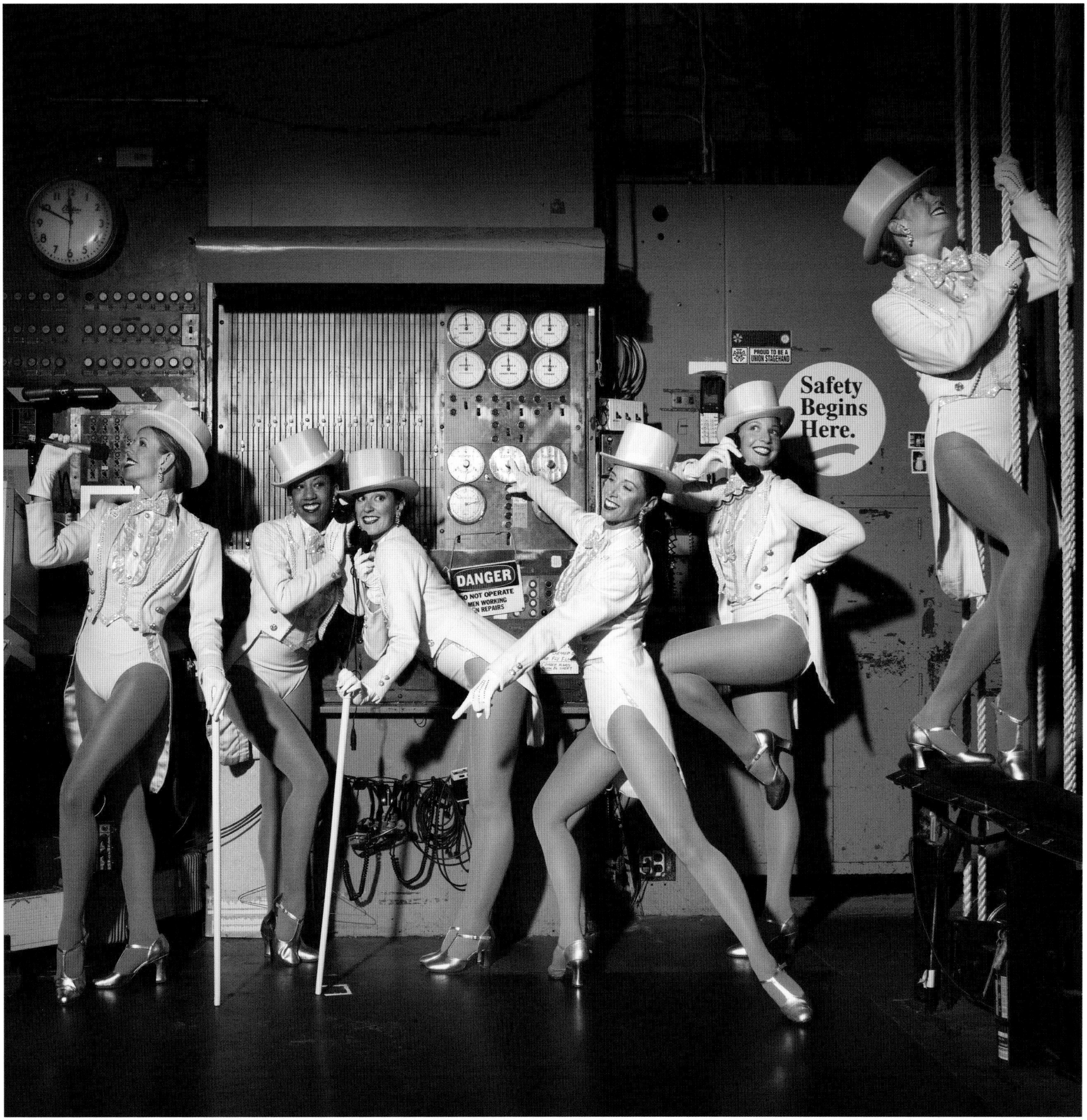

Measuring 144 feet across, The Great Stage is the width of a full city block. From his control board, the stage manager cues the stagehands and talent throughout the shows.

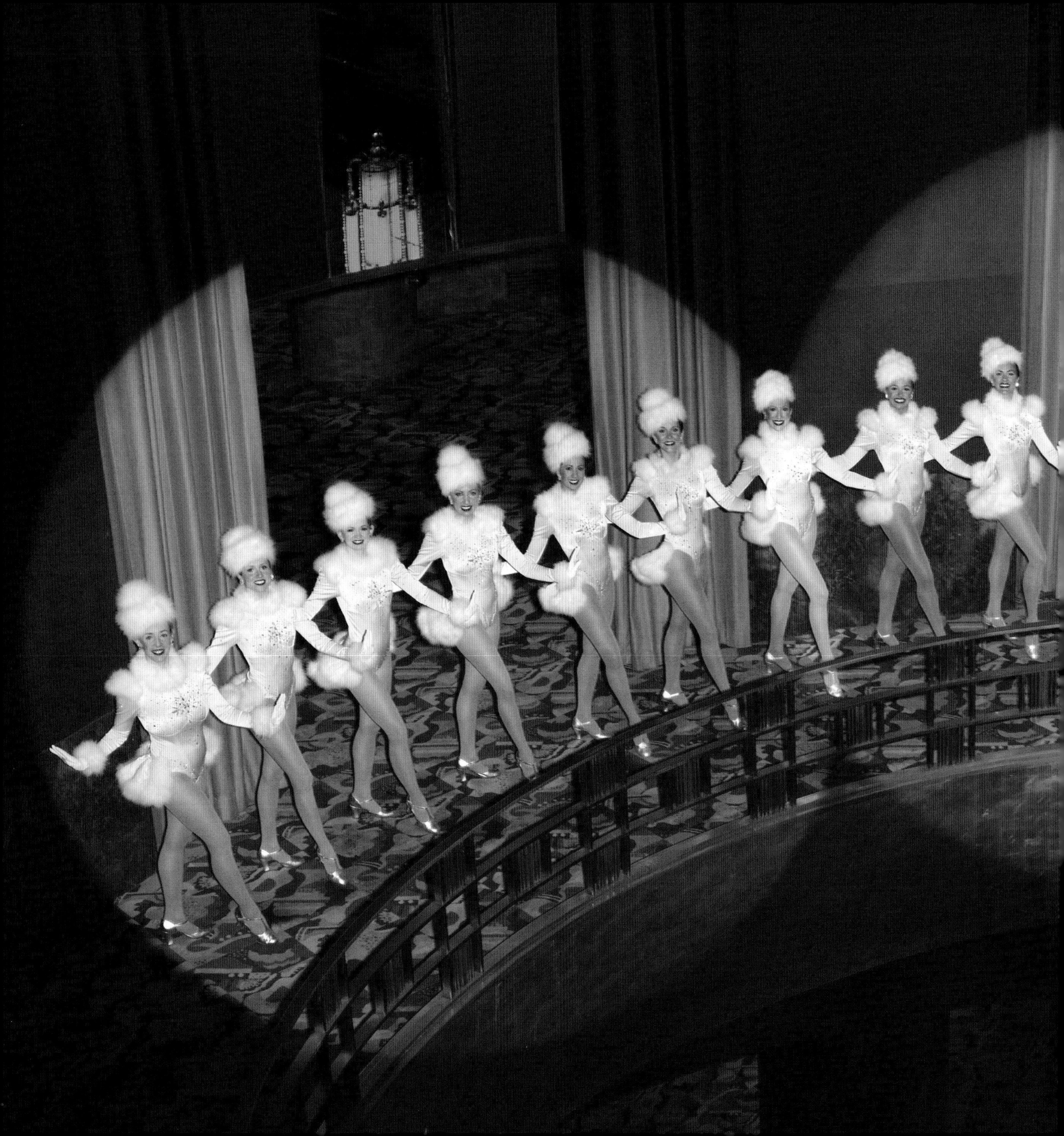

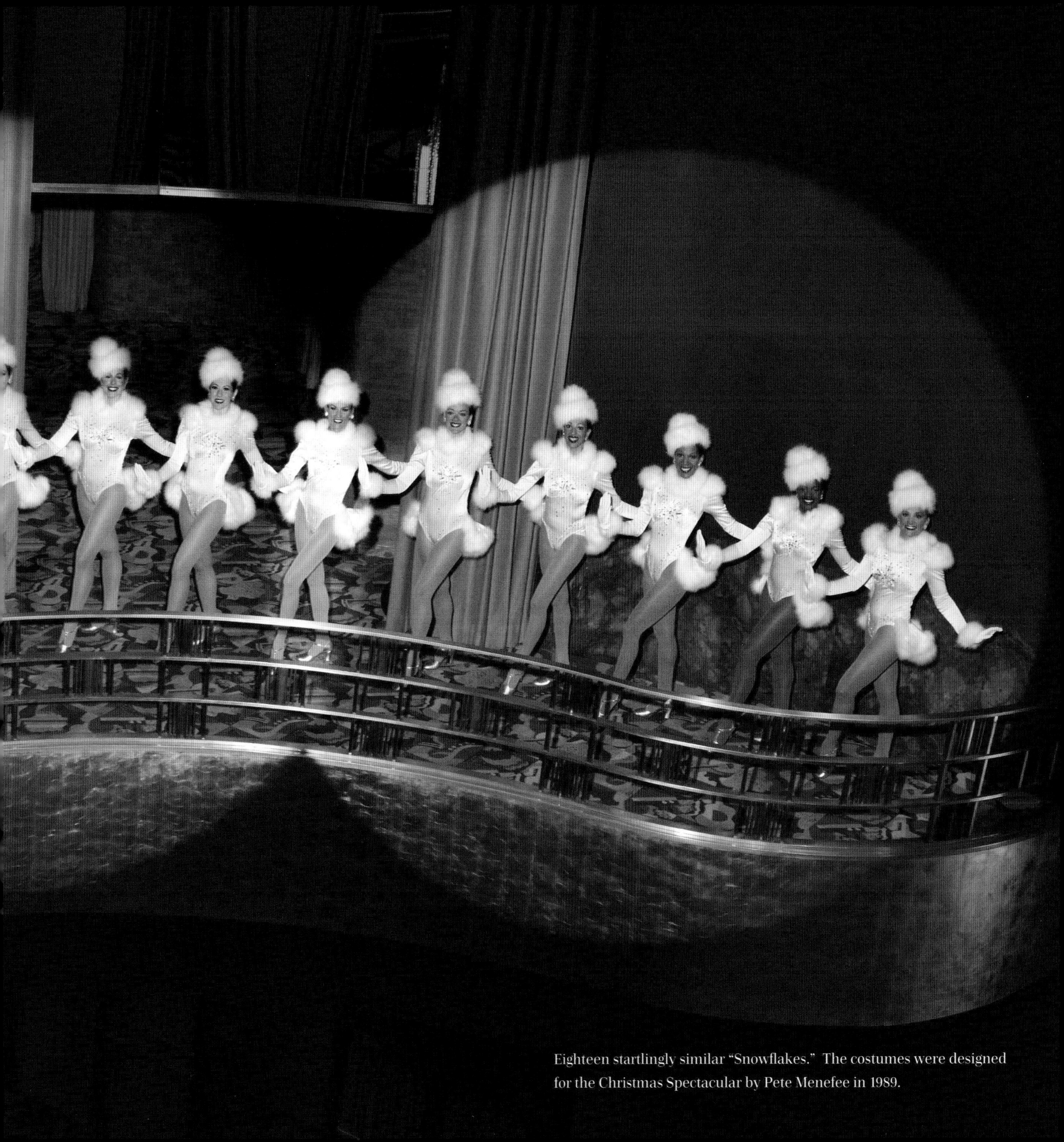

Eighteen startlingly similar "Snowflakes." The costumes were designed for the Christmas Spectacular by Pete Menefee in 1989.

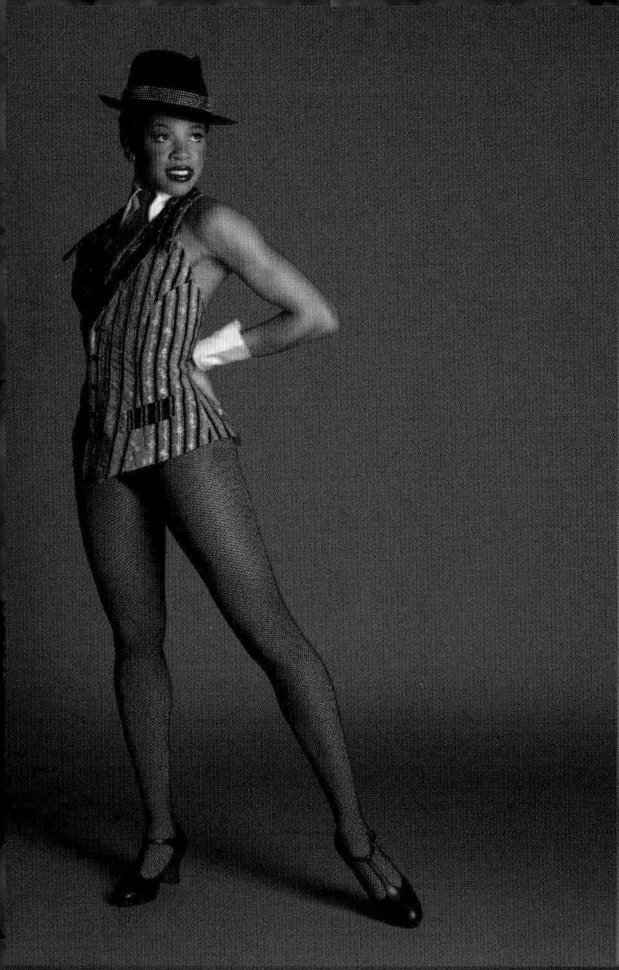
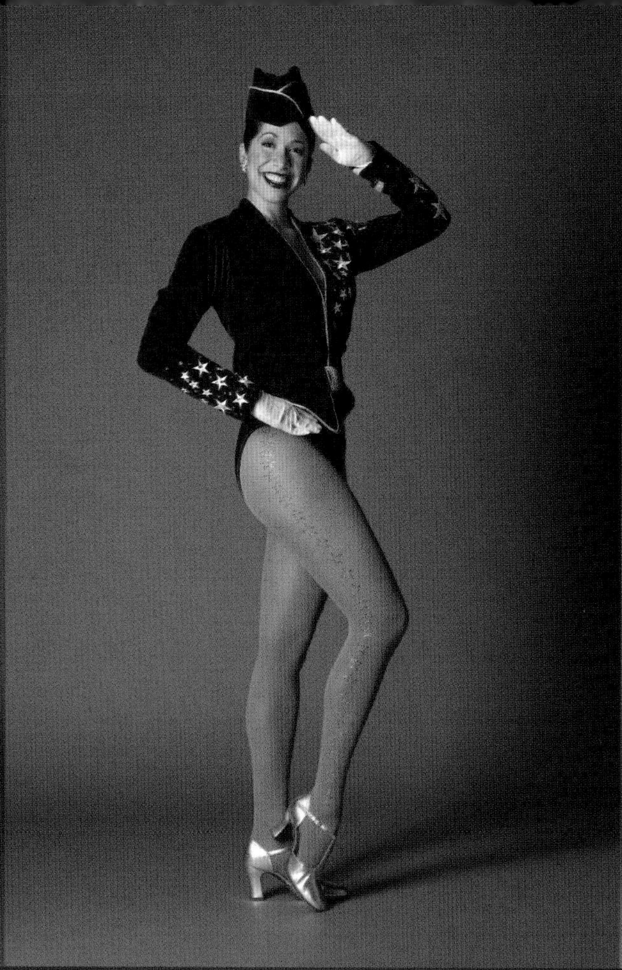
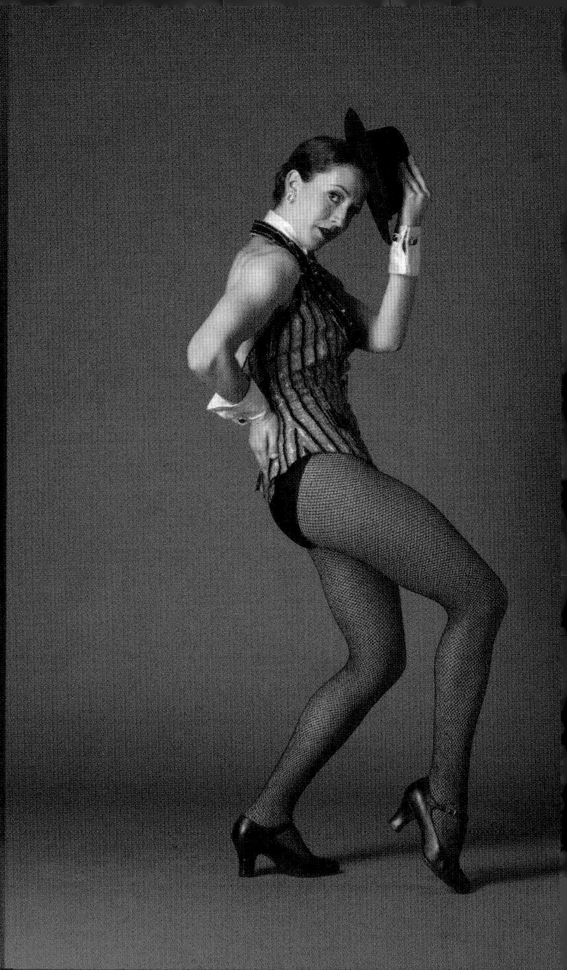
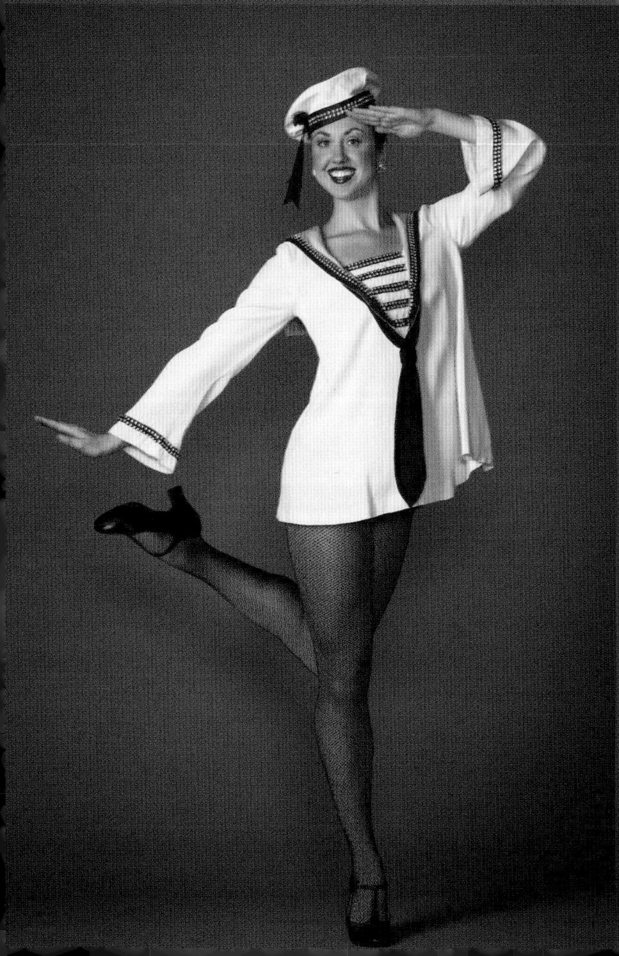
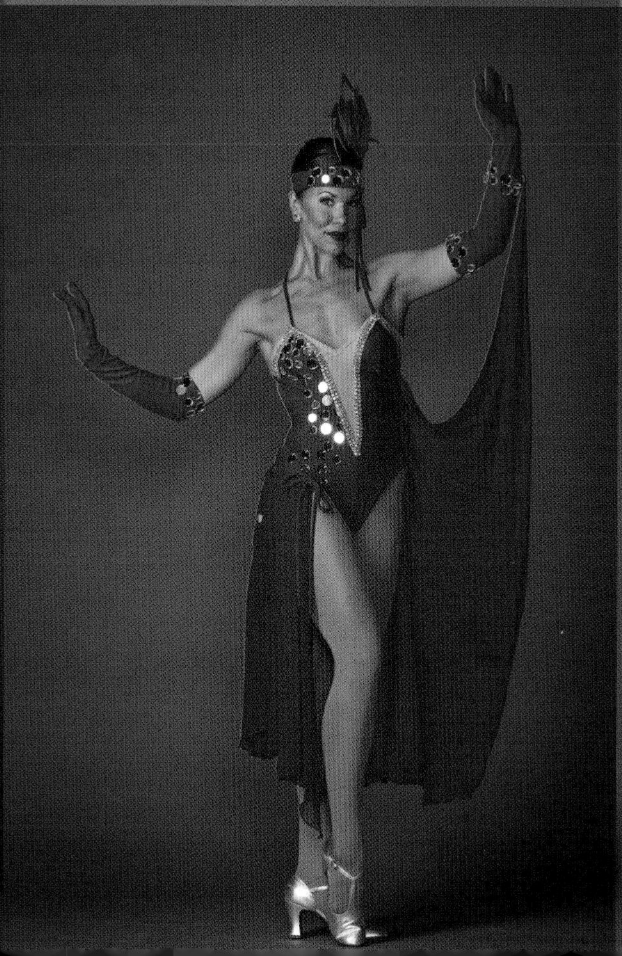
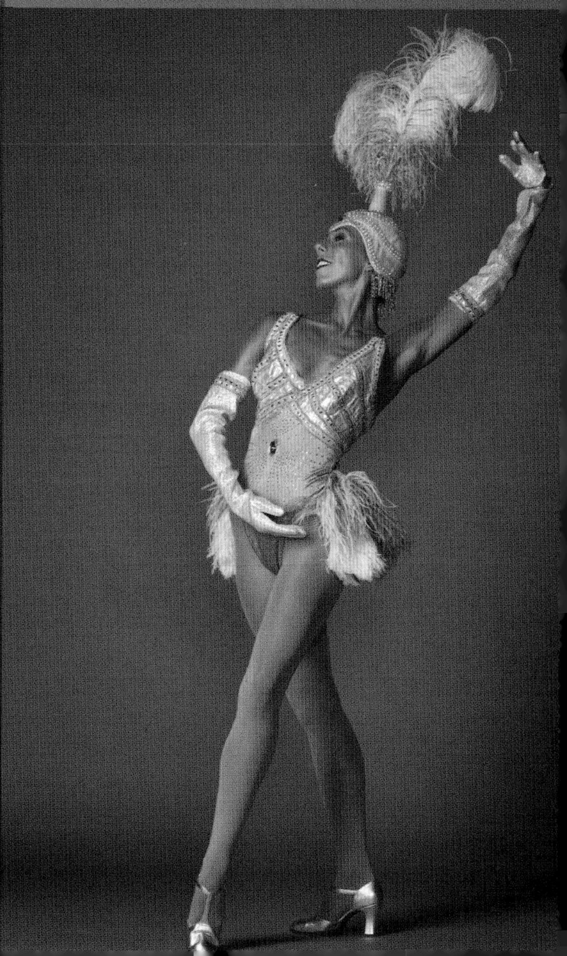

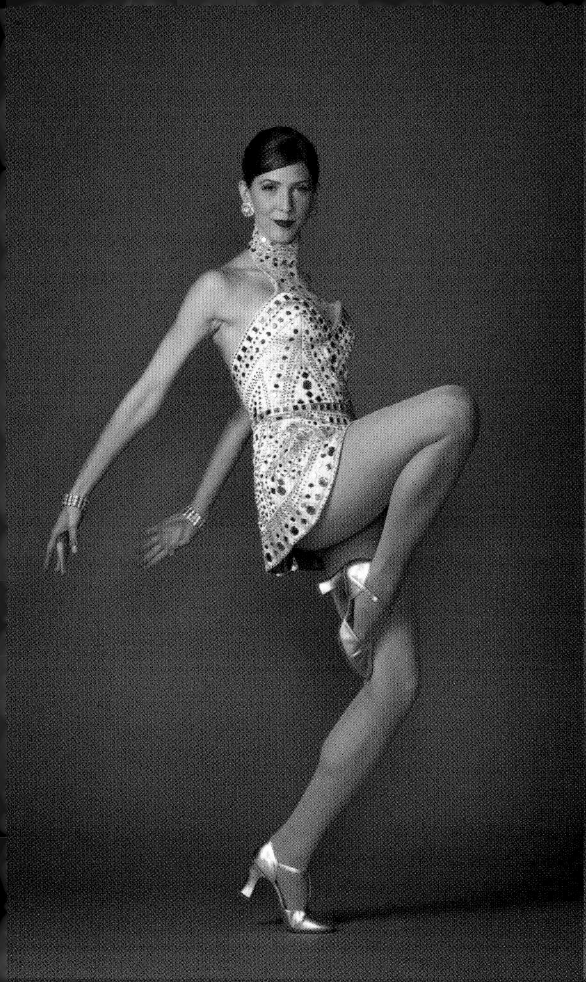
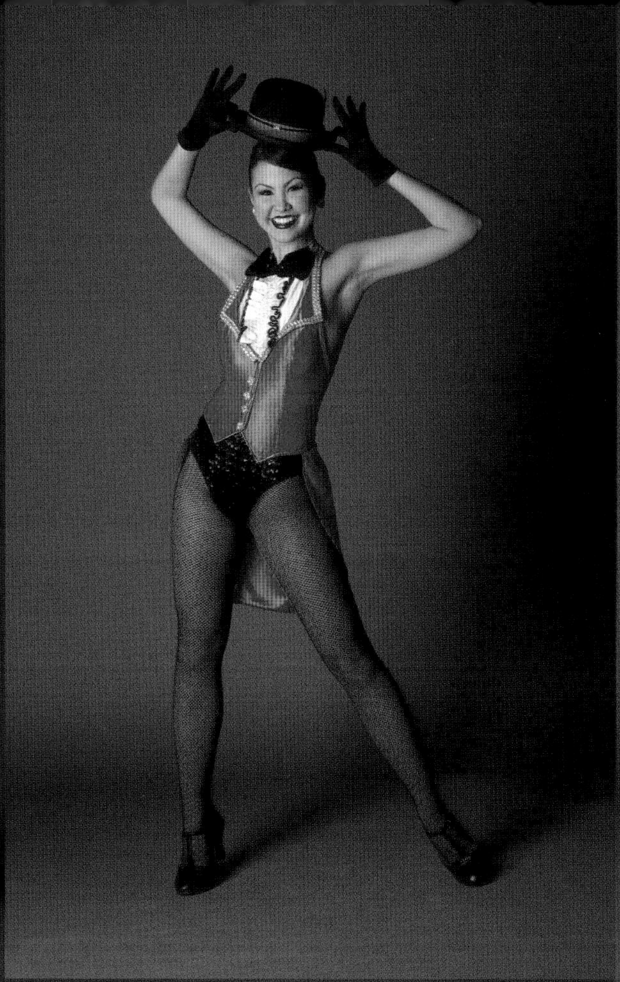
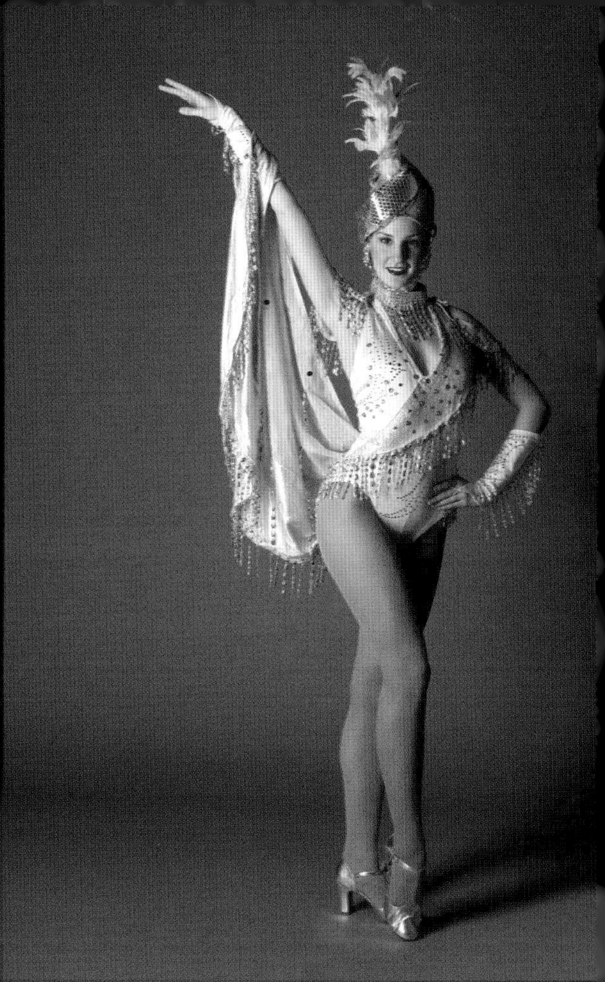
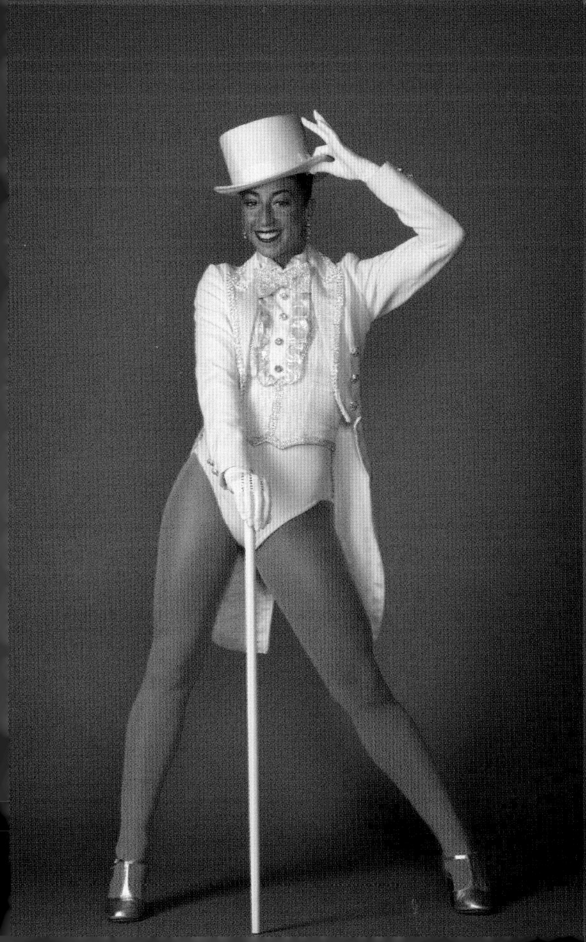
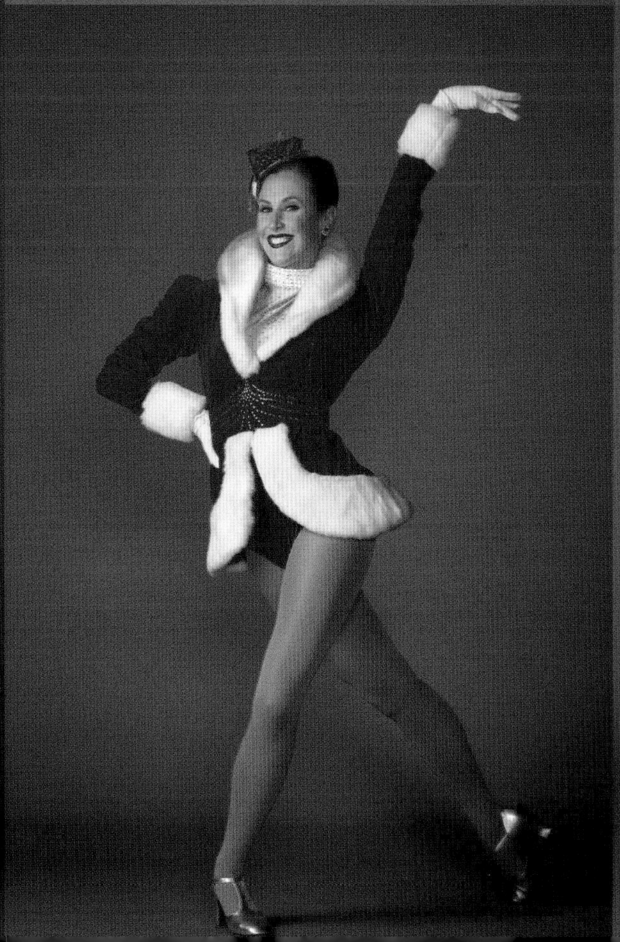
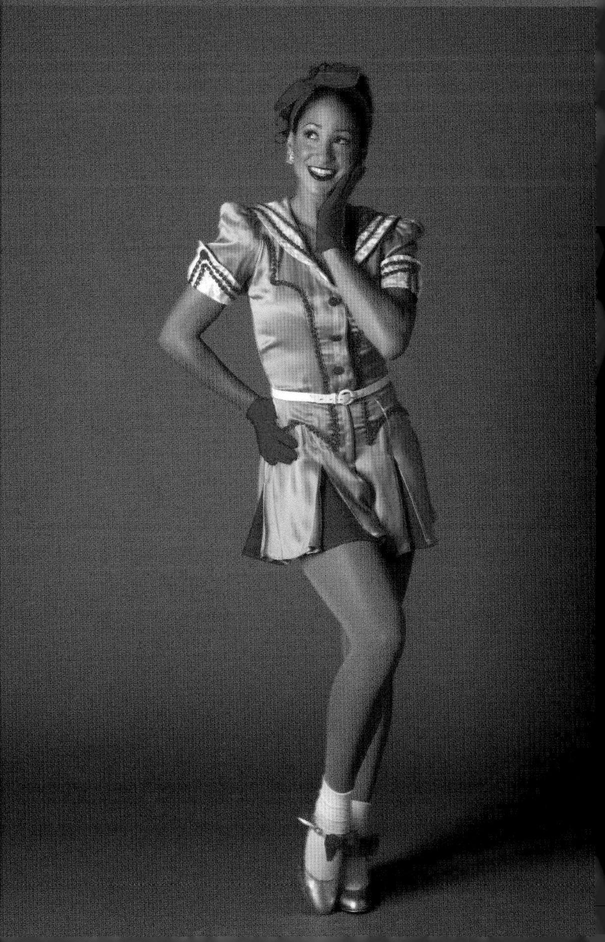

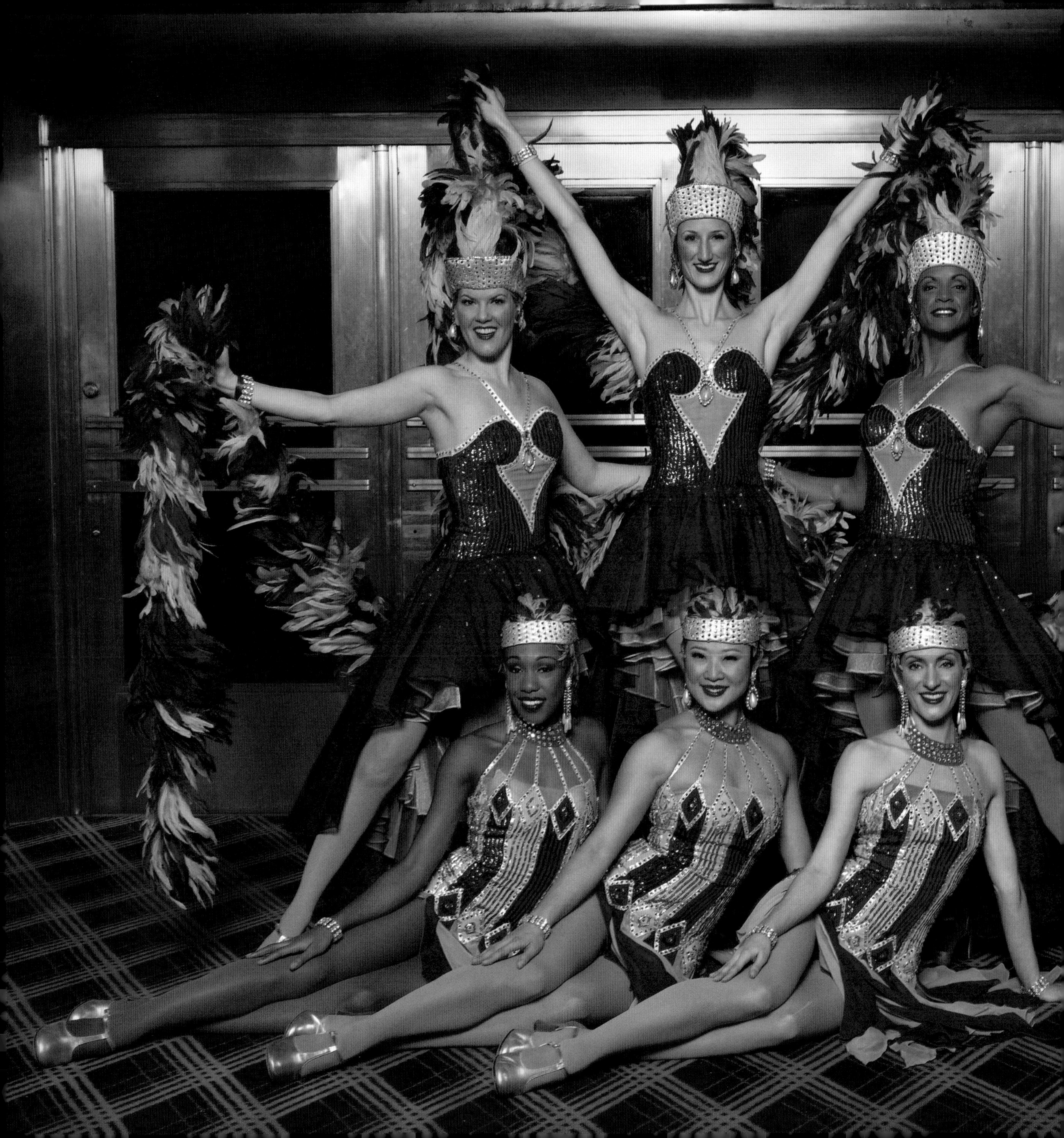

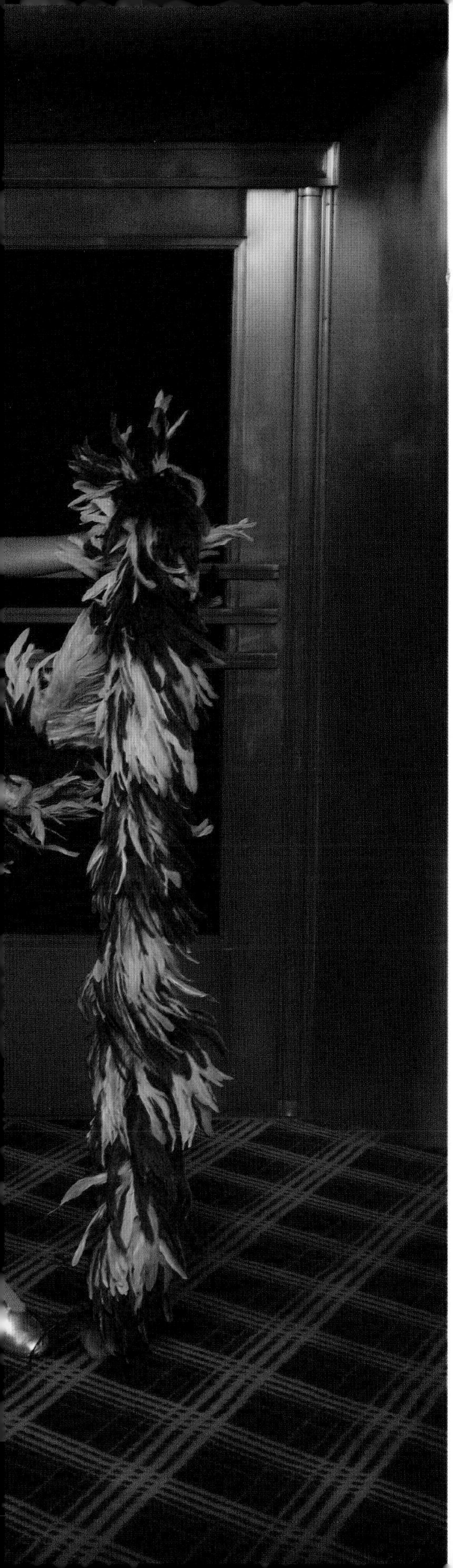

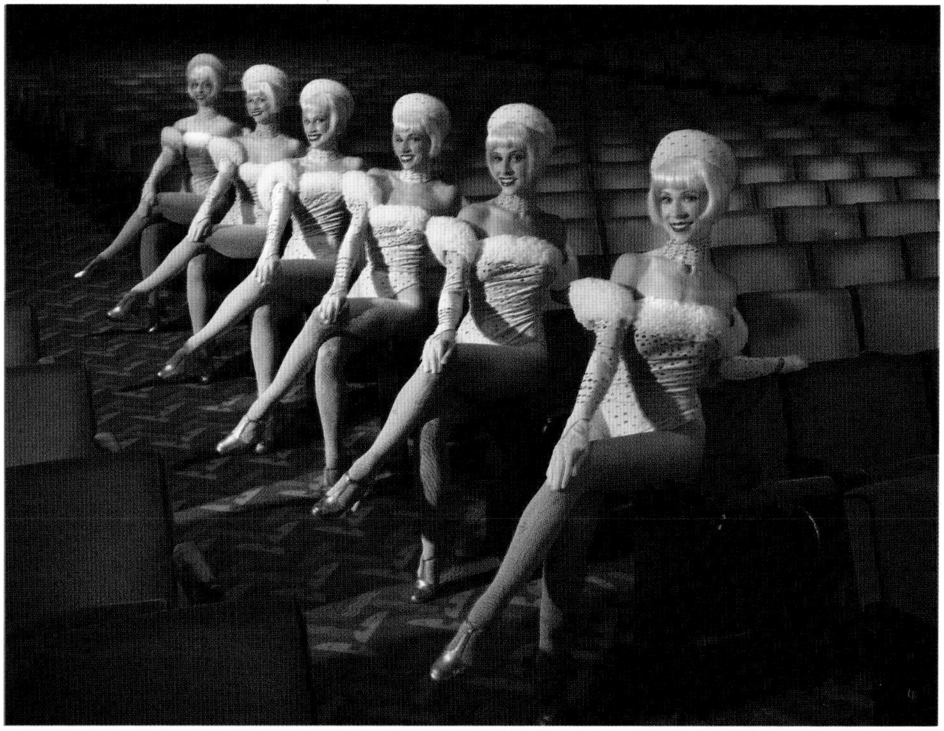

The Music Hall seats 5,931, making it one of the world's largest theatres!

On the left, this year's Rockettes feature costumes designed by Erté in 1990 for the Gershwin number in the Easter show.

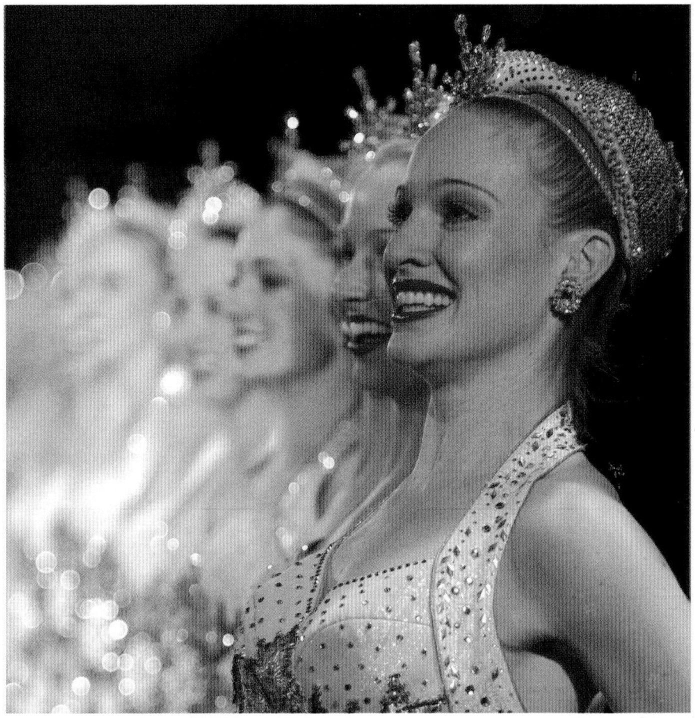

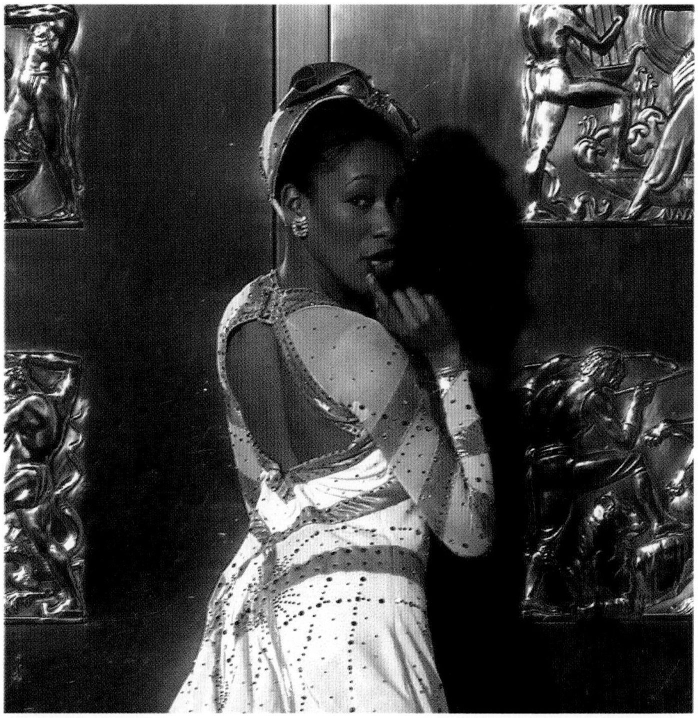

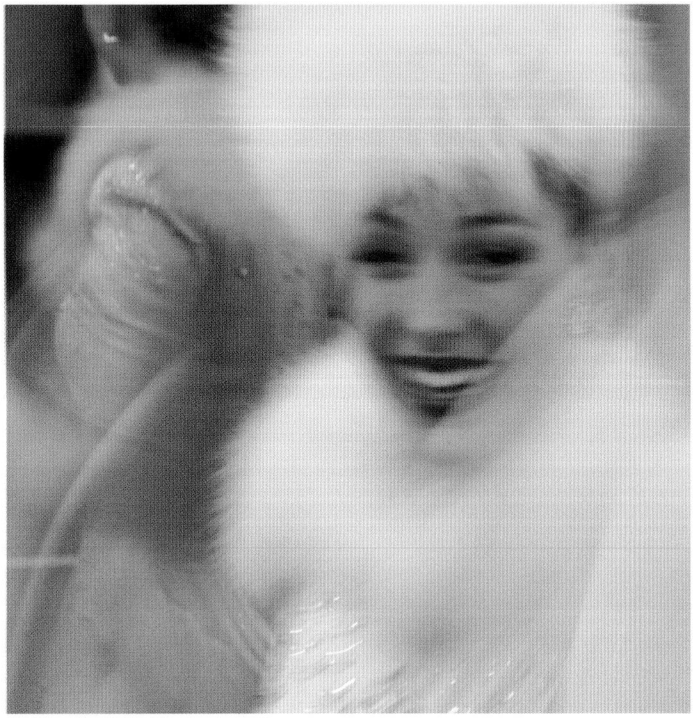

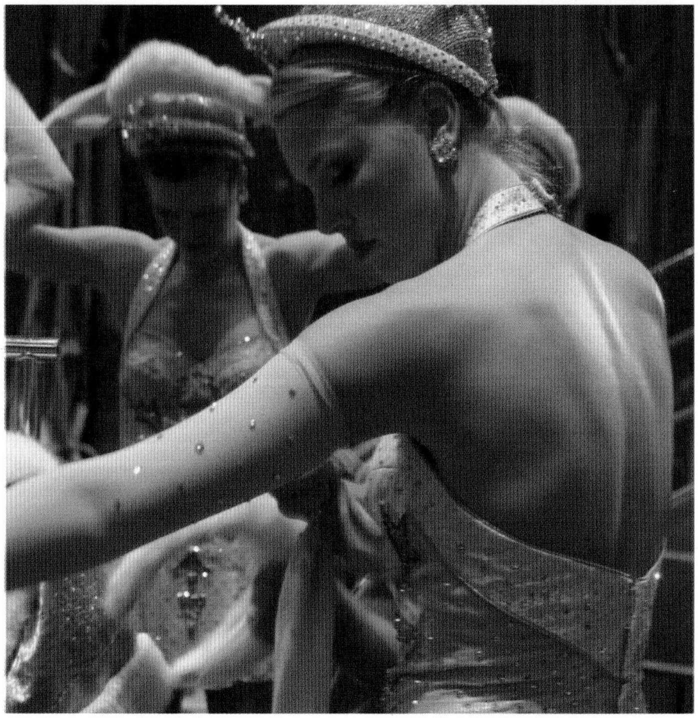

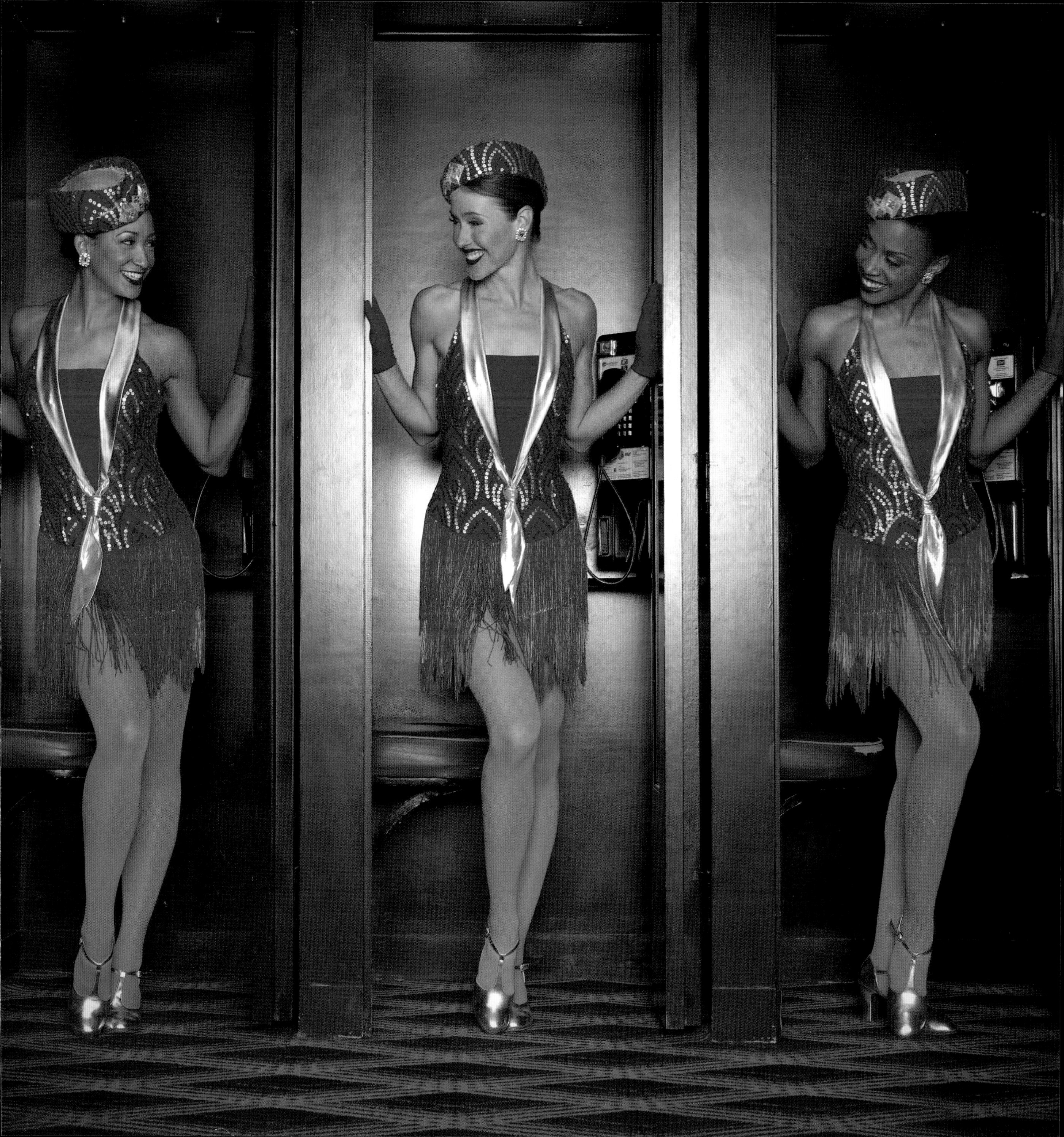

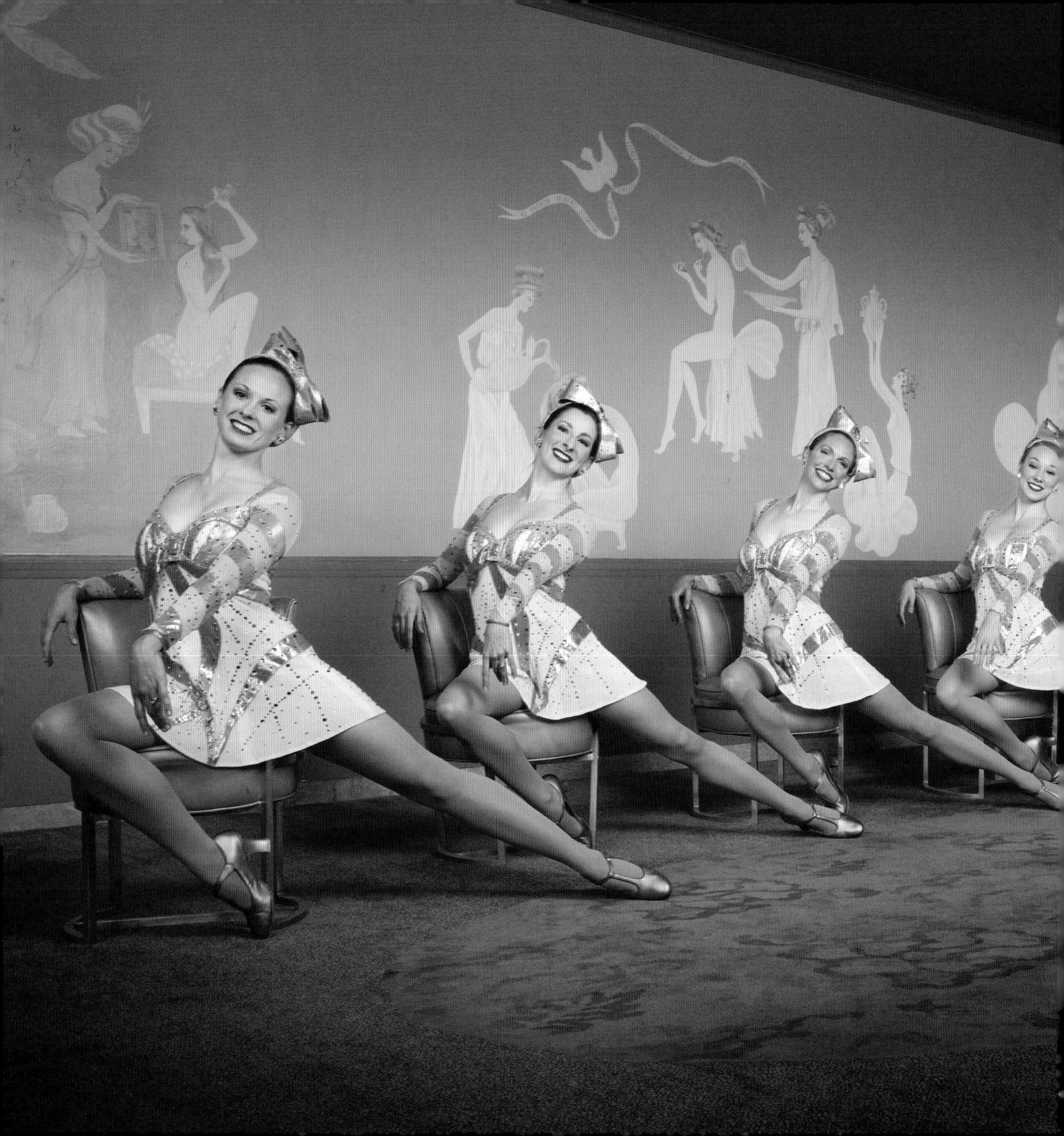

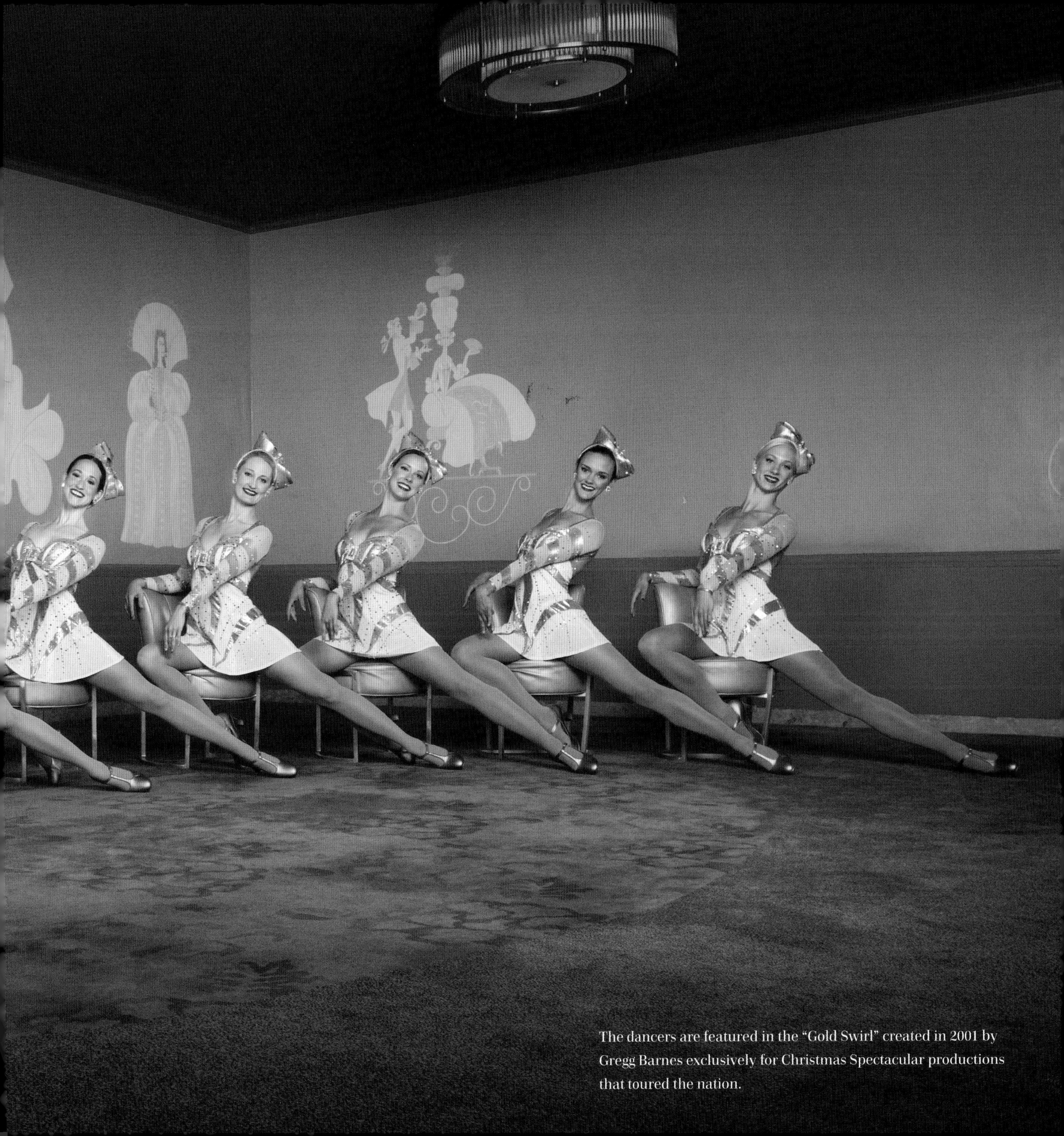

The dancers are featured in the "Gold Swirl" created in 2001 by Gregg Barnes exclusively for Christmas Spectacular productions that toured the nation.

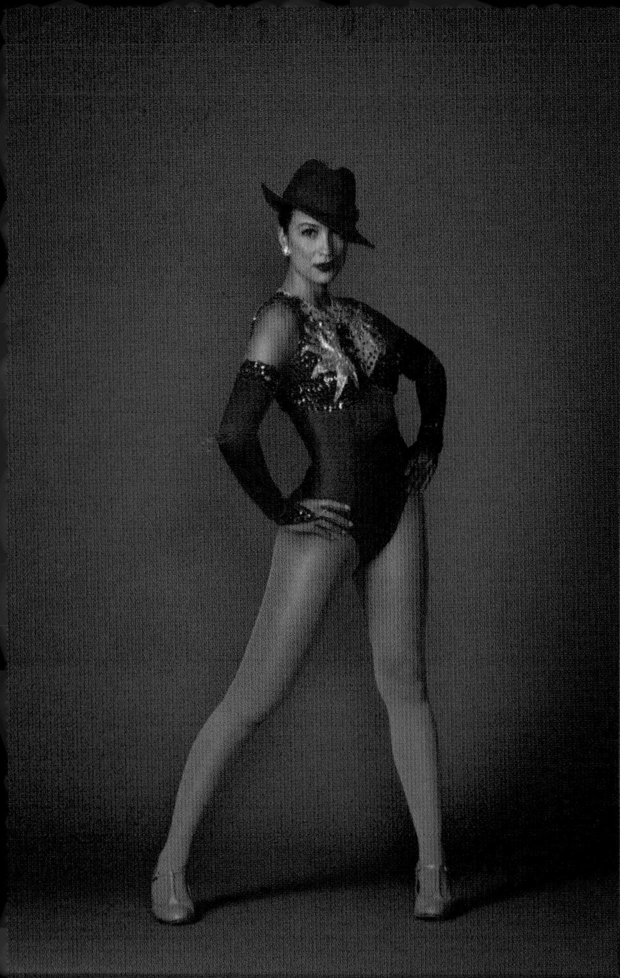
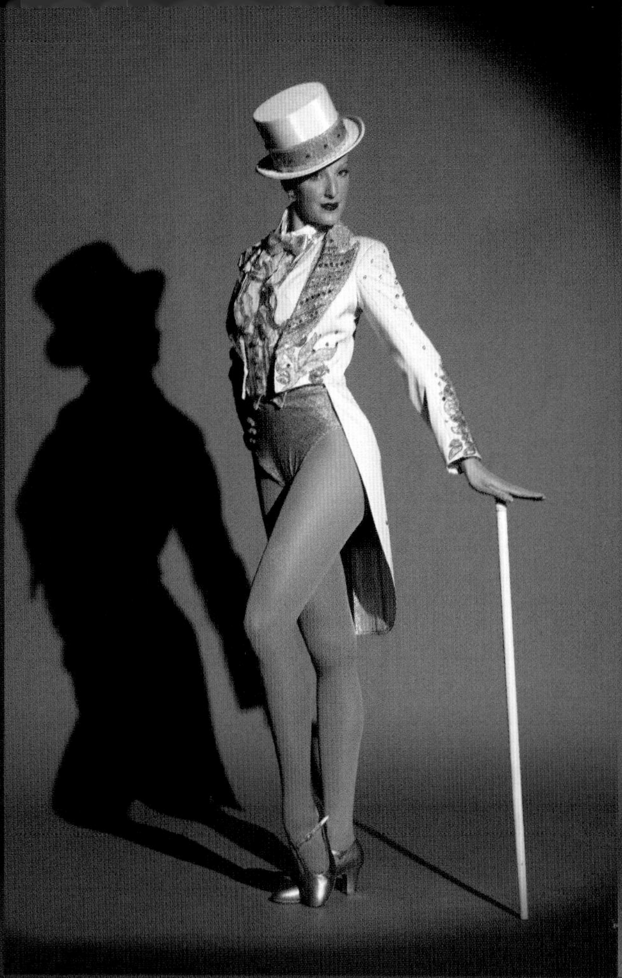
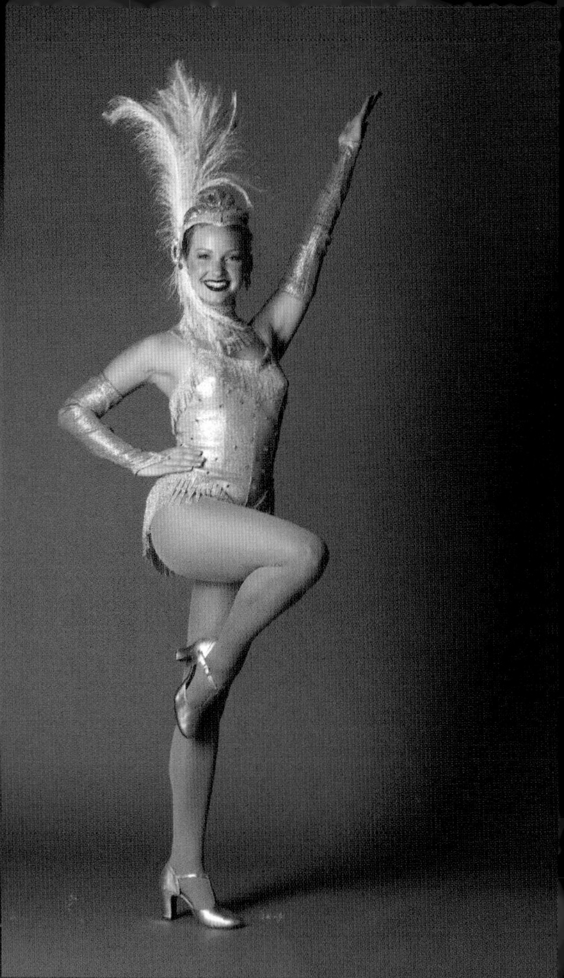
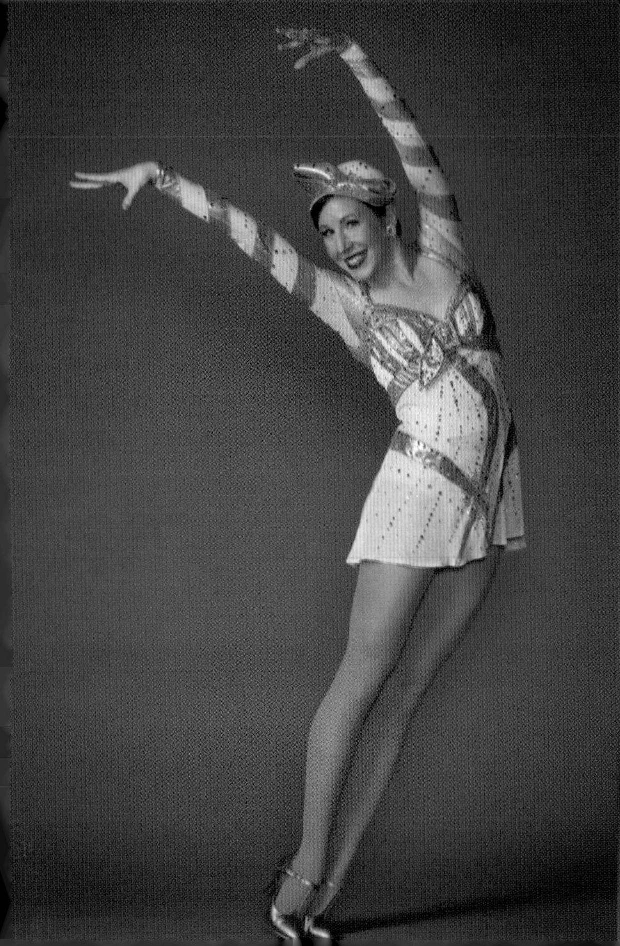
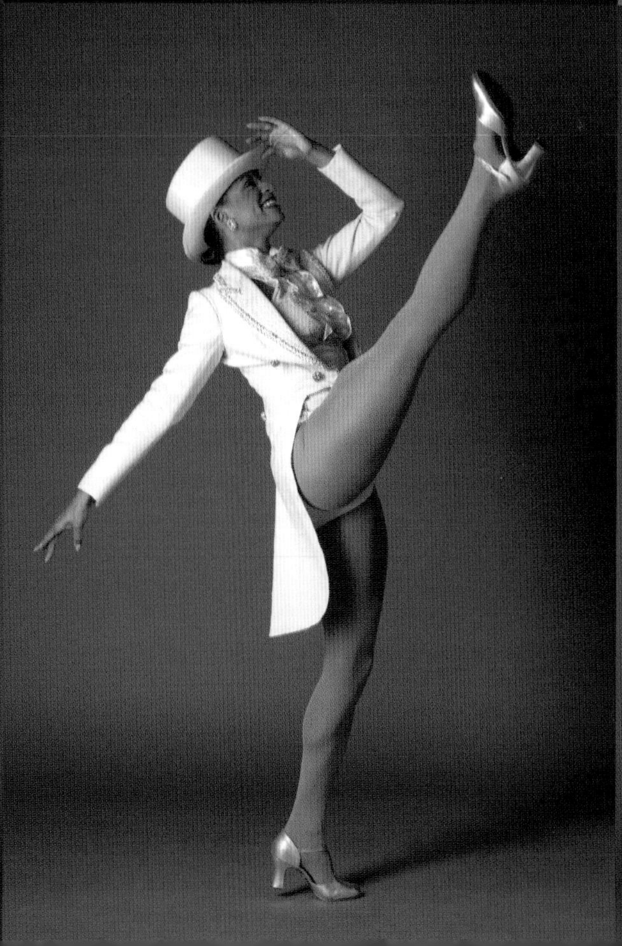
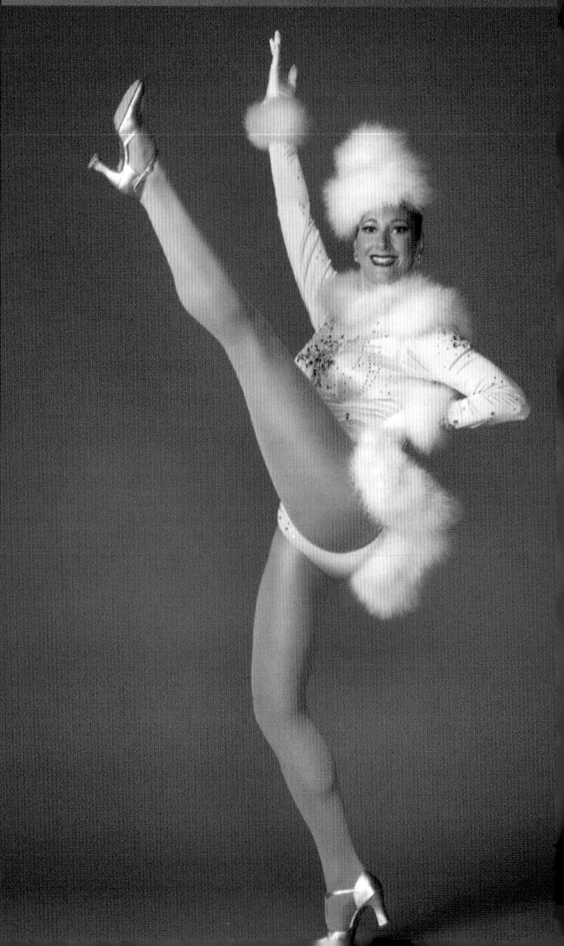

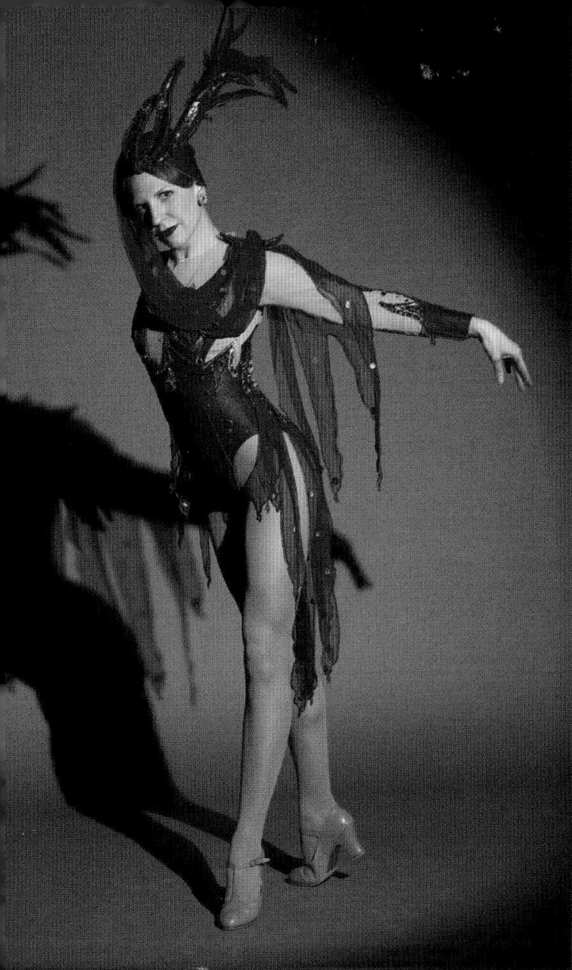
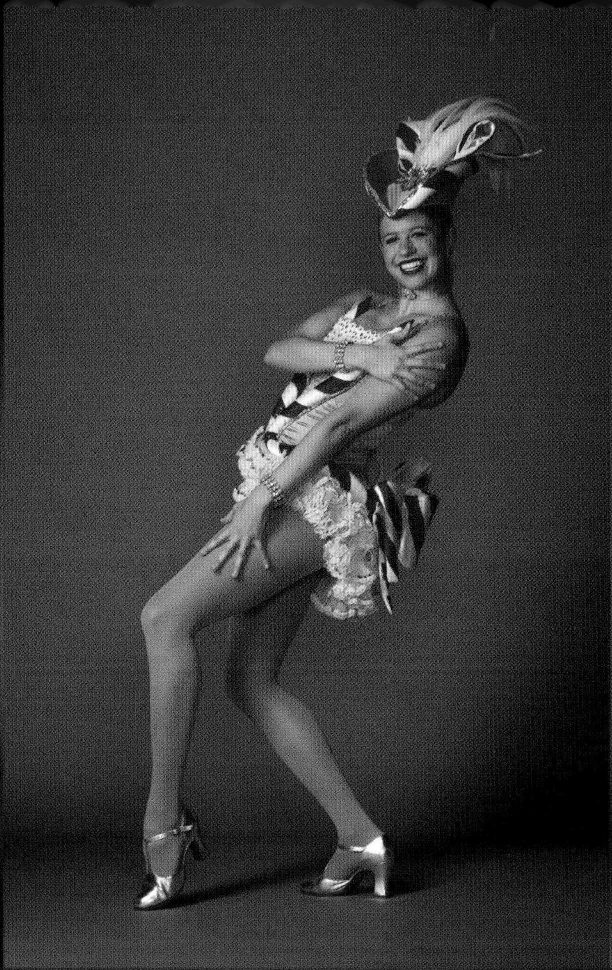
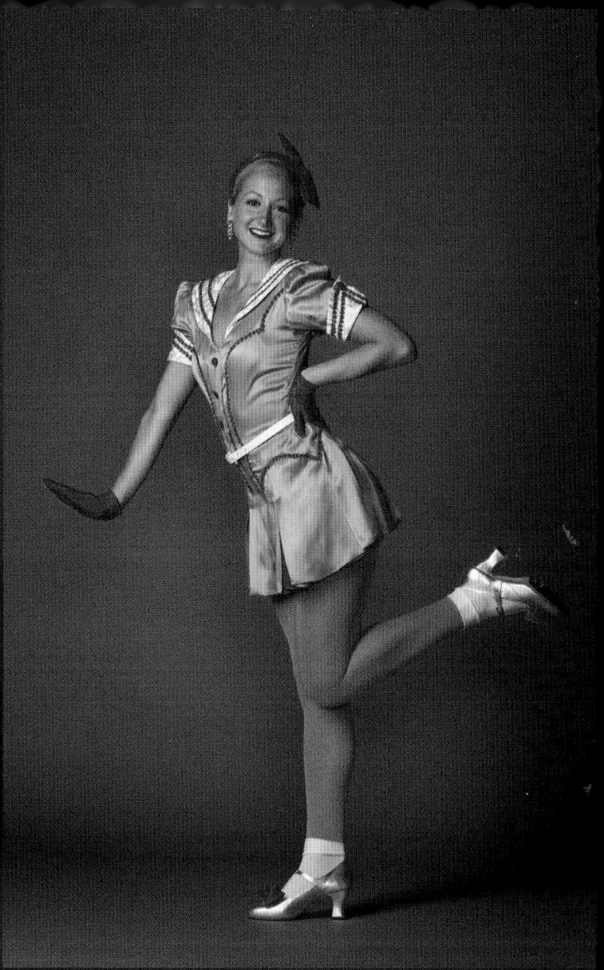
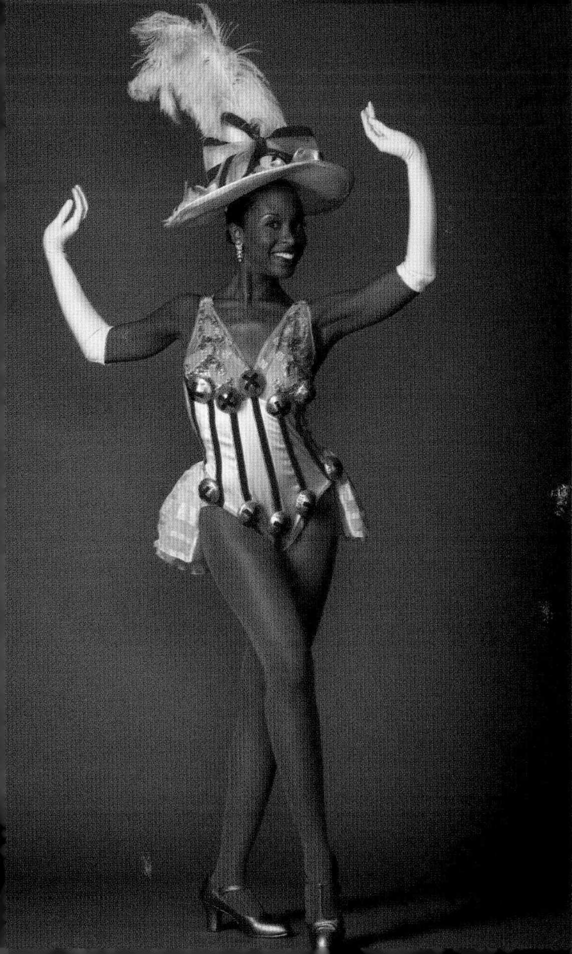
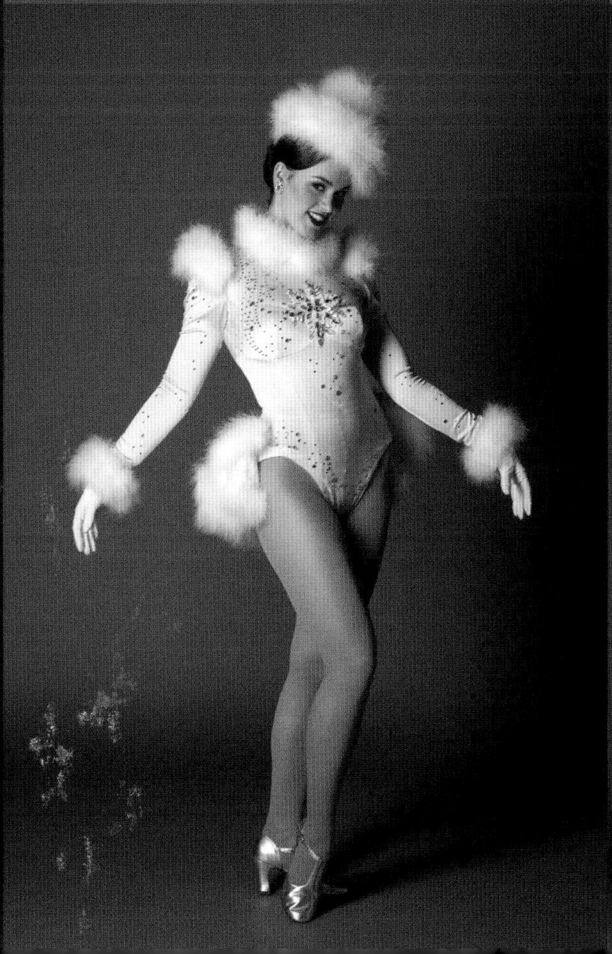
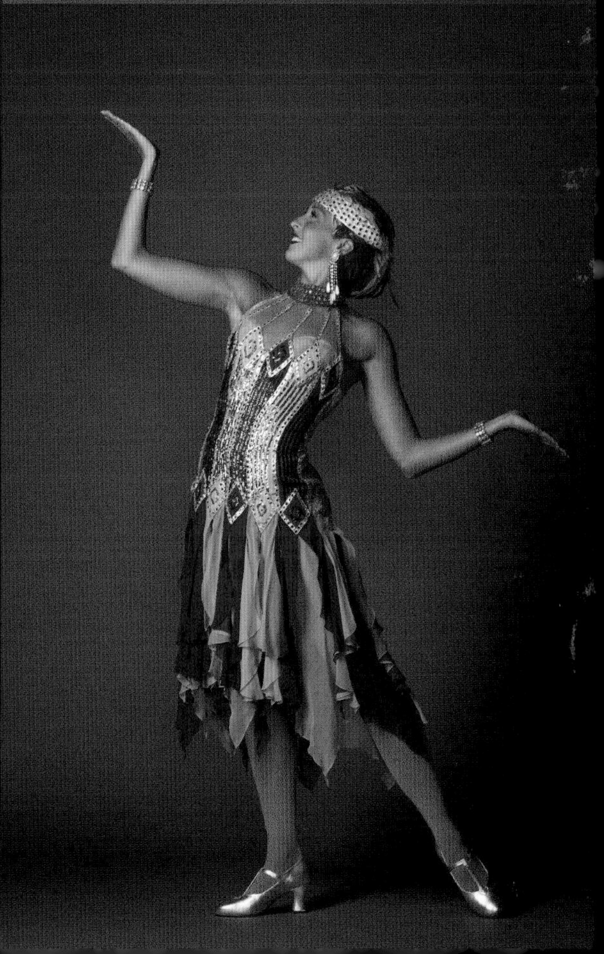

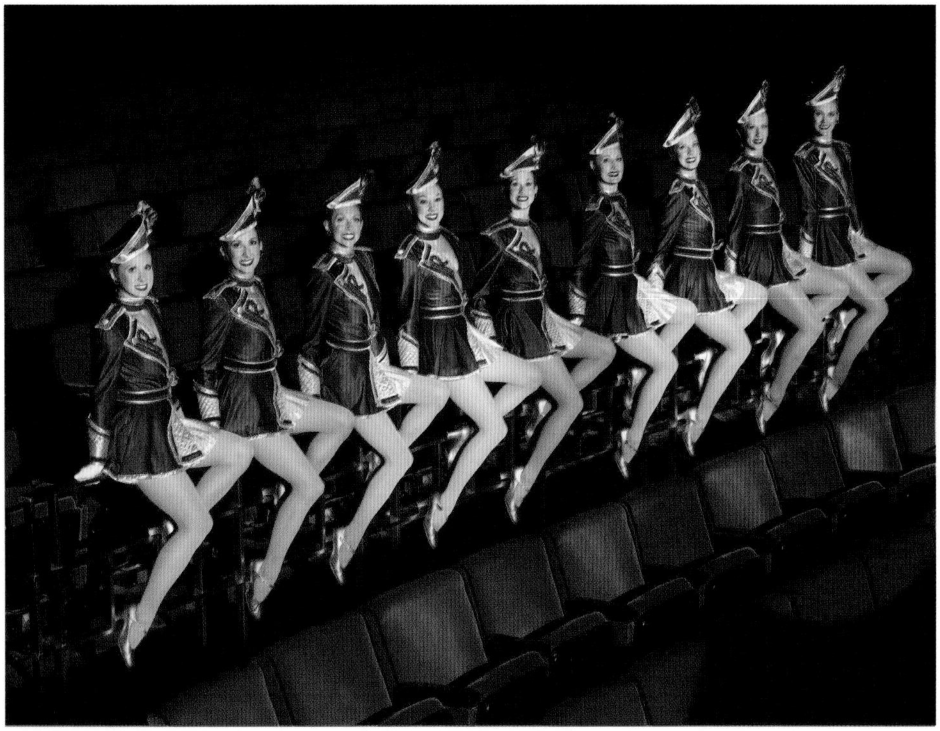

One of the most celebrated auditoriums ever created, the entire space takes up 1.8 million cubic feet.

On the right, the towering arches that frame the stage curve down from the ceiling in a sweeping 180-degree arc and most commonly radiate in golden hues when lit prior to a show.

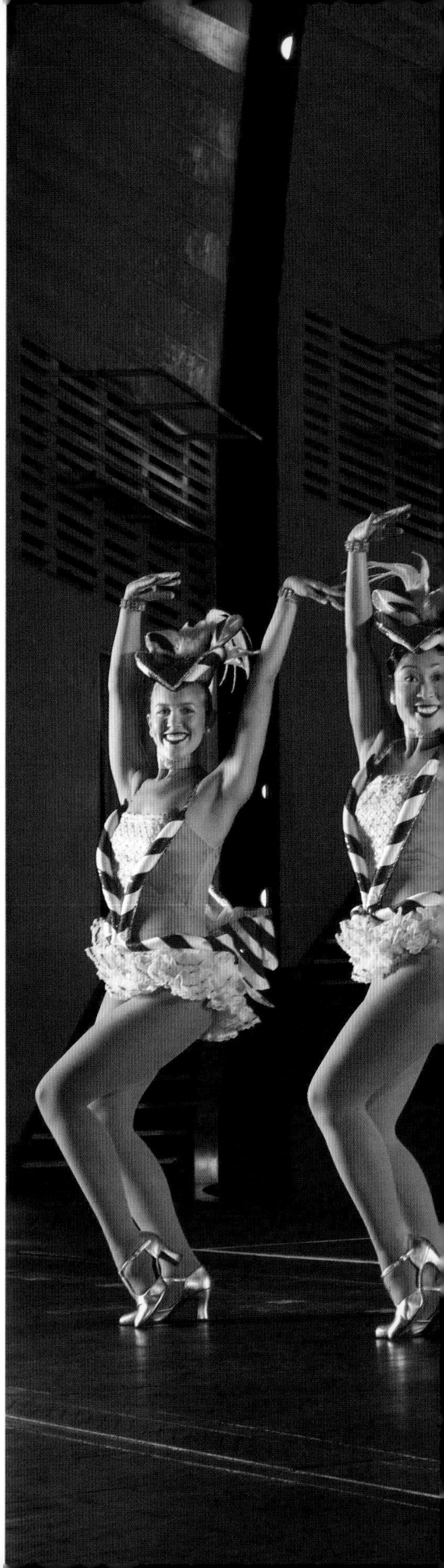

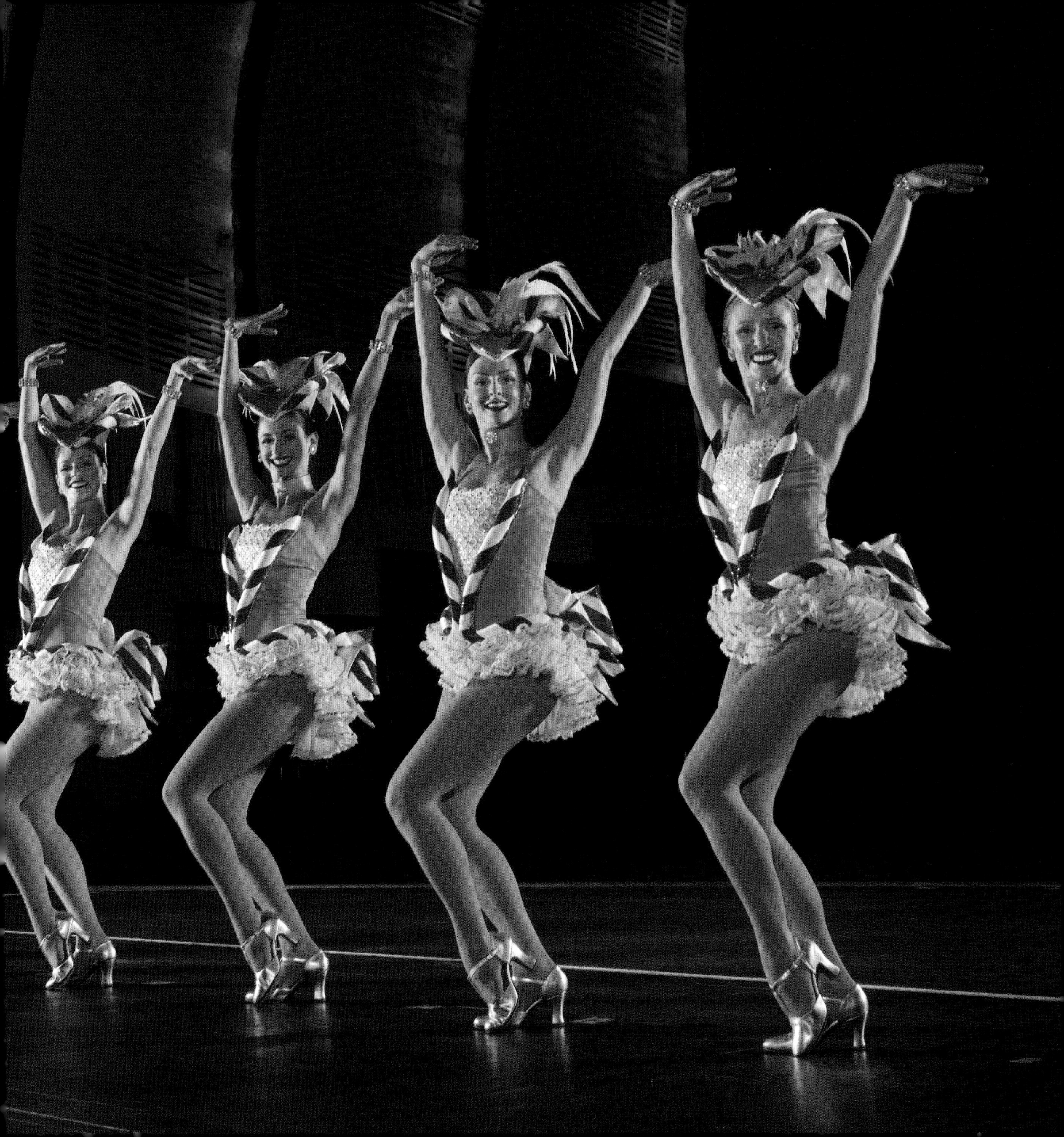

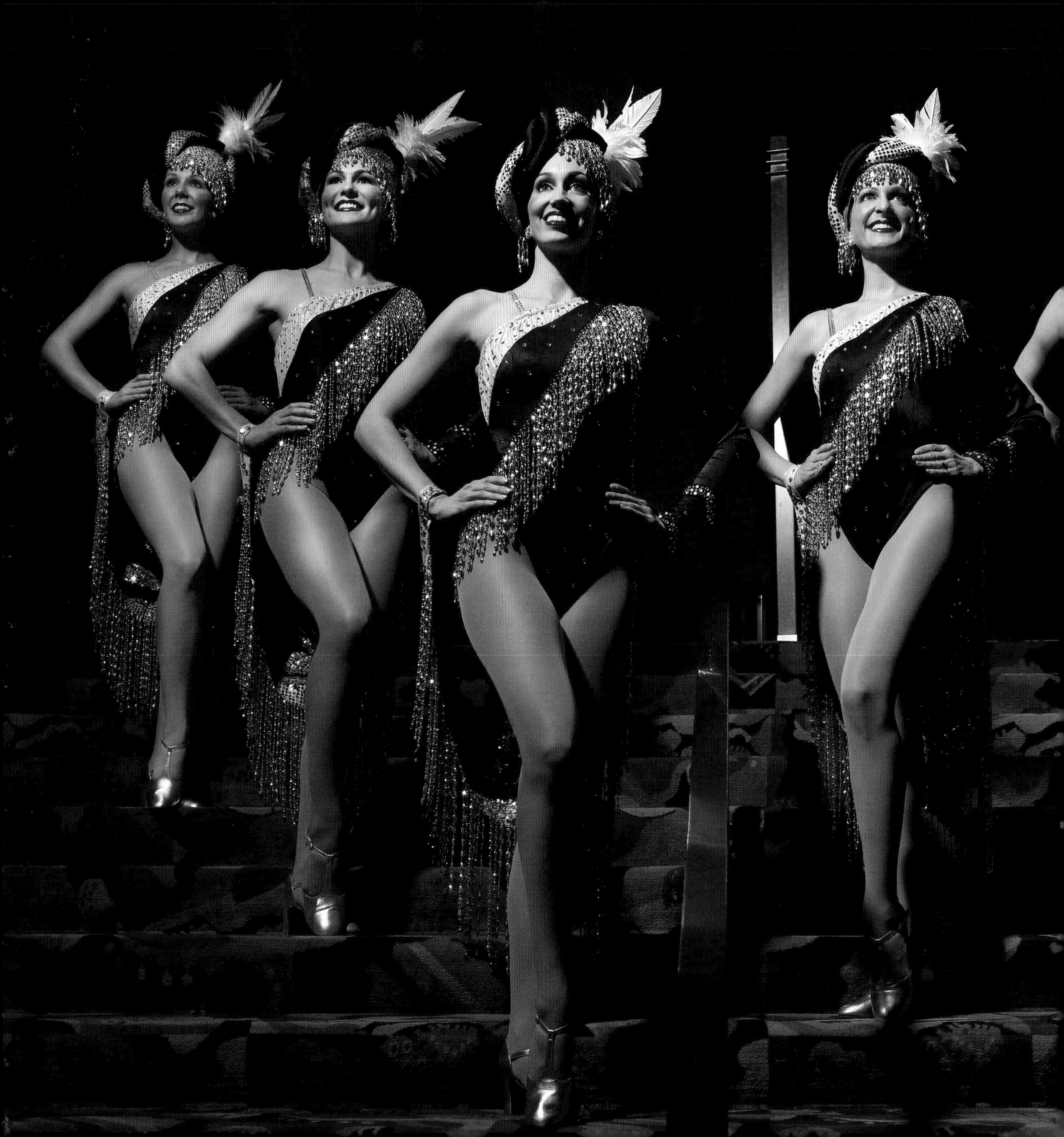

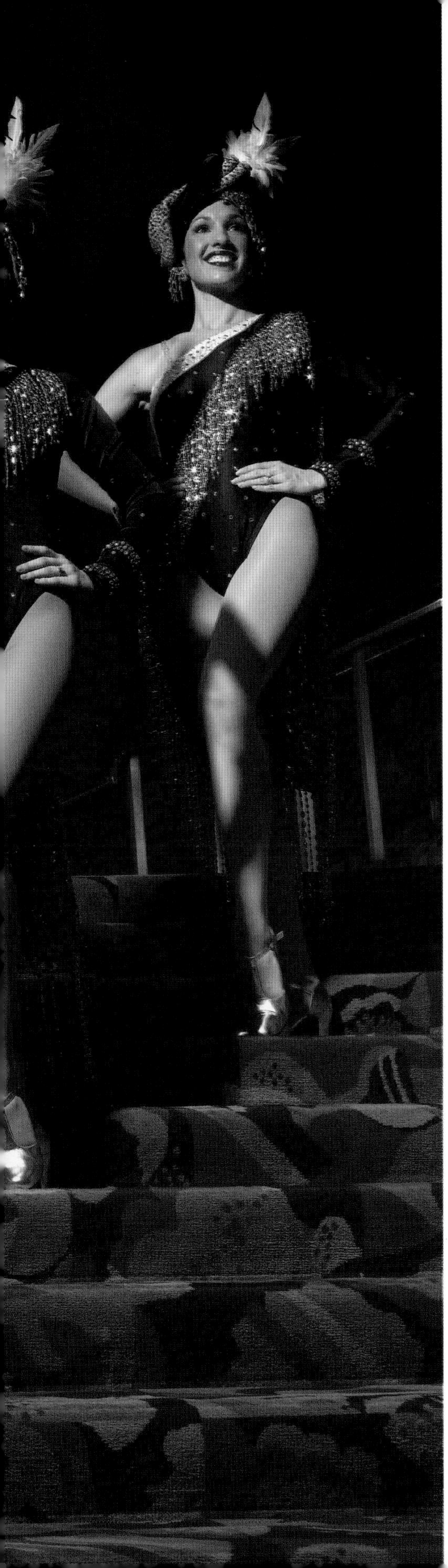

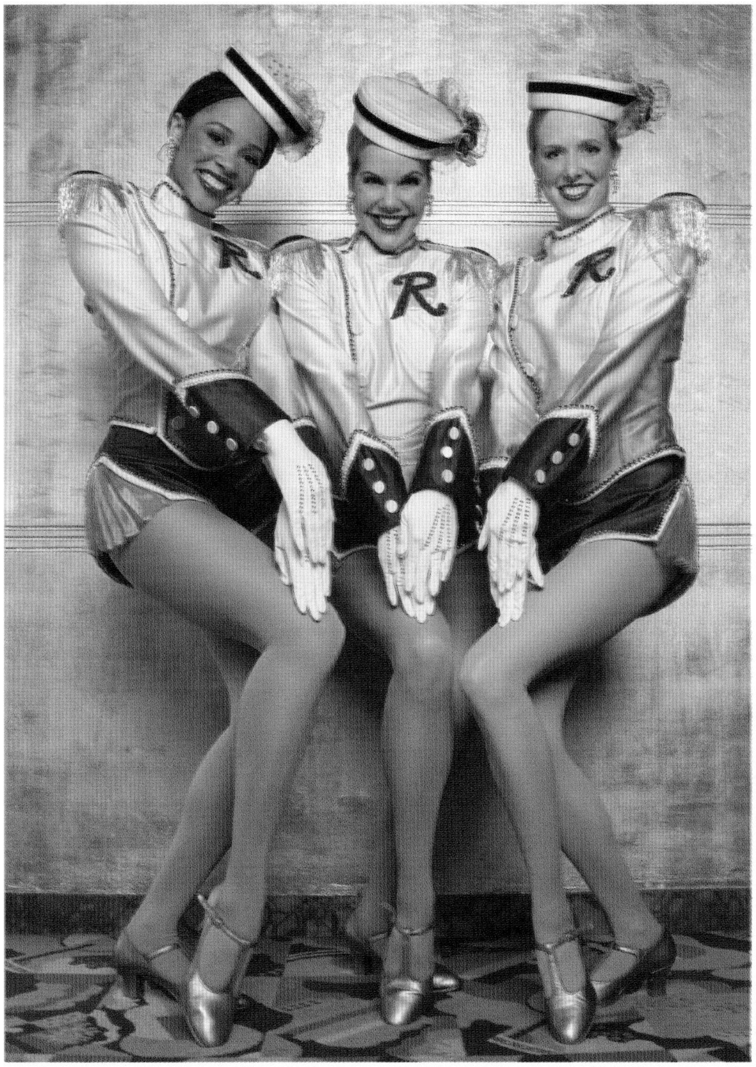

To add to the opulence of the Music Hall, 675,000 sheets of metal leaf were used to cover the ceilings of the Grand Foyer, promenades, and staircases.

At left, Bob Mackie designed this costume in 1982 called "Dancing in Diamonds."

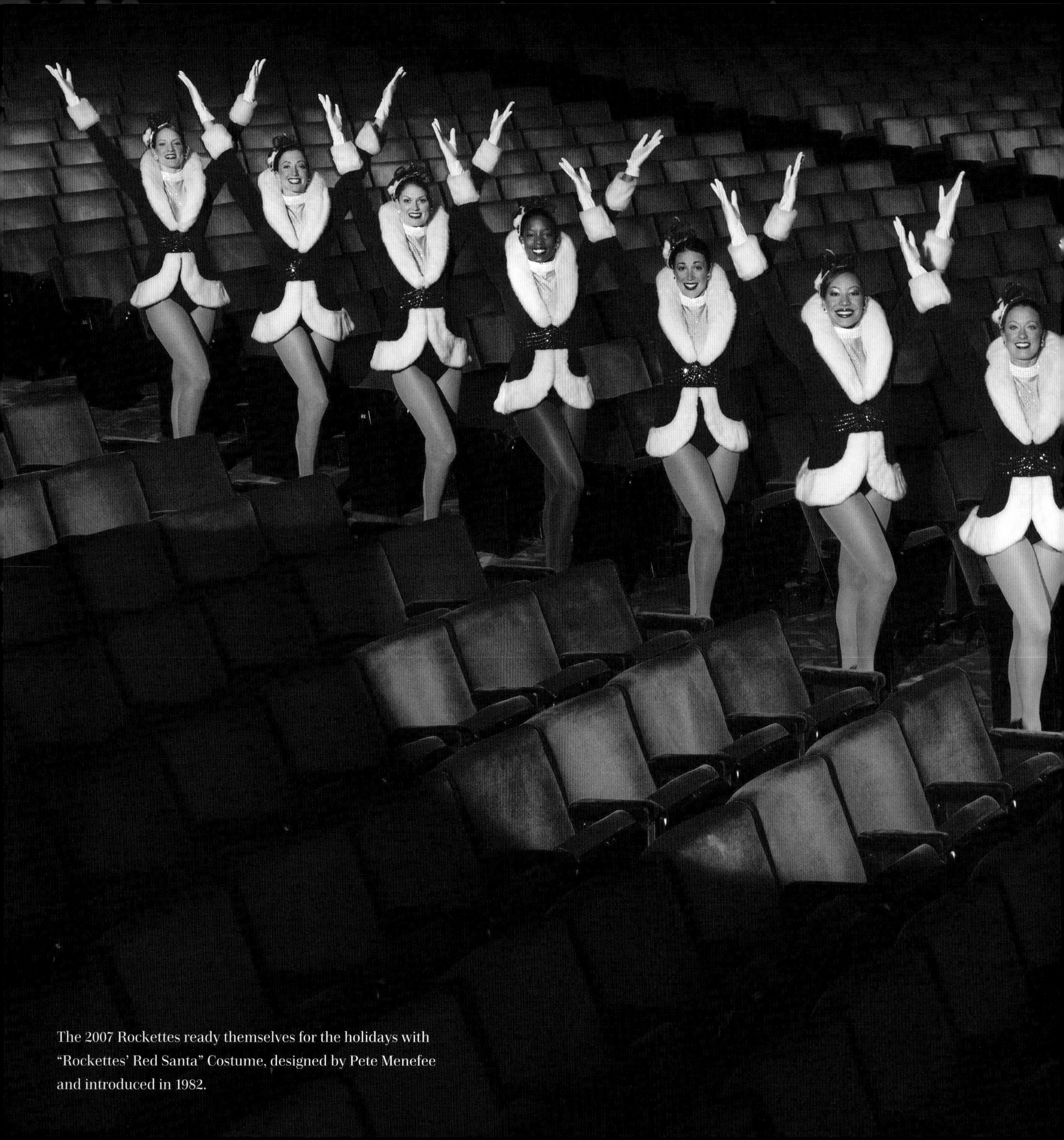

The 2007 Rockettes ready themselves for the holidays with "Rockettes' Red Santa" Costume, designed by Pete Menefee and introduced in 1982.

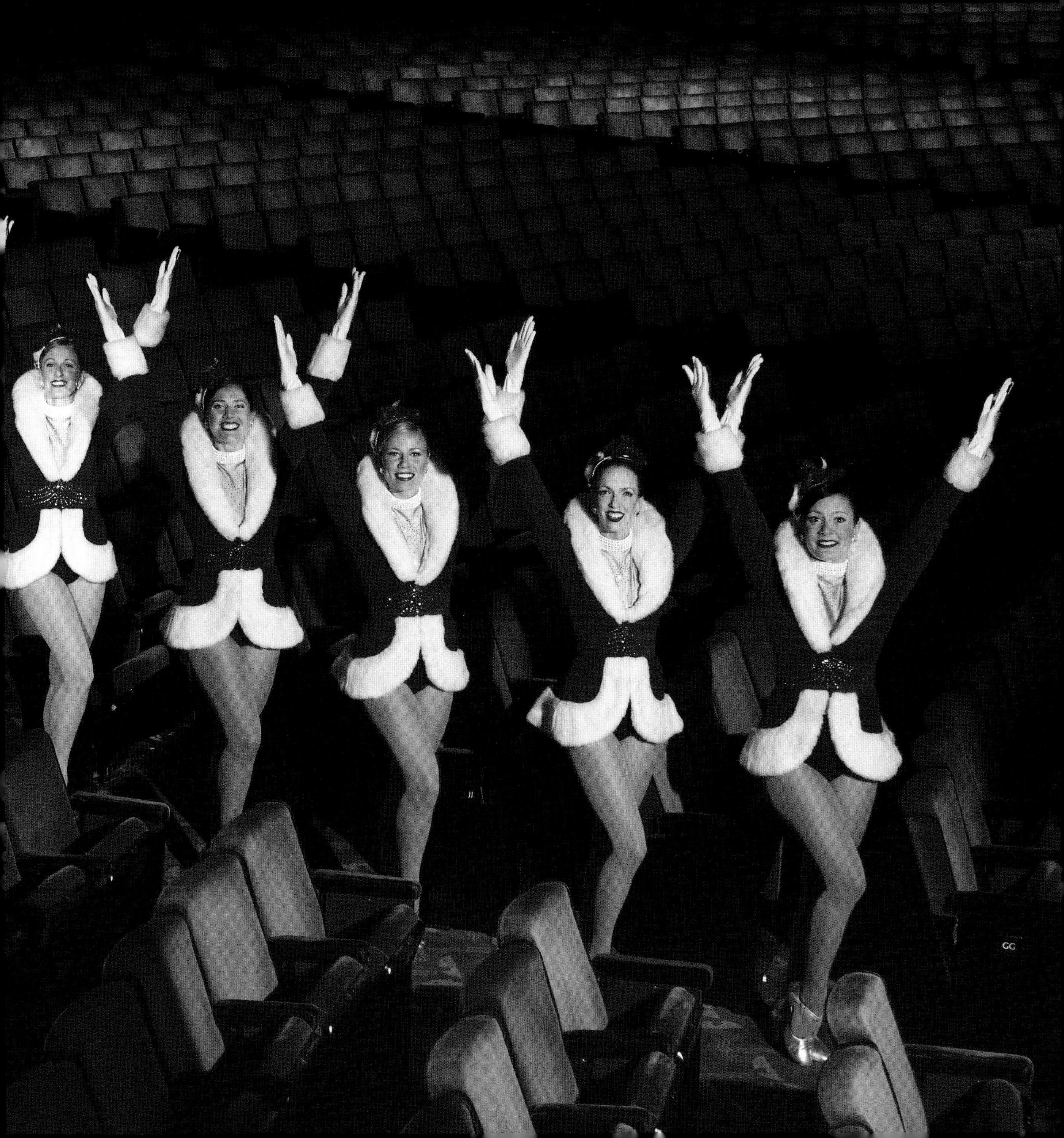
GG

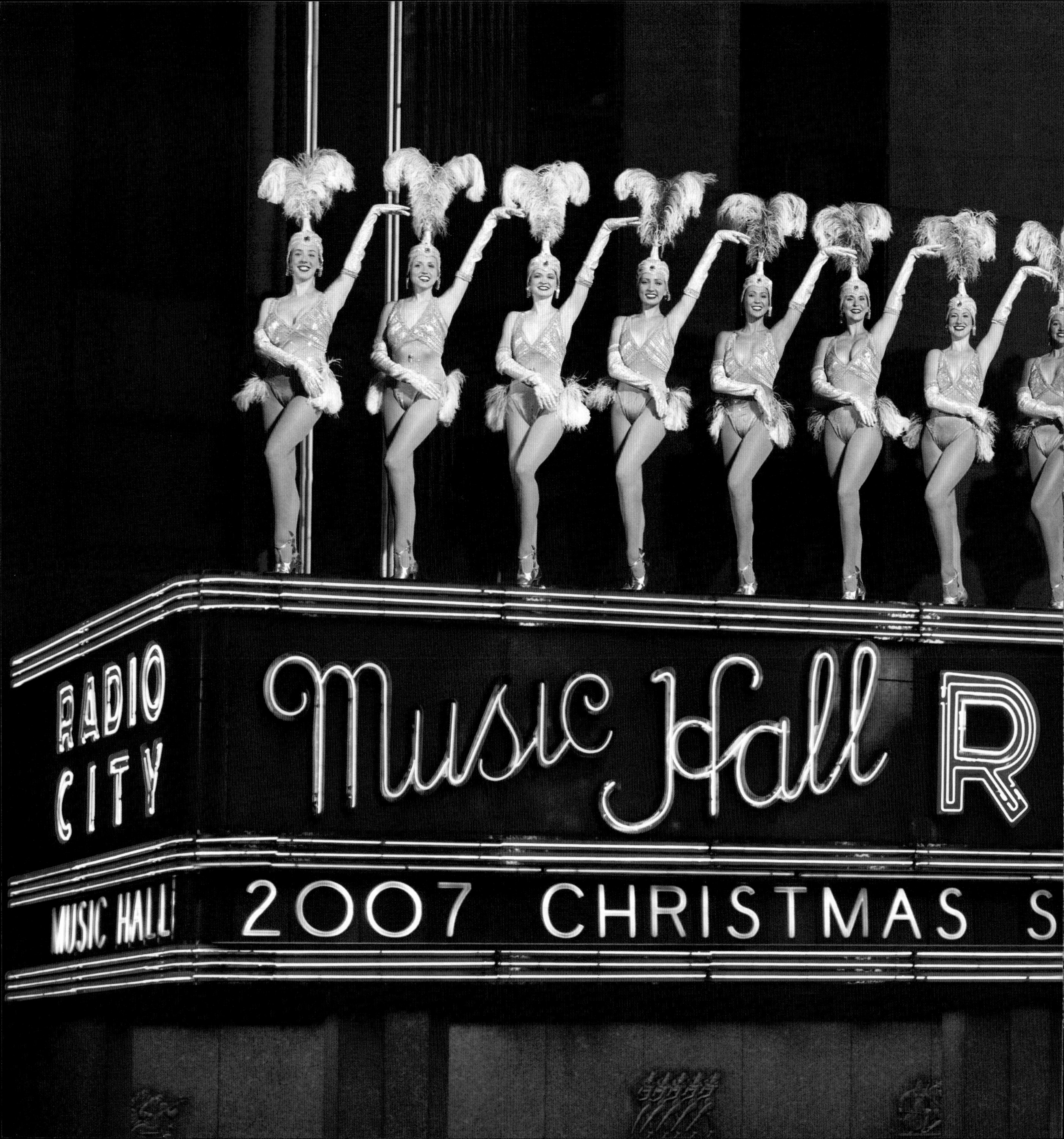
RADIO CITY
Music Hall R
MUSIC HALL
2007 CHRISTMAS S

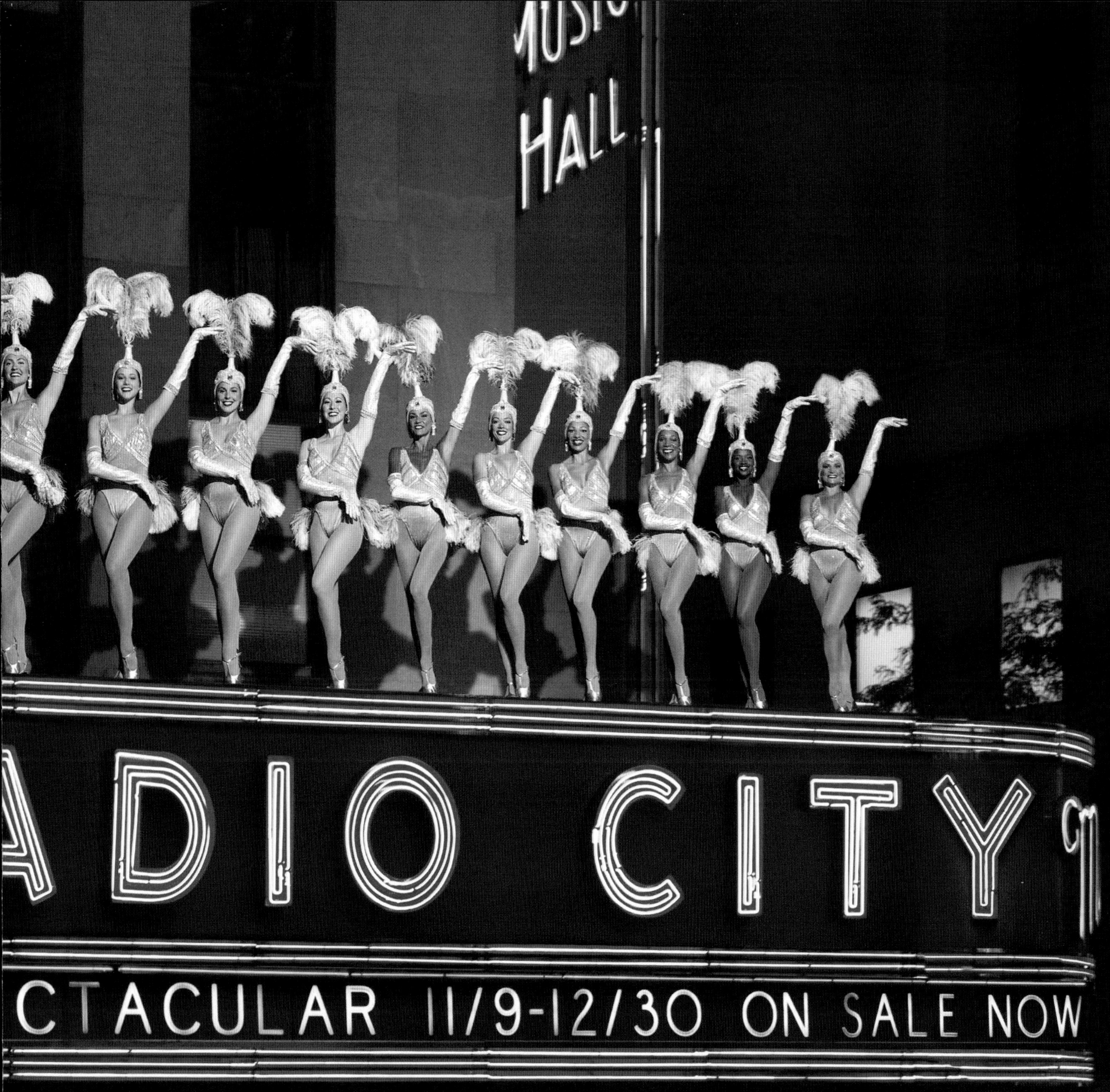
HALL
ADIO CITY
CTACULAR 11/9-12/30 ON SALE NOW

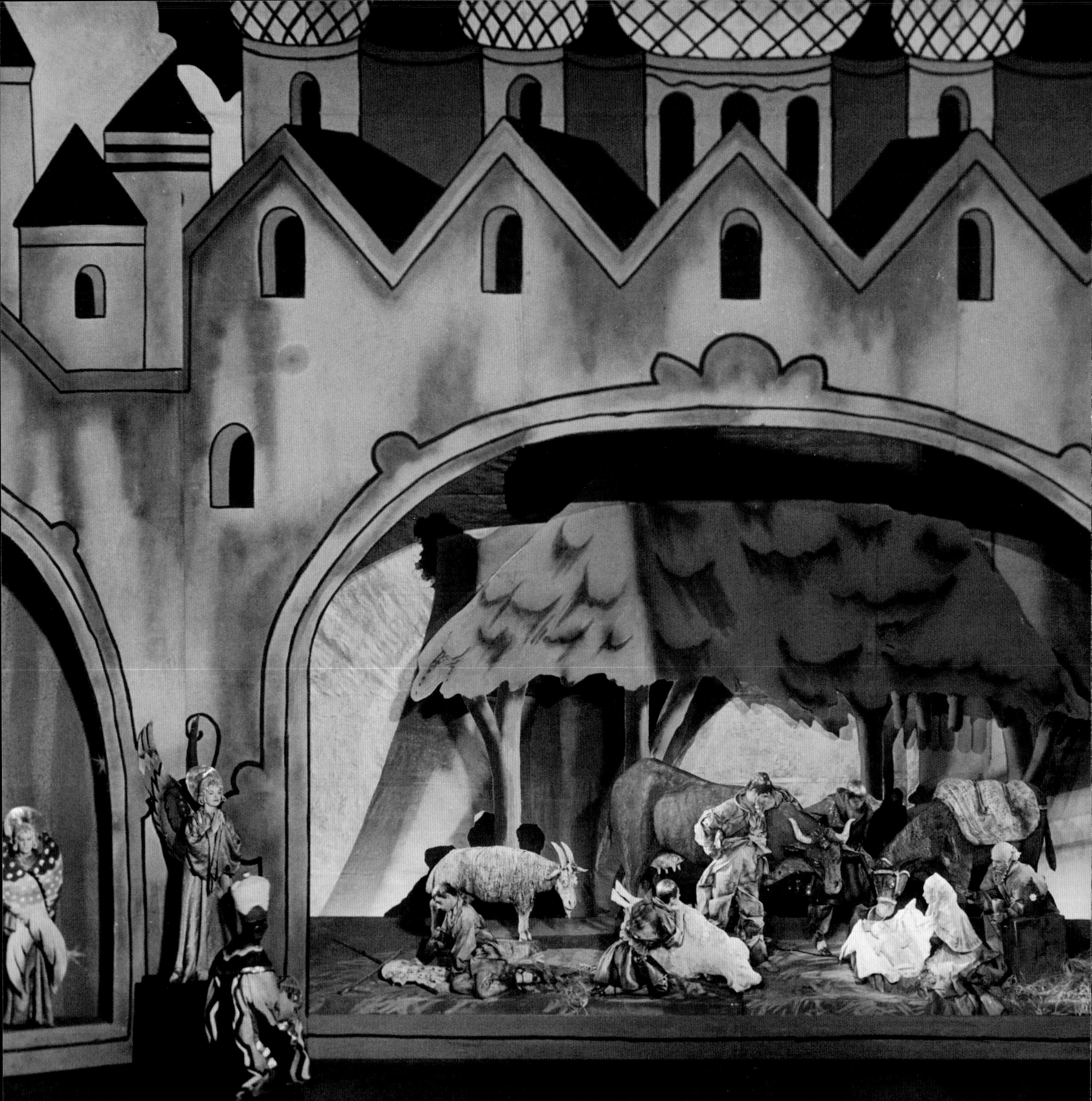

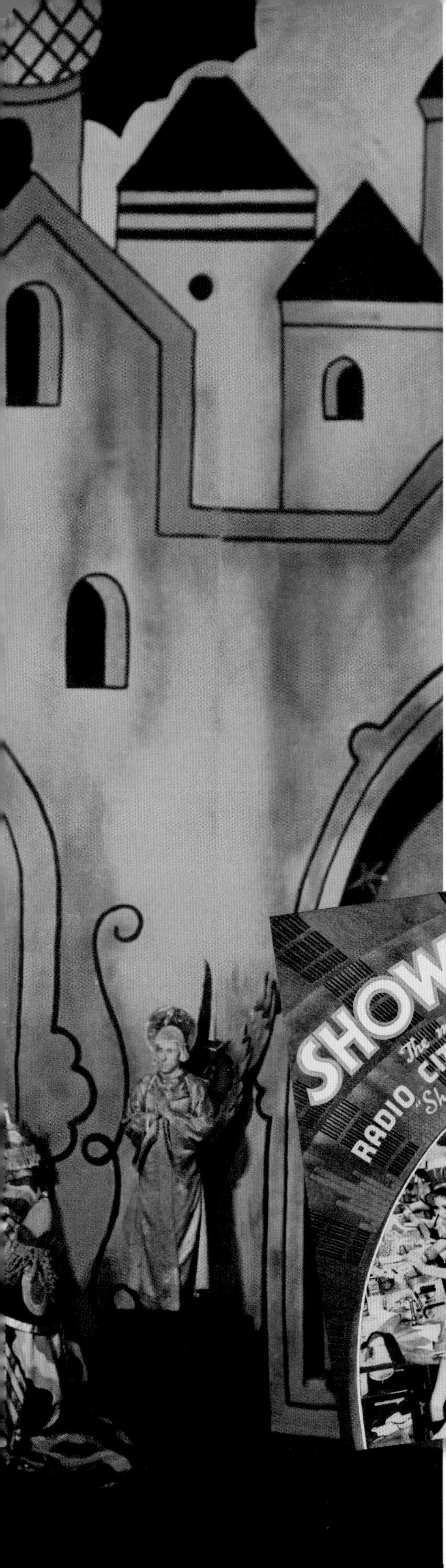

HISTORY OF THE CHRISTMAS SPECTACULAR

Every year, more than a million visitors make the *Radio City Christmas Spectacular* part of their holiday festivities. The eight-week show has been a sellout success since its debut. The original 1933 production was a holiday gift to the movie-going audiences. The show's legendary "Parade of the Wooden Soldiers" and the "Living Nativity" (*left*) scenes were developed and choreographed by Rockettes' founder Russell Markert.

The *Christmas Spectacular* continued to be presented annually as a live performance coupled with the top movie premiere of the day for decades to come. In 1978, Radio City Music Hall was slated to close due to financial problems. The Rockettes led the crusade to save the theatre. In 1978, the Music Hall was designated a New York City Landmark (it was designated a National Historic Landmark in 1987). The movie-and-stage-show format remained a Radio City signature until 1979, when the mass showcasing of new films called for a different focus and full feature productions were re-introduced, such as the *Radio City Christmas Spectacular*.

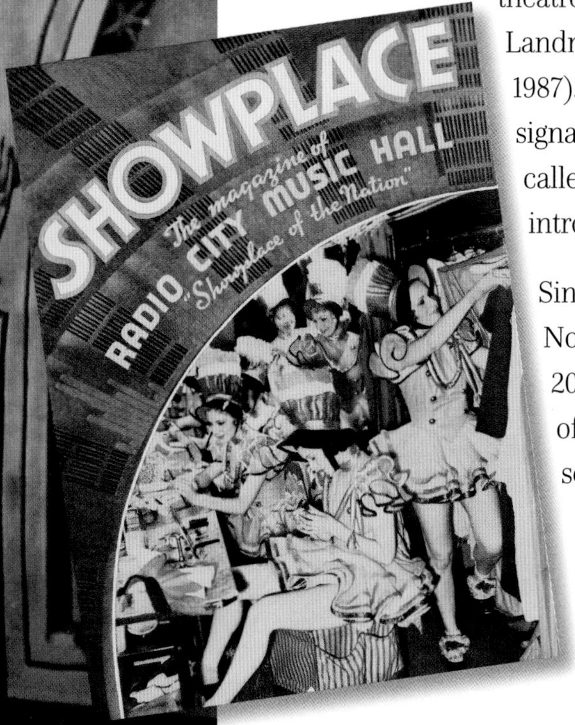

Since 1994, the *Christmas Spectacular* has gone on the road. Now, it plays to enthusiastic audiences across the country. In 2007, the *Radio City Christmas Spectacular* celebrates 75 years of continuous celebration of Christmas and the holiday season in New York City.

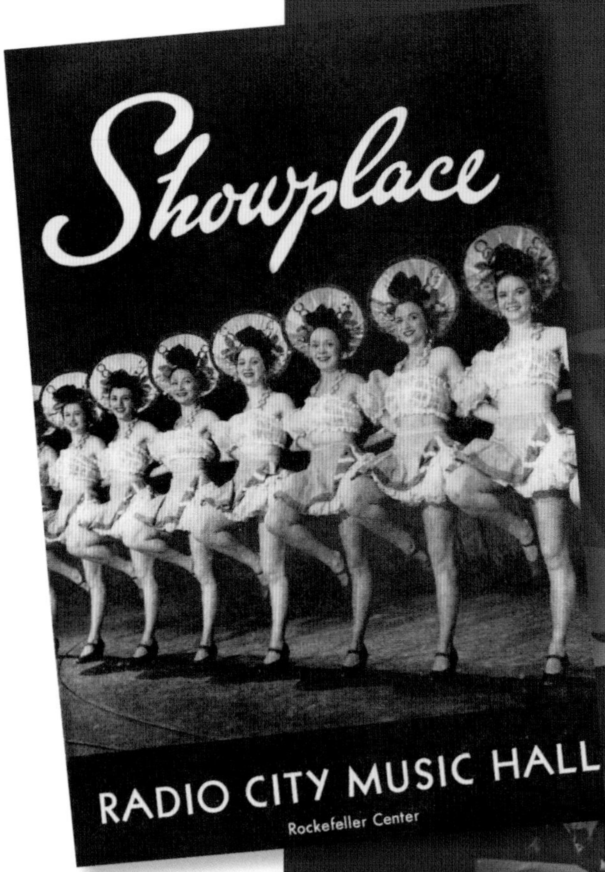

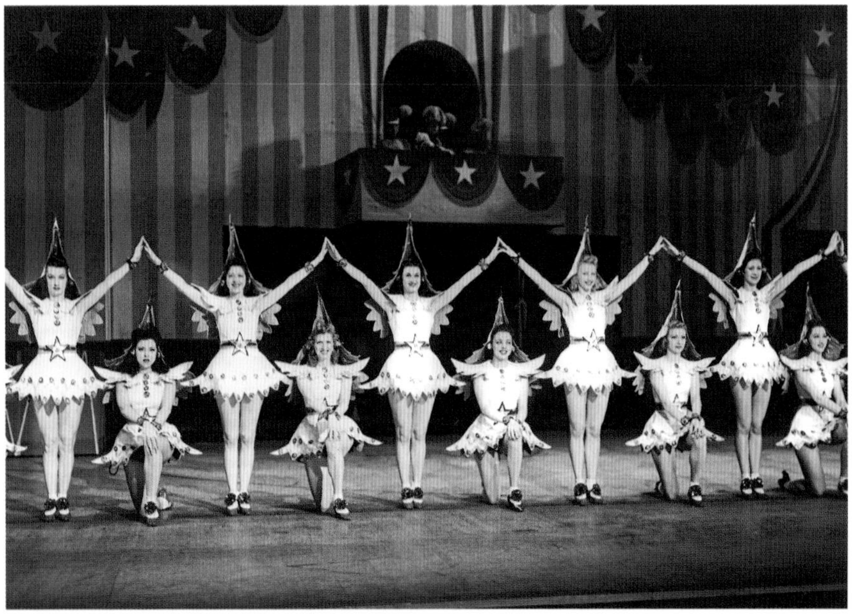

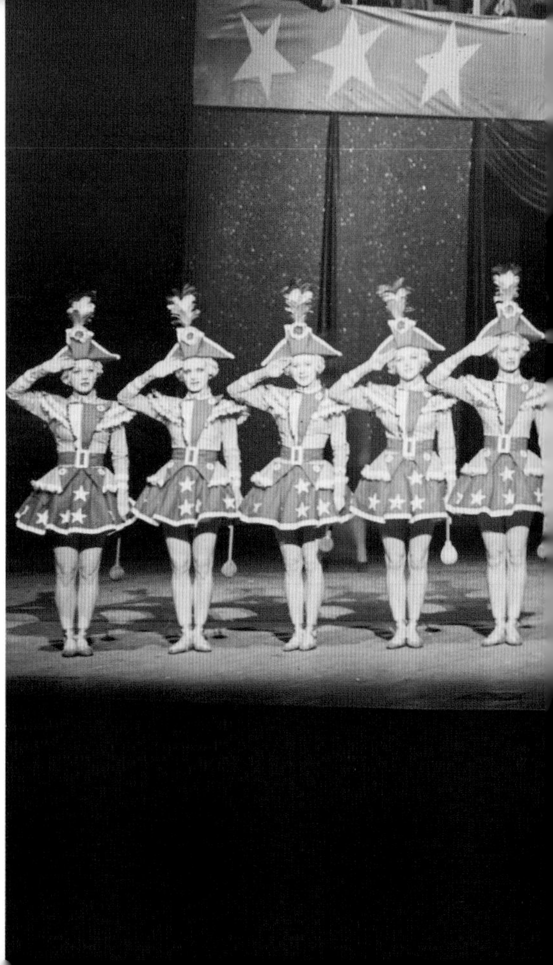

The glittering production of the "Star Bright" is presented here in this 1944 photo.

On the right is a photo of "Kris Kringle's Carnival." The Rockettes are captured with the year's Christmas salute.

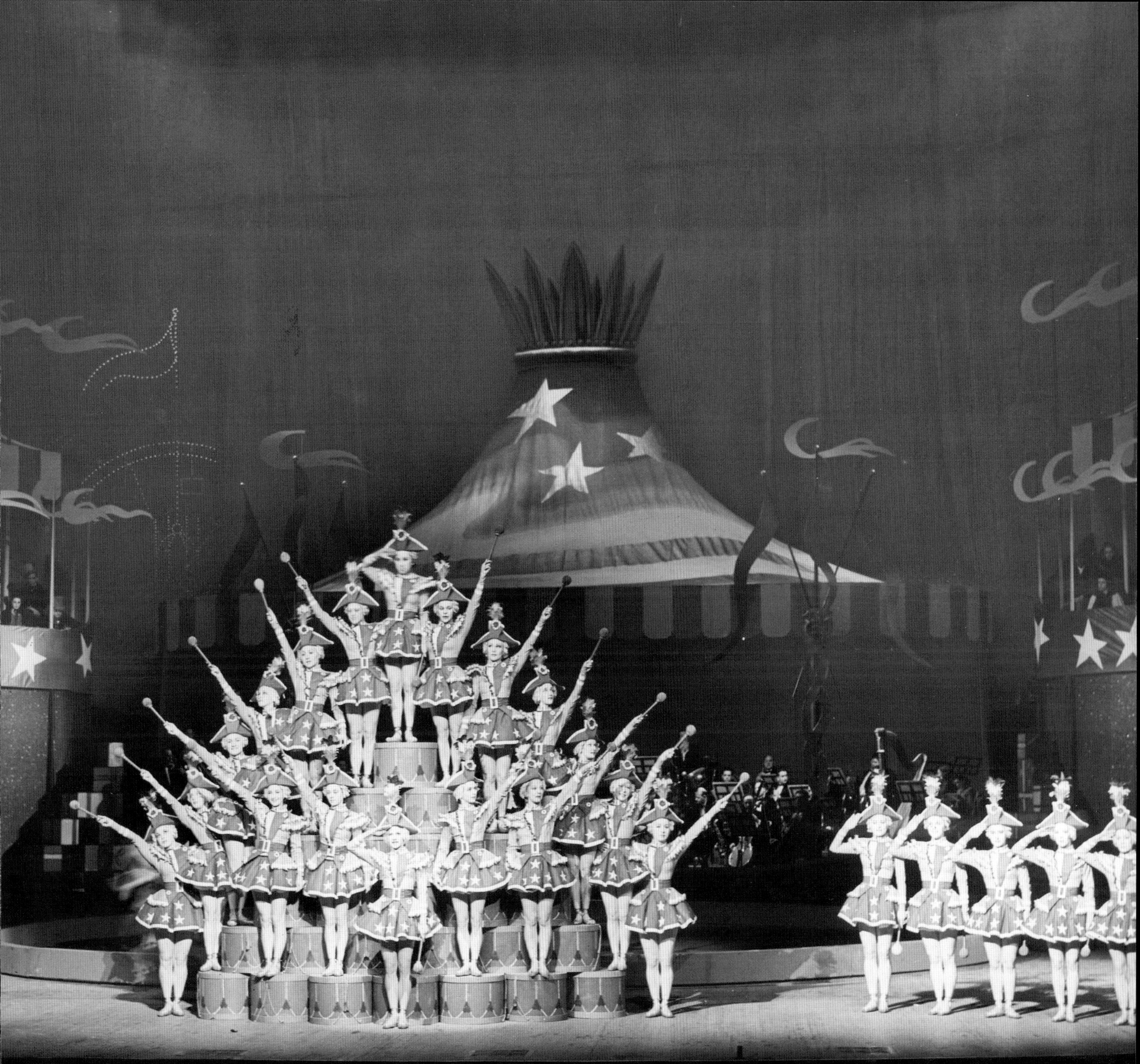

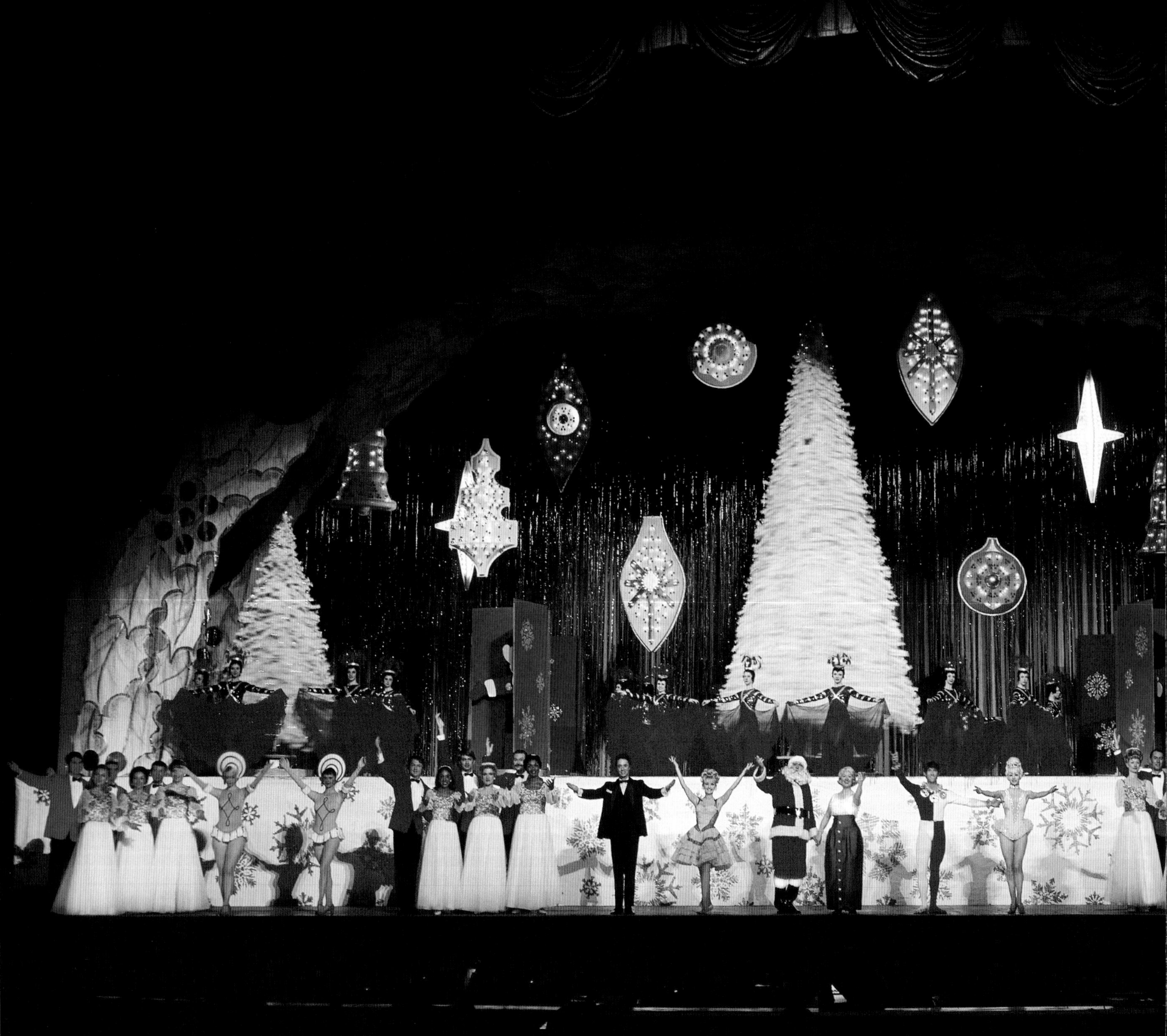

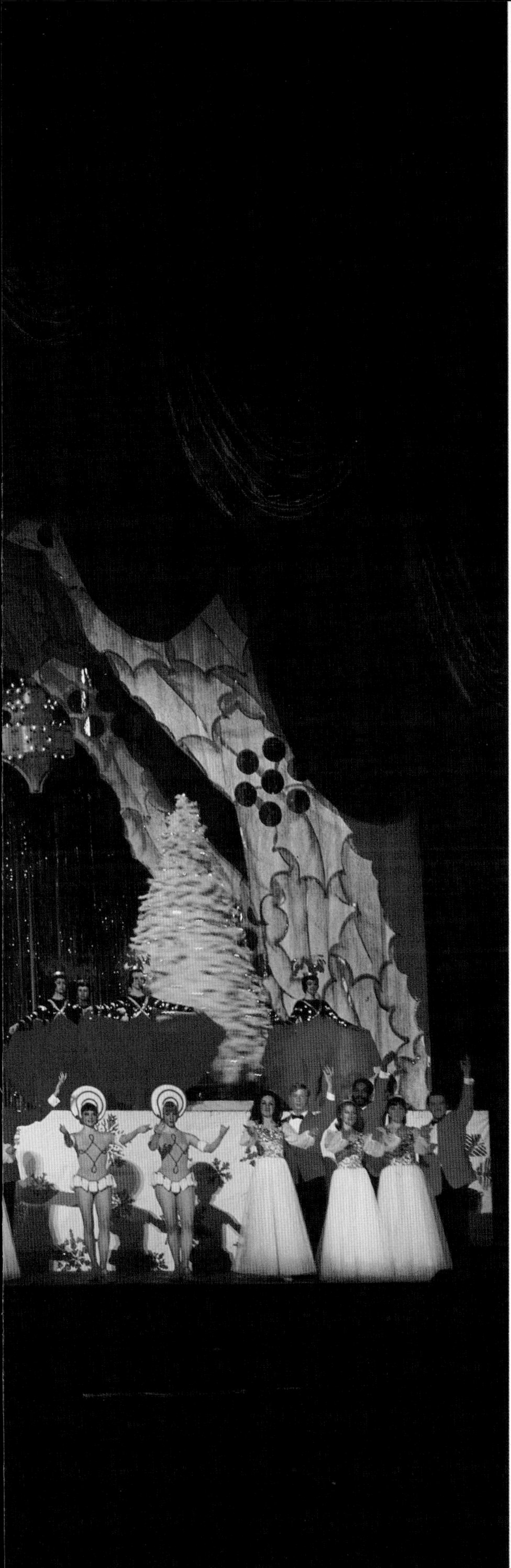

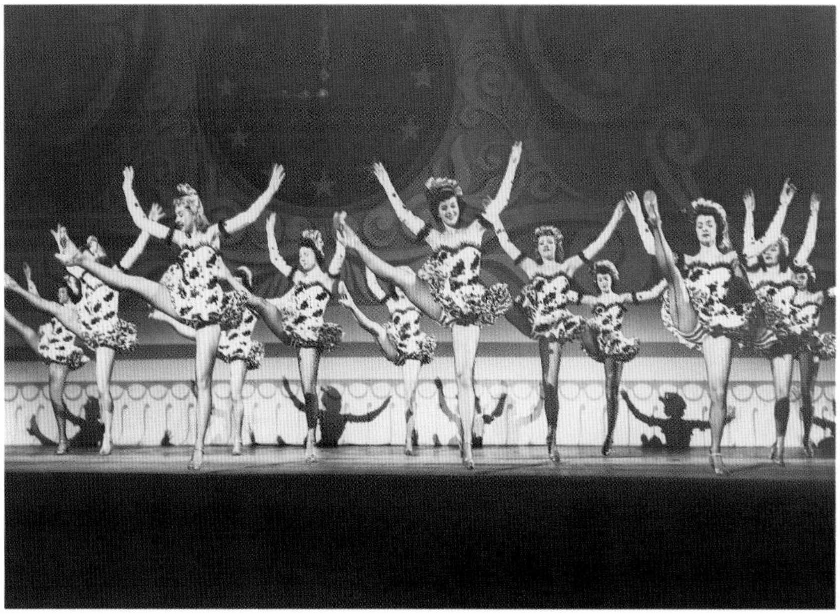

Vincente Minnelli's "Kismet" charmed the audience this Christmas and Radio City welcomed back its original art director, who created the costumes and sets for which Radio City became known.

On the left is the 1958 Chistmas Show Grand Finale scene including Santa Claus and all the trimmings. The film feature for that year was *The Impossible Years.*

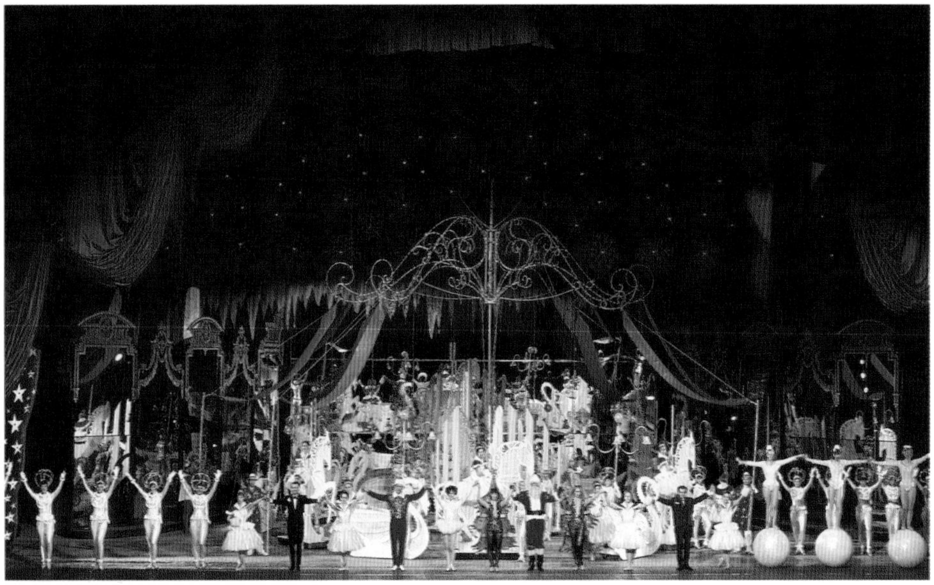

In 1960, Deborah Kerr and Robert Mitchum's high drama The Sundowners *premiered this Christmas season and our live stage show was produced by the Rockettes' one and only, Russell Markert.*

On the right, the inimitable Ray Bolger starred in this holiday treat, "Babes in Toyland," along with Annette and Ed Wynn. Bolger had an earlier history with Radio City, having performed in the opening night gala that Roxy produced. Also starring in that show, besides the Rockettes, Ballet Company, and all the other Radio City regulars, were the Martha Graham Dancers, The Flying Wallendas, and many, many others.

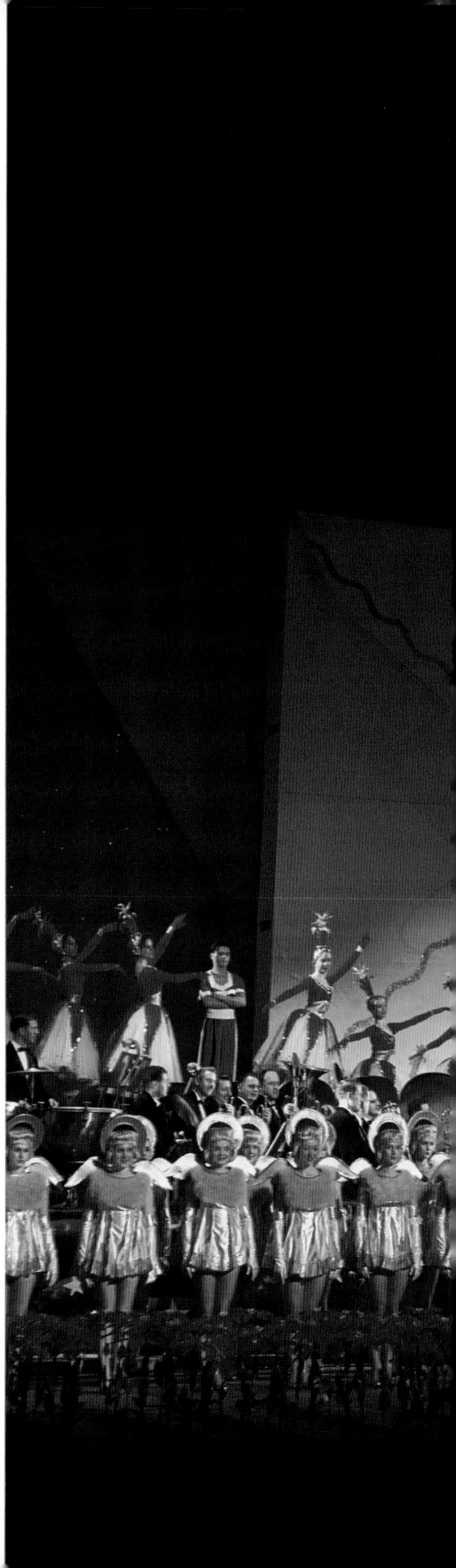

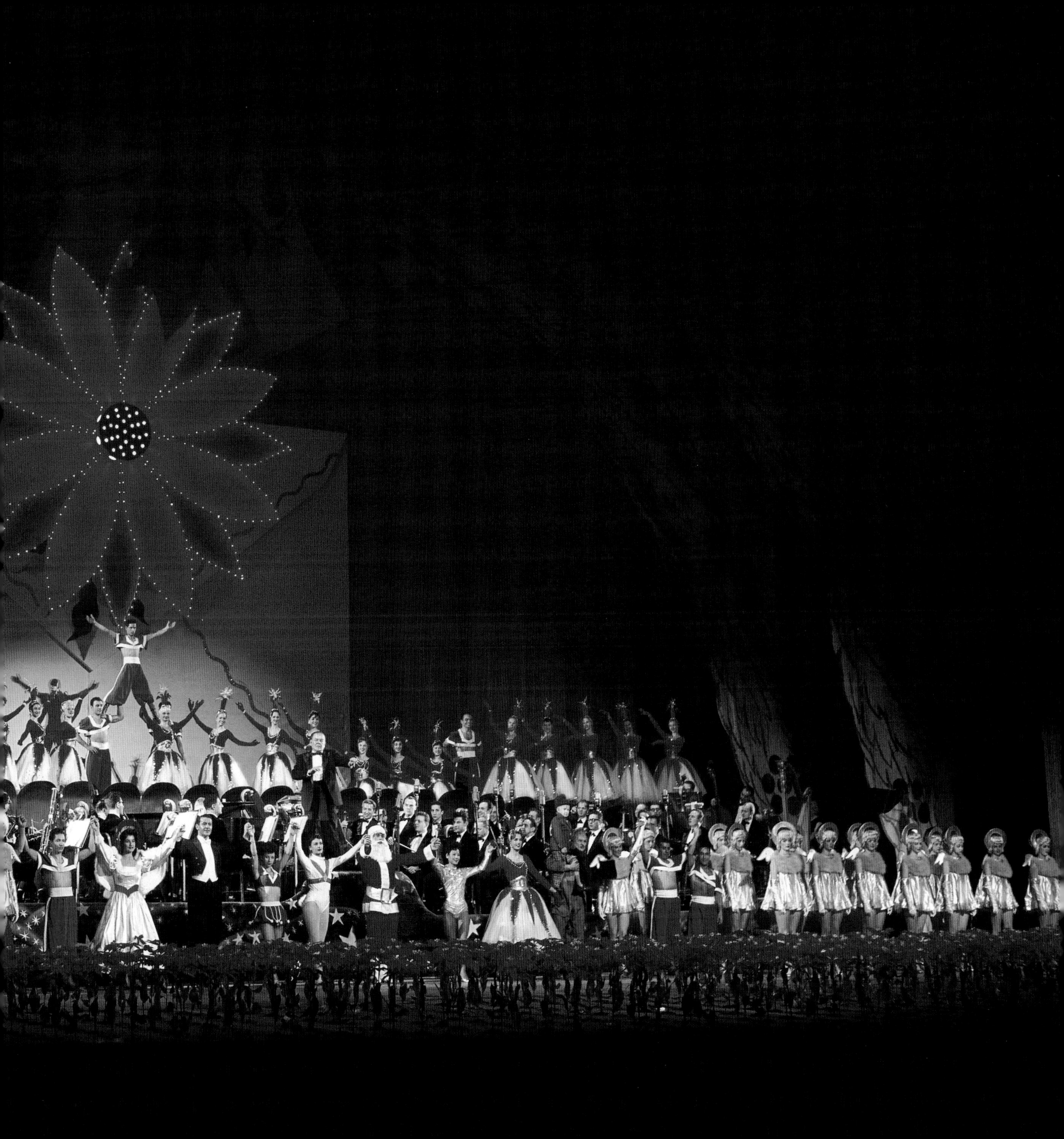

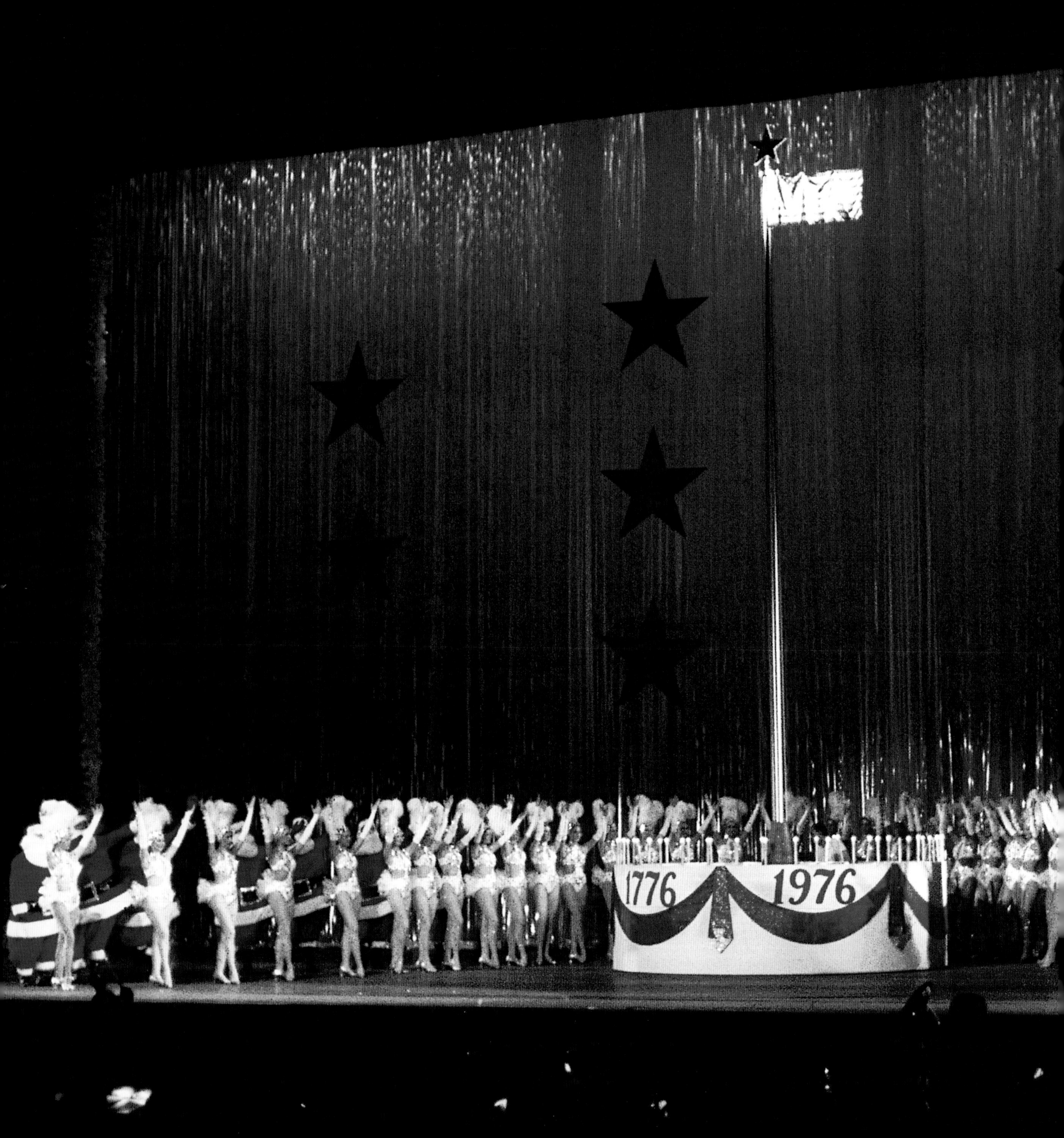
1776
1976

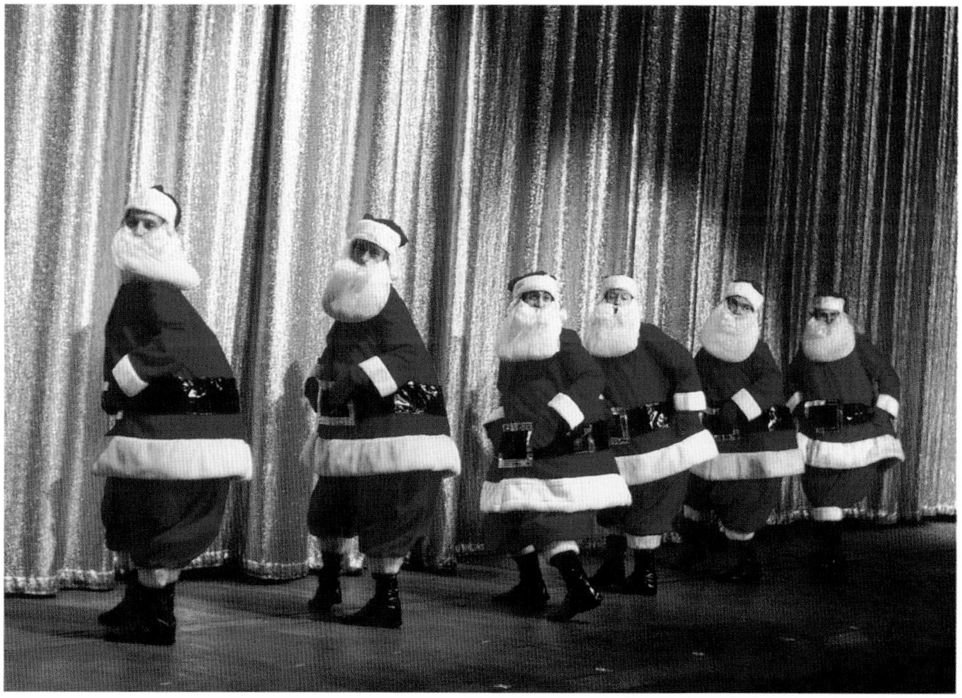

The 90-minute all-live Christmas Show that the public now knows and loves began in 1979. Radio City did not miss one year of celebrating this greatest of seasons with its patrons.

On the left, "1776" lit up the Music Hall with a live stage show entitled "Greetings," inspired by themes of Hallmark Cards. The Salvation Army "Femail" Carriers and a comedian named "Will B. Able" performed the Christmas Show this year.

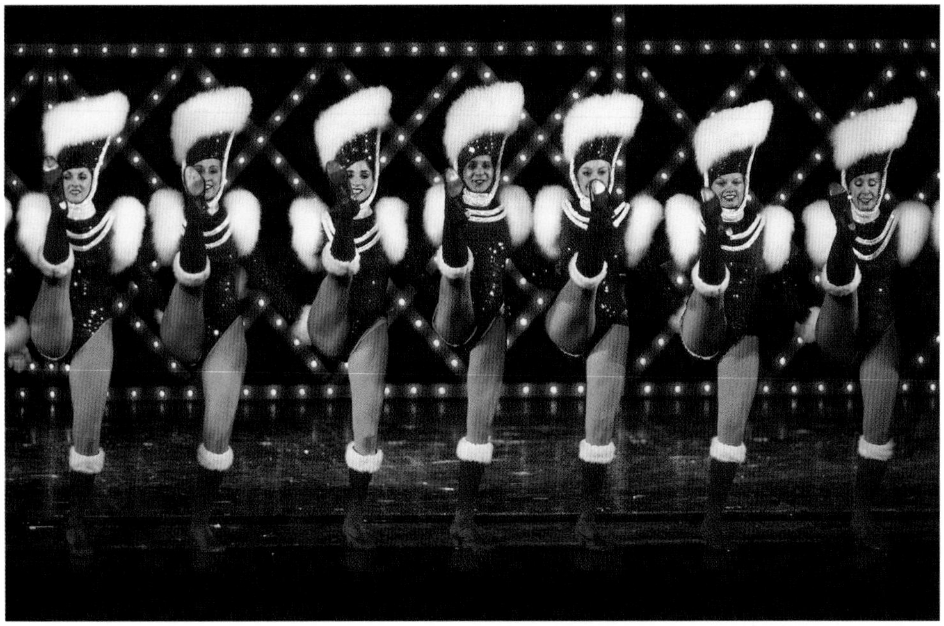

In 1994, the Christmas Show was "on the road." This was the first year the production was held outside of New York and Branson, Missouri was the first location.

In 1997, Radio City Music Hall had reached another crisis period in its history and was at risk to close. The Music Hall needed a new lease on life and that lease came in the form of a 25-year lease by Cablevision Systems, who not only kept the Christmas Show running and the Rockettes kicking, but closed the theater after the 1997 Christmas Show for a complete theater restoration, to reopen in October of 1999 with a gala celebration never seen before in the annals of Radio City history.

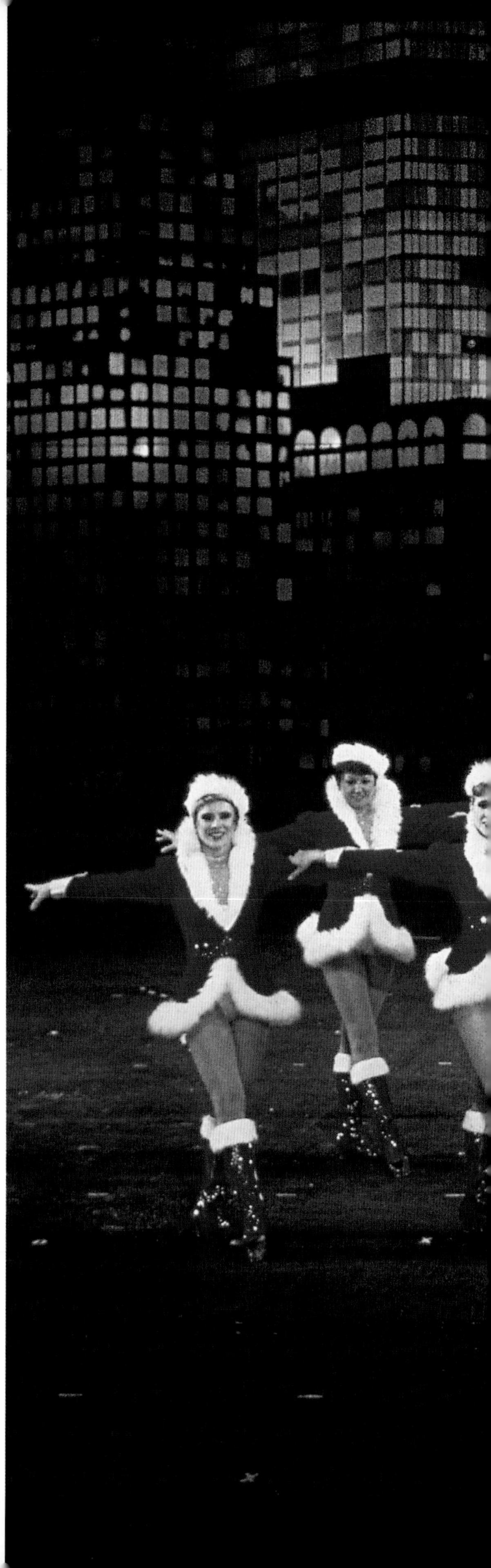

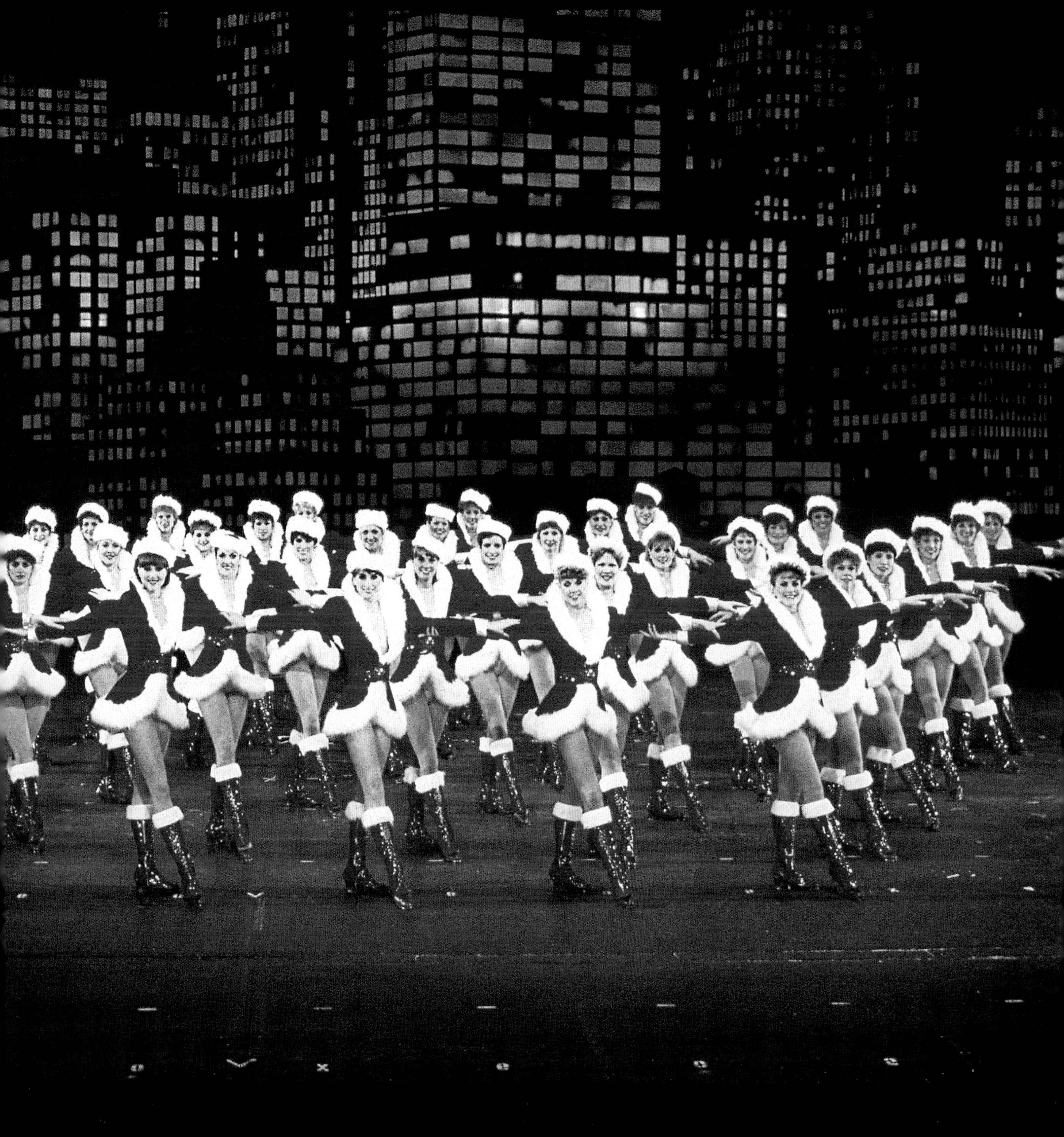

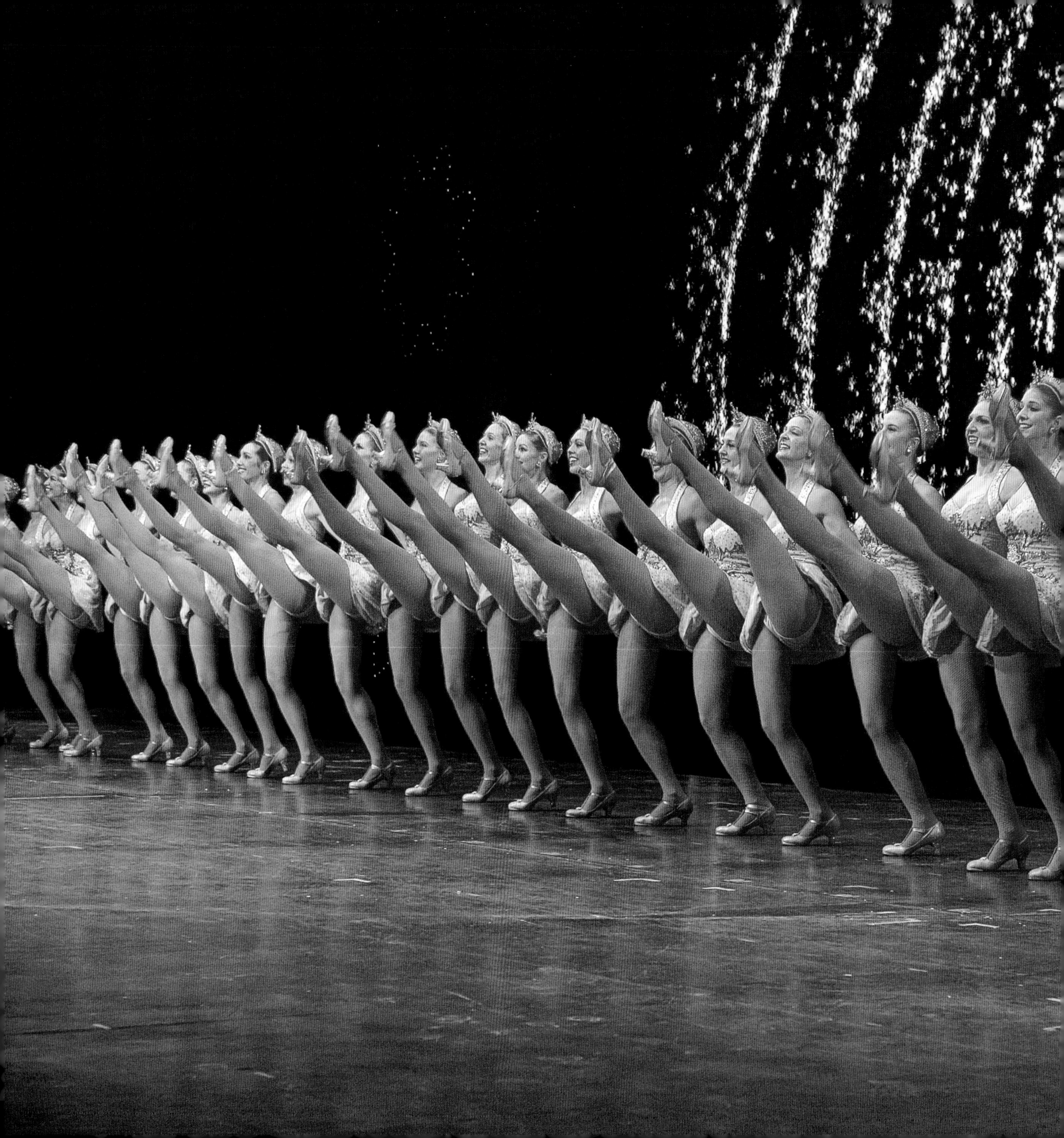

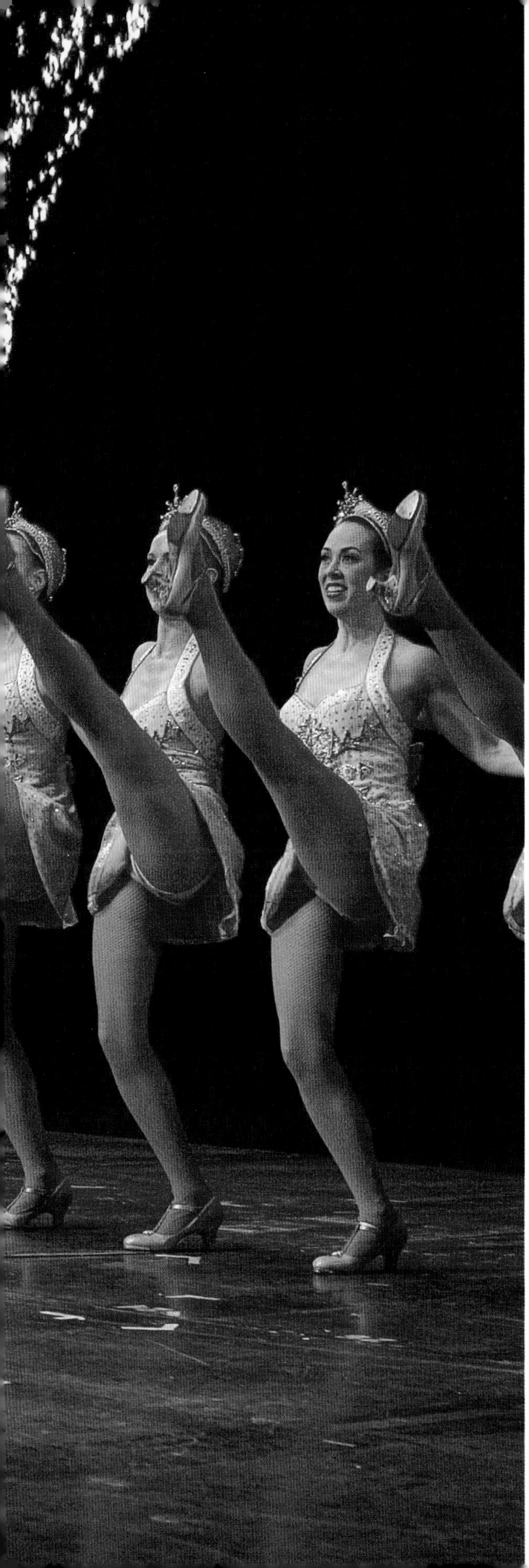

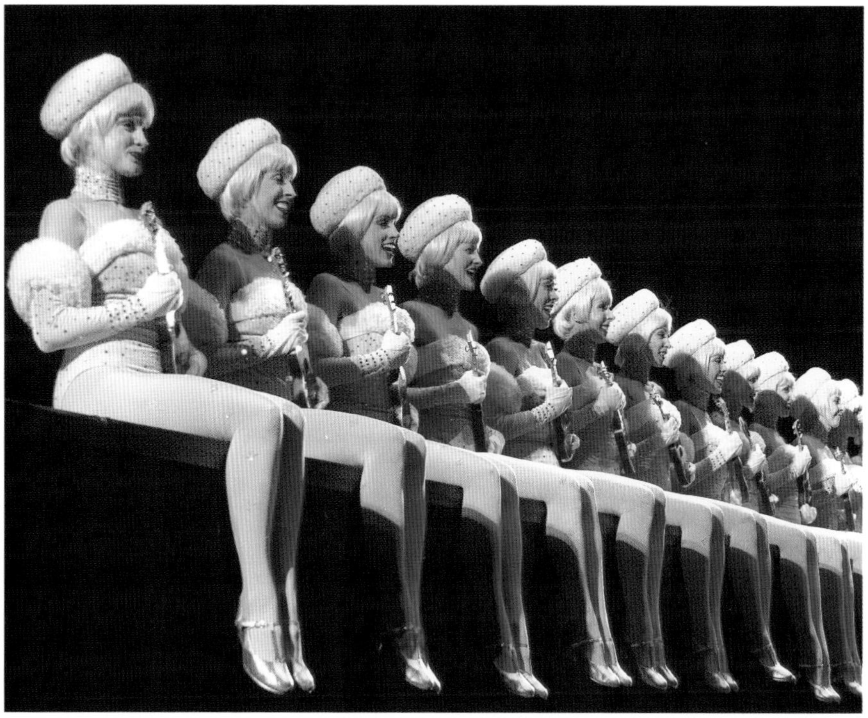

Through the years the holiday production has provided joy and entertainment to the millions of audiences that have come to celebrate the Christmas tradition.

In 2006, Radio City proudly announced that the director of the Radio City Christmas Show would be Linda Haberman, the first female director of the Christmas production.

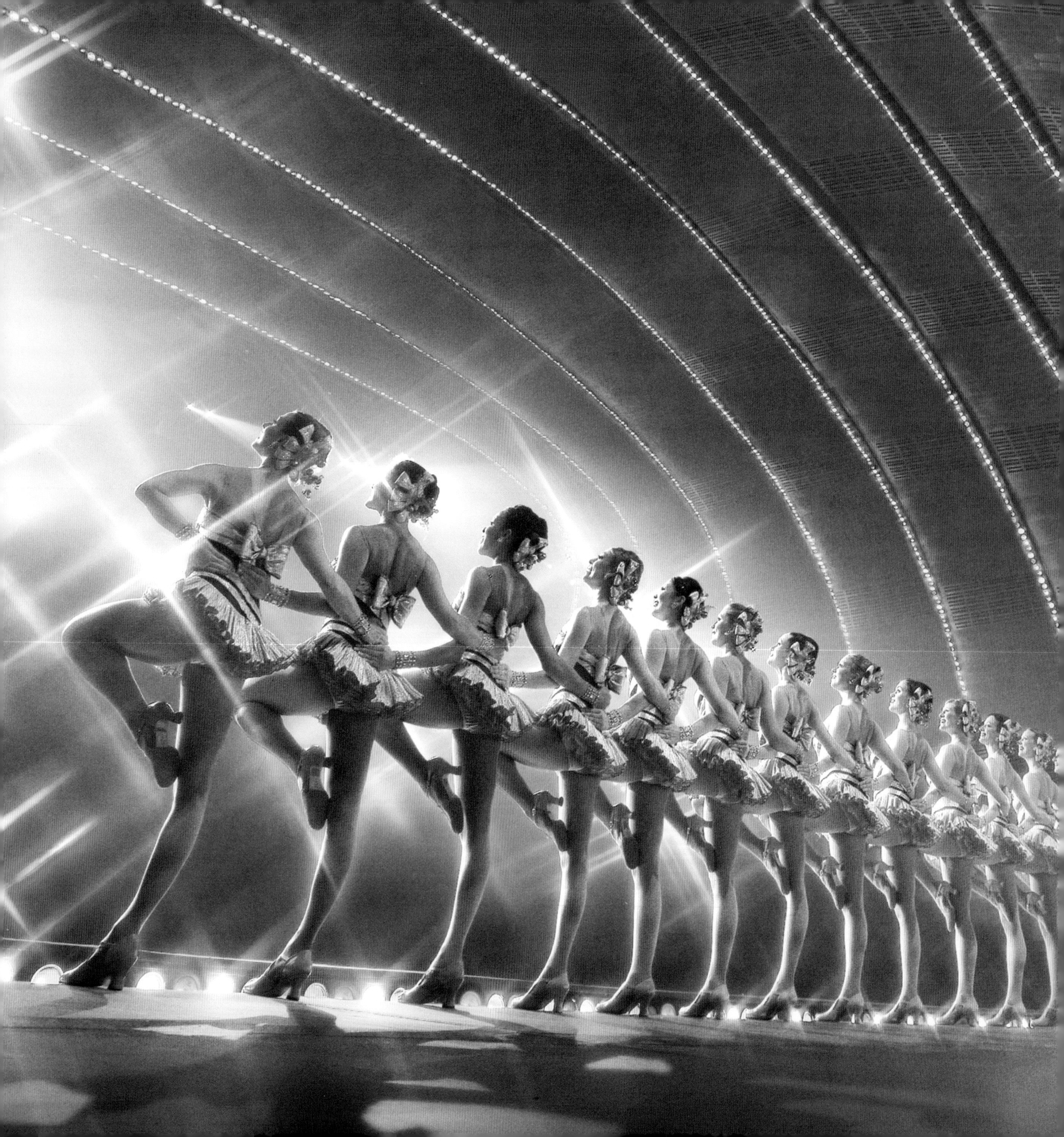

THE 75TH YEAR OF THE CHRISTMAS SPECTACULAR

Only the Radio City Christmas Spectacular can feature a holiday celebration 75 years in the making! The 2007 edition of the Radio City Christmas Spectacular is the most dramatic re-imagining of America's #1 holiday show in 75 years. The re-imagined show features new scenes and Rockette performances, with 10 all-new costumes and breathtaking special effects on stage such as fireworks that light up the New York City skyline and Santa flying over the Great Stage!

Audiences who have come to love the Christmas Spectacular over the decades will find themselves immersed in the Christmas magic only Radio City Music Hall can make from the moment they walk in the doors. This year, traditional favorites that never grow old such as the "Parade of the Wooden Soldiers" and the "Living Nativity" will meet new, incredibly intricate and modern takes on this classic American tradition.

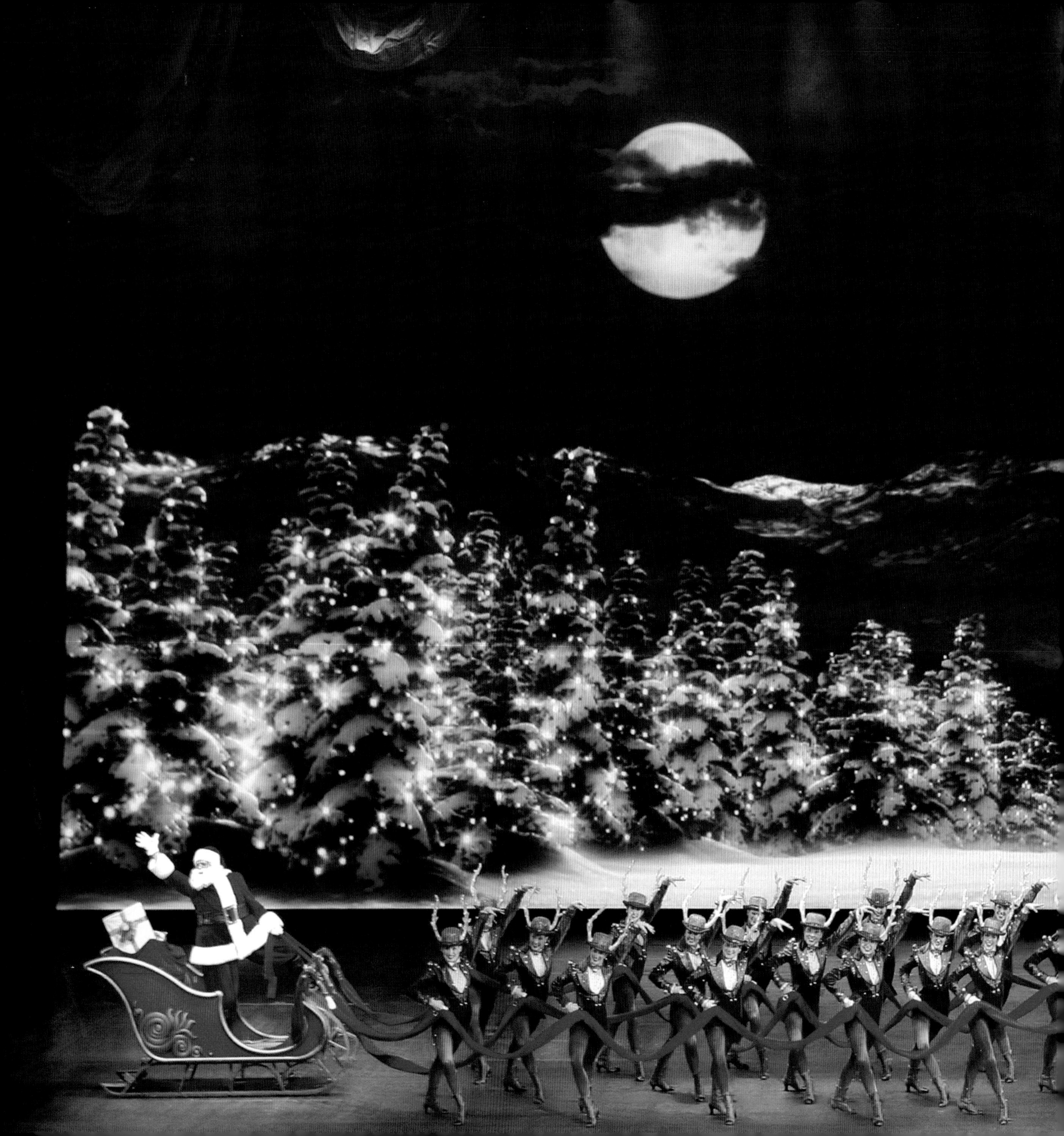

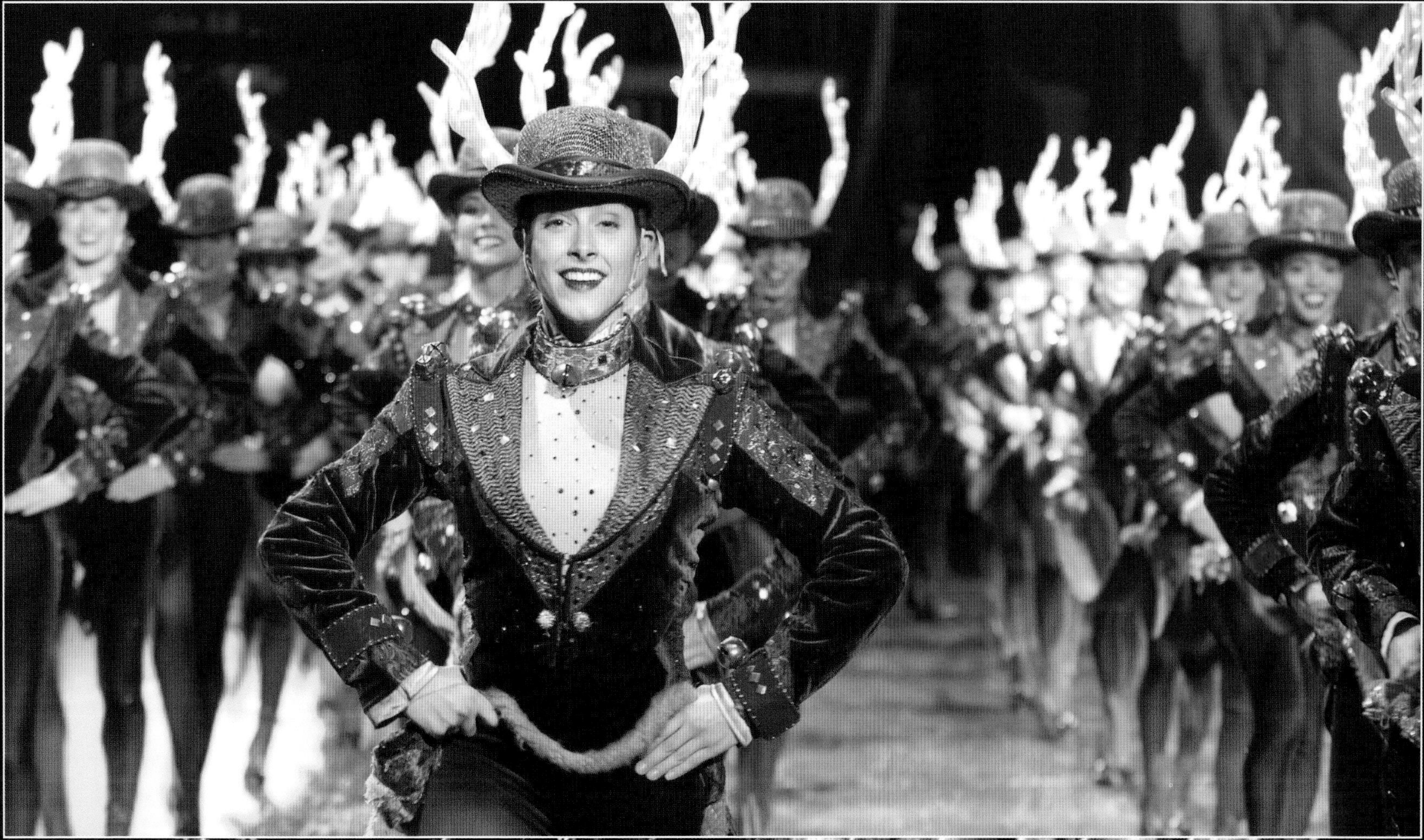

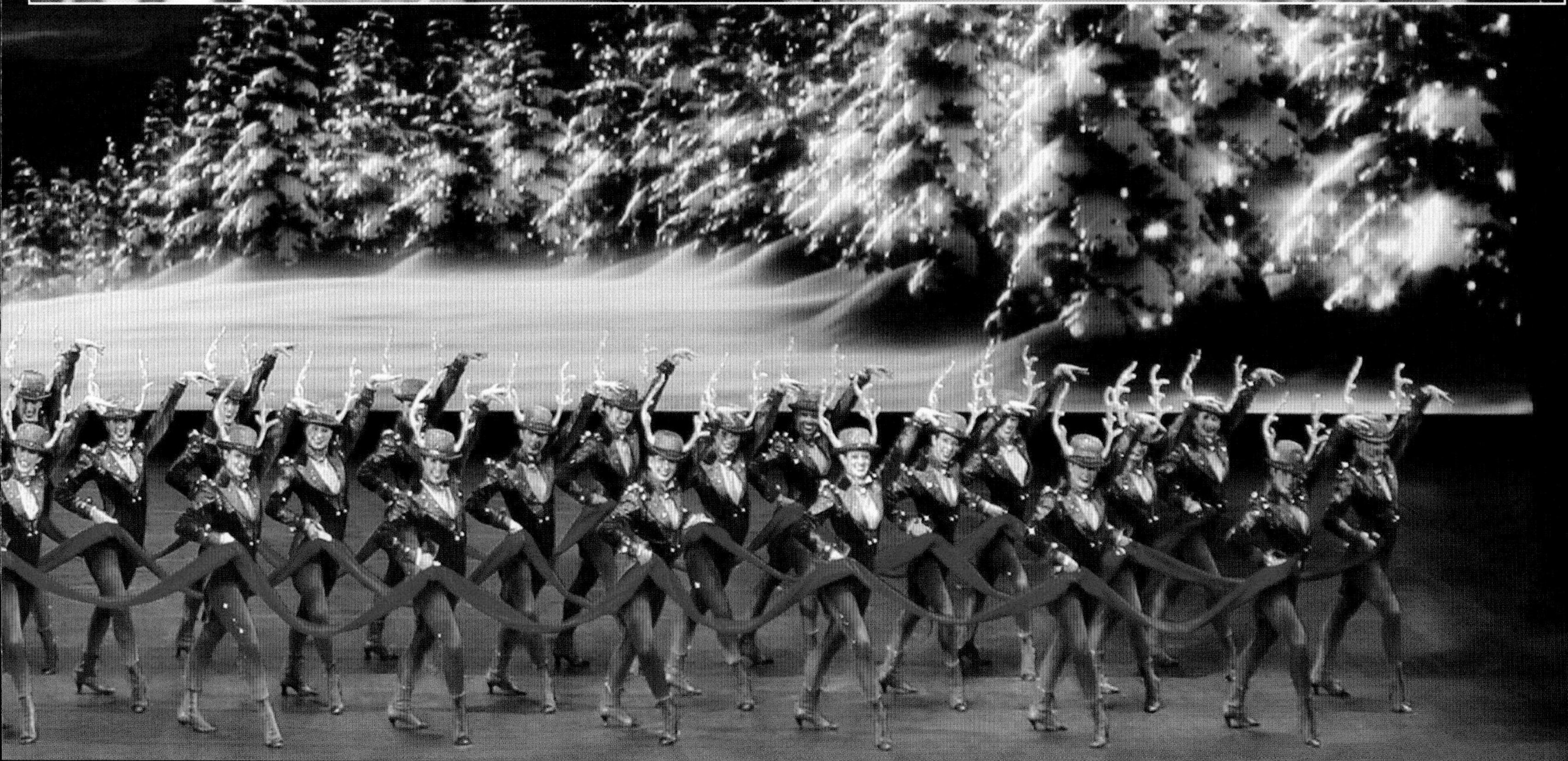

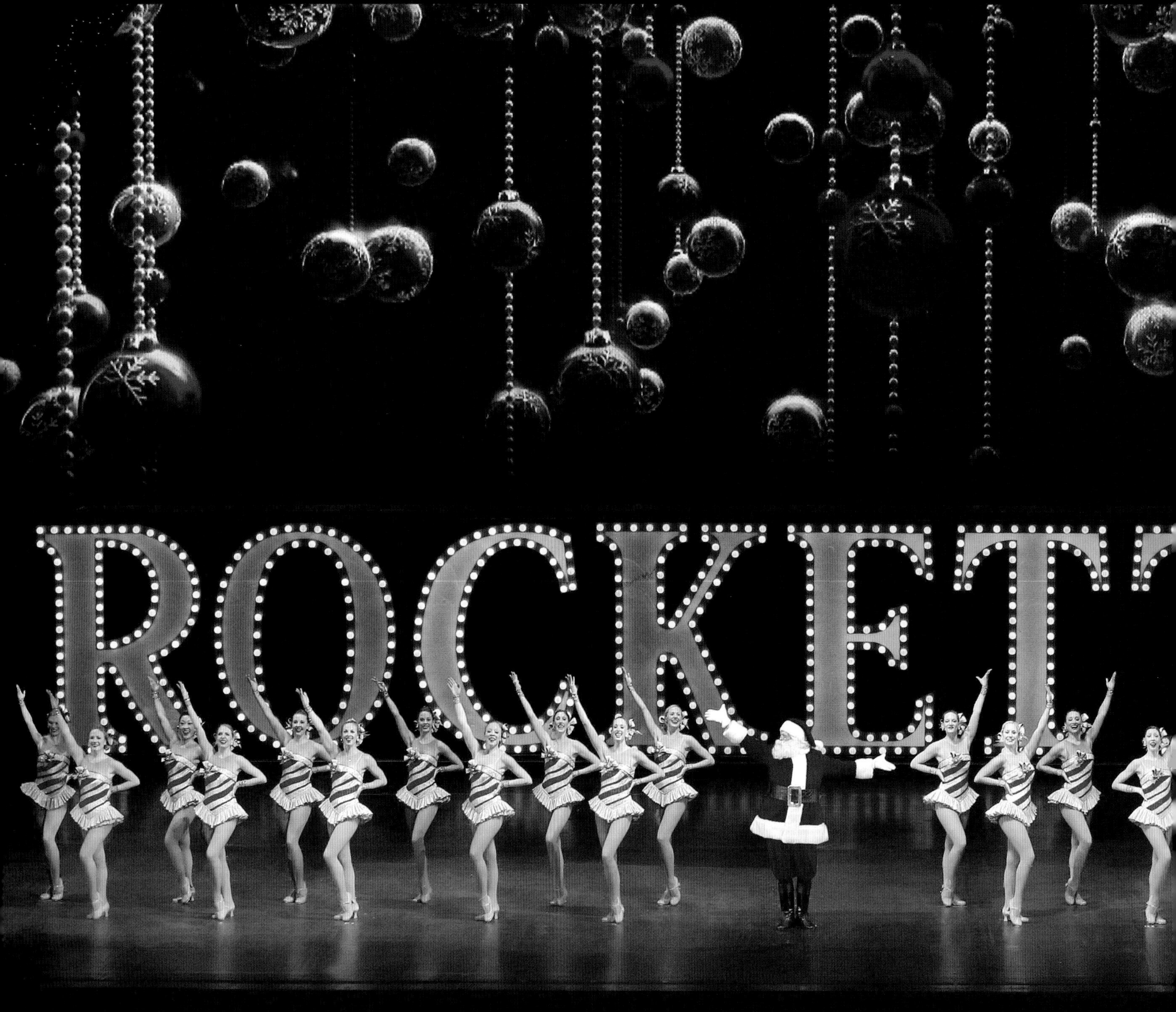
ROCKET

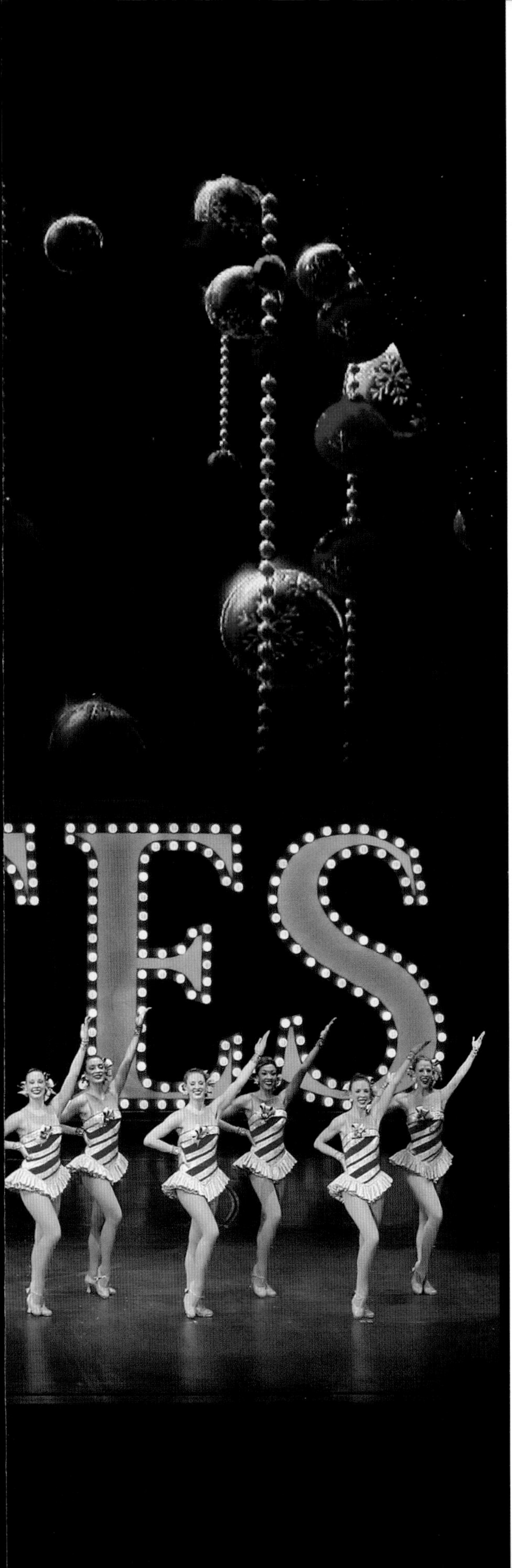

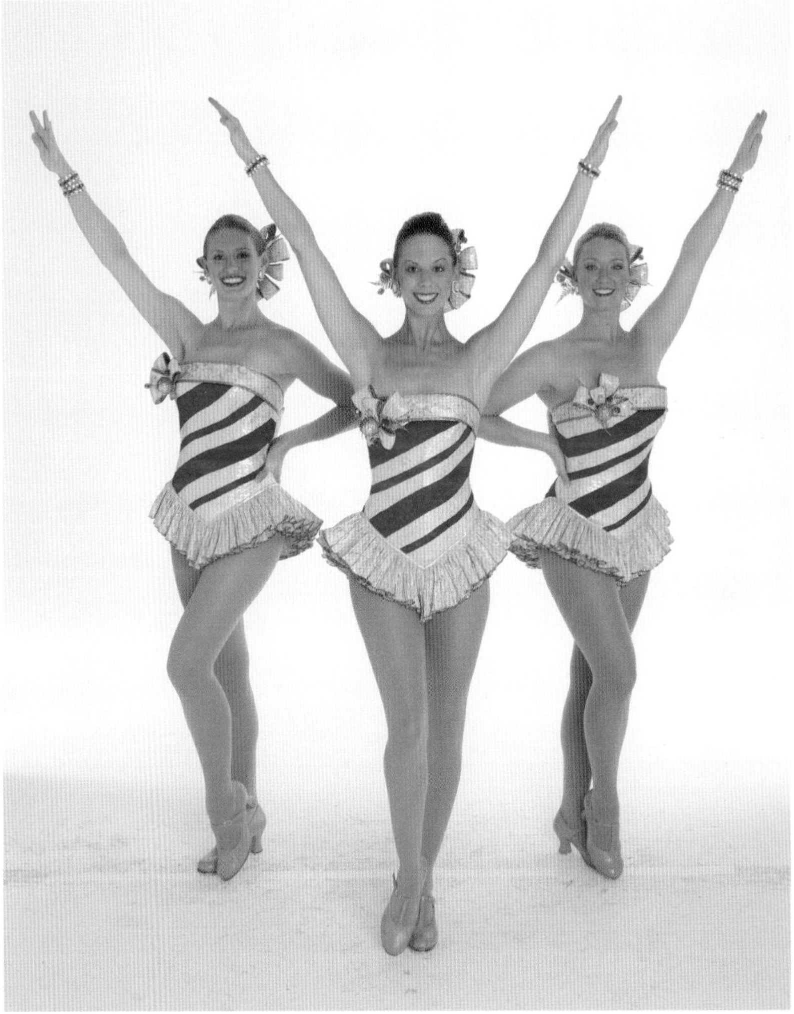

The Rockettes premiered the "Twelve Days" costume in 2006. Designed by Frank Krenz, these striking costumes are perfect for the tour de force tap number, "Twelve Days of Christmas."

On the left, in a riveting, rousing tap rendition of the beloved carol, Santa presents the first gift of Christmas.

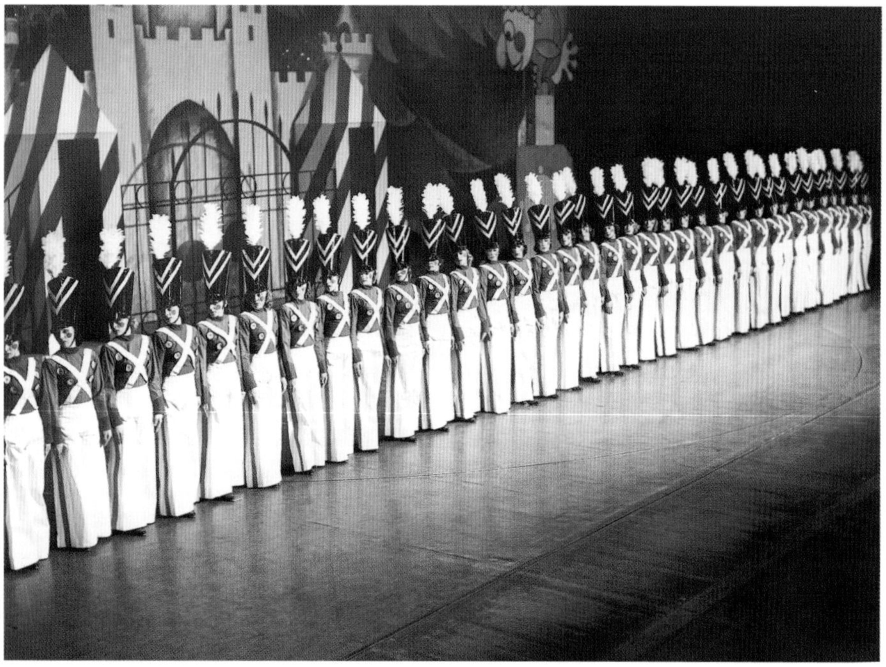

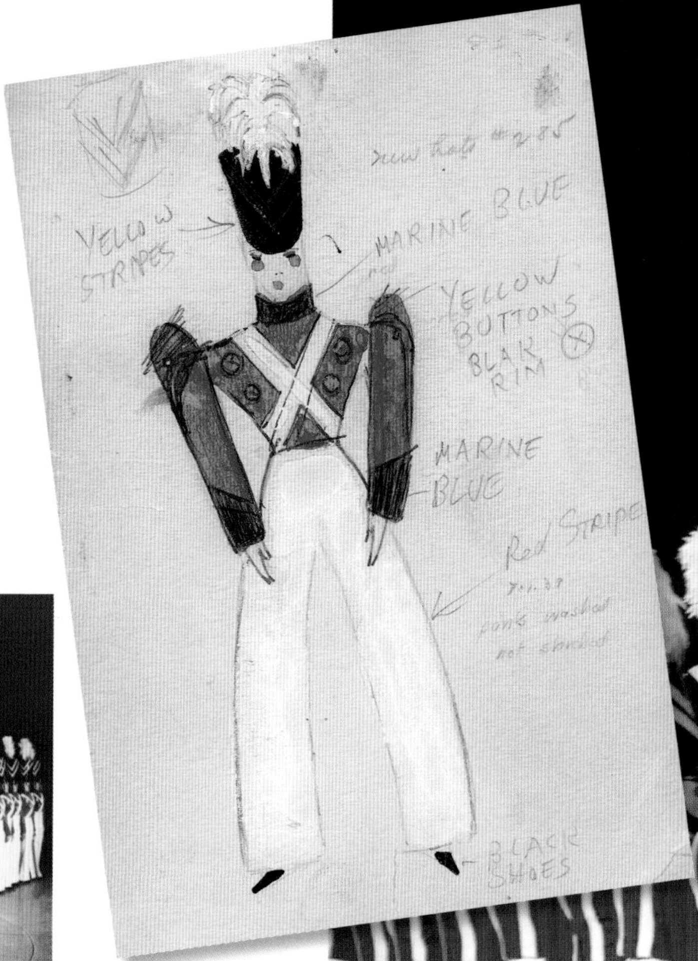

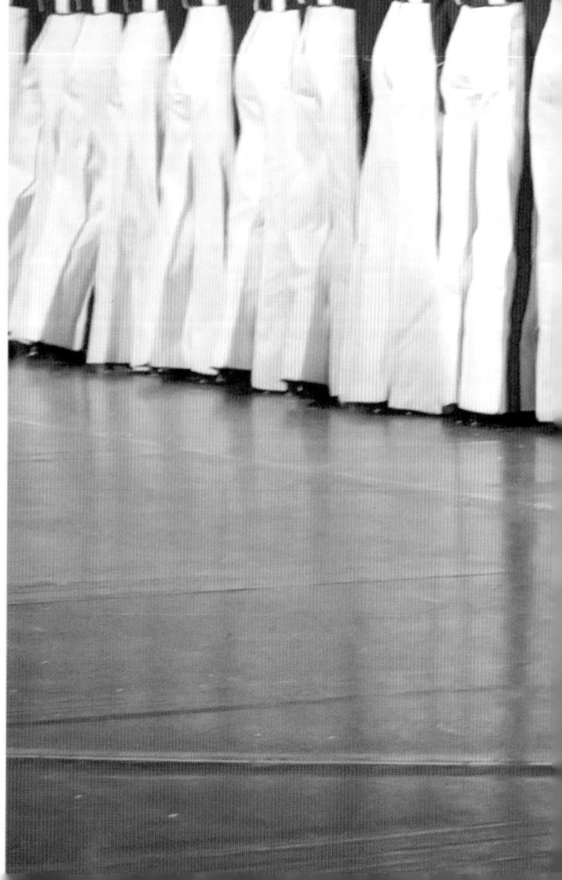

The "Parade of the Wooden Soldiers" continues to set the standard as the signature Rockette number for precision performance.

The iconic toy-soldier costumes of the *Christmas Spectacular* are the authentic 1933 Vincente Minnelli design that he modeled after a porcelain doll; the outfits have remained unchanged since their debut. The hats are nearly three feet tall, the pants are stiffly starched, and the red jackets button narrow and high. The show-stopping finale is the domino fall. A cannon blast starts the fall, and the entire line of Rockettes cascades backwards. The "Parade of the Wooden Soldiers," which has been in the show since 1933, remains a vital part of the 2007 show's core. (*following page*)

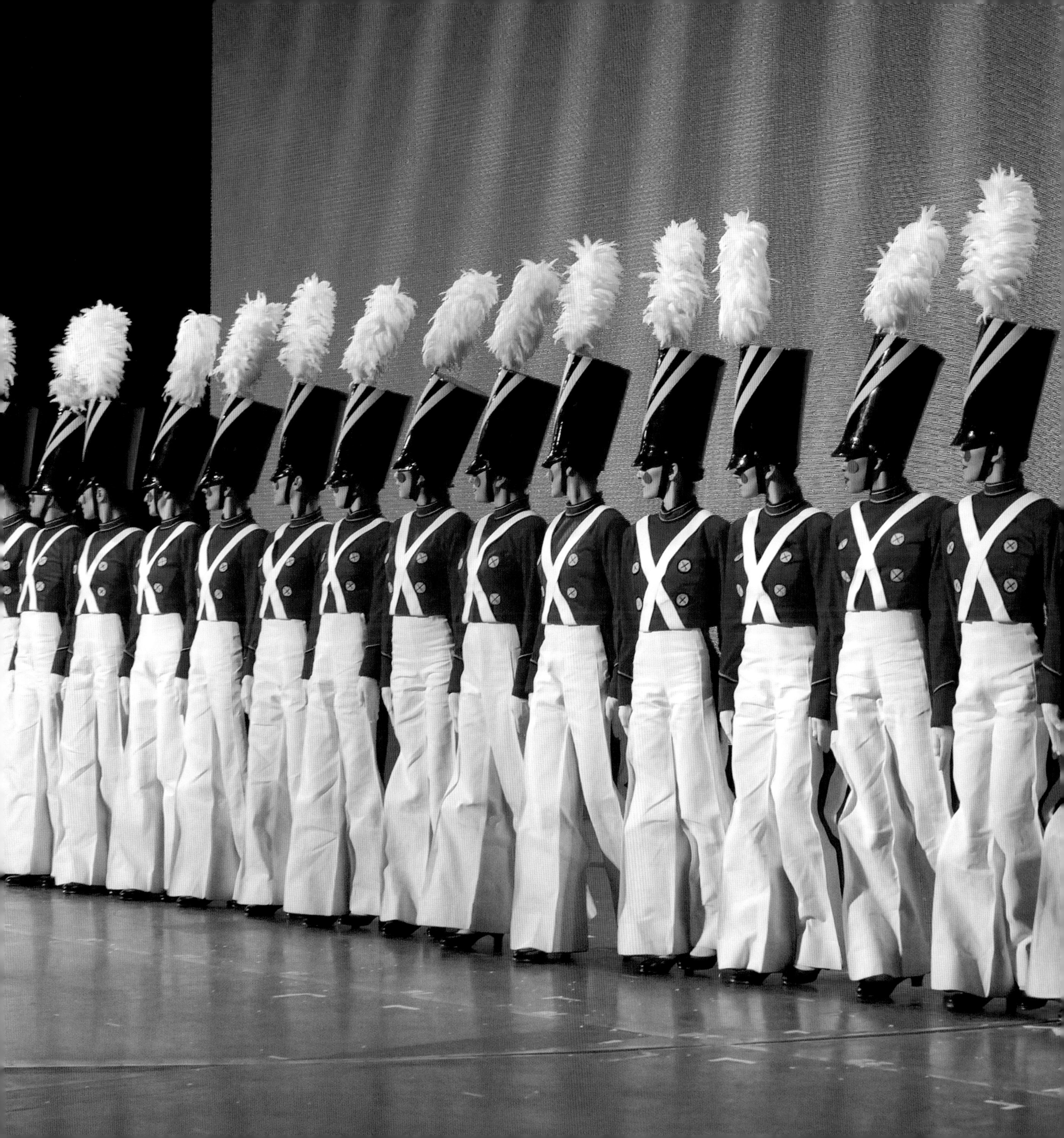

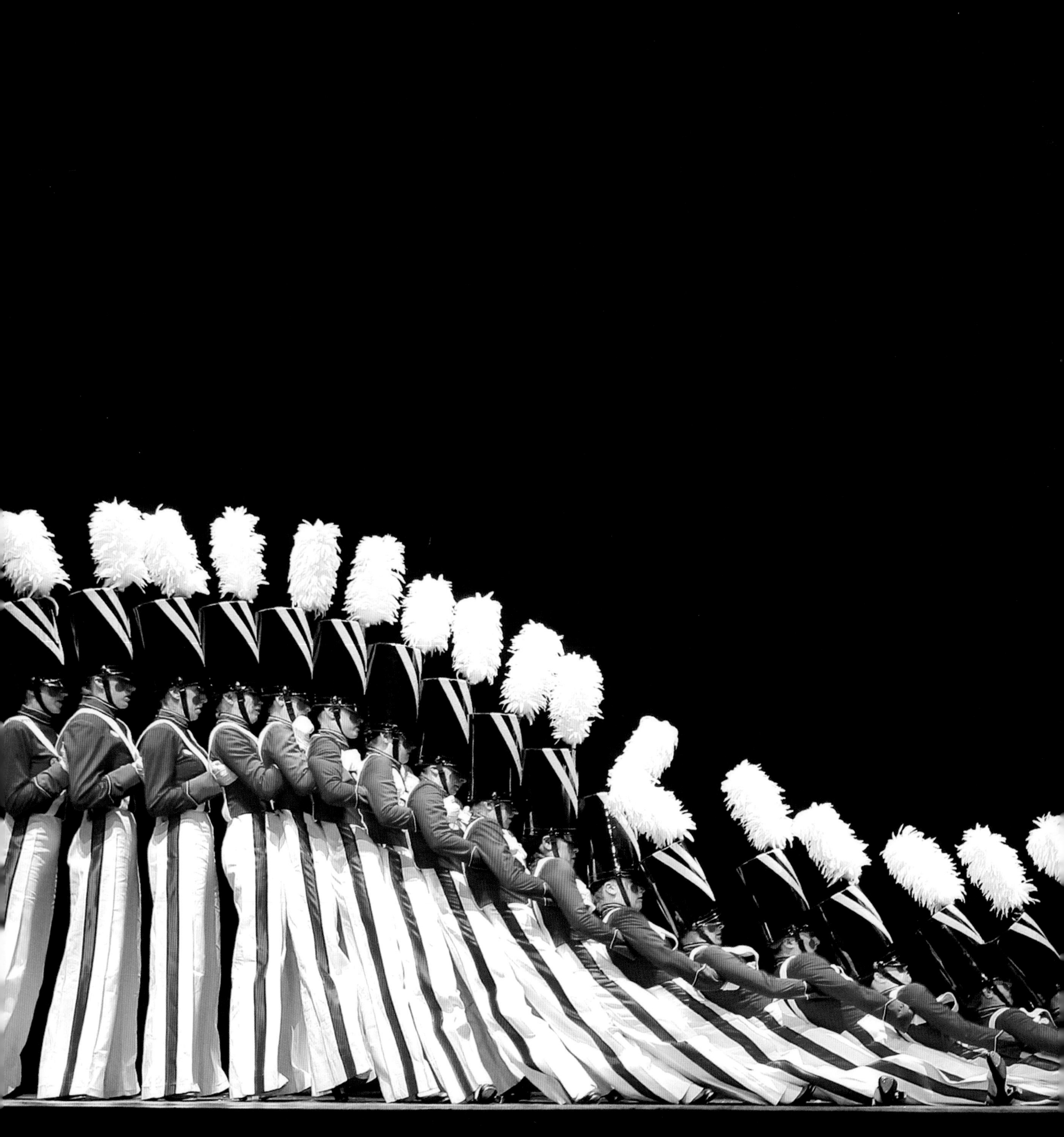

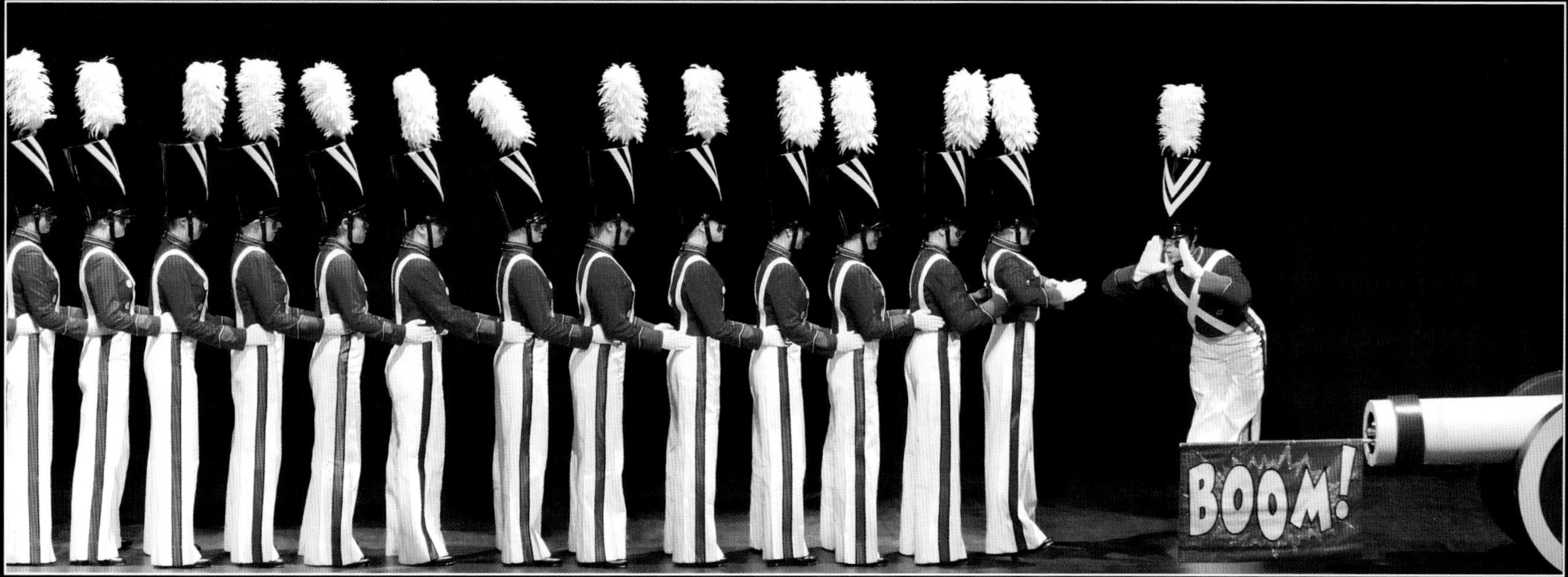
BOOM!

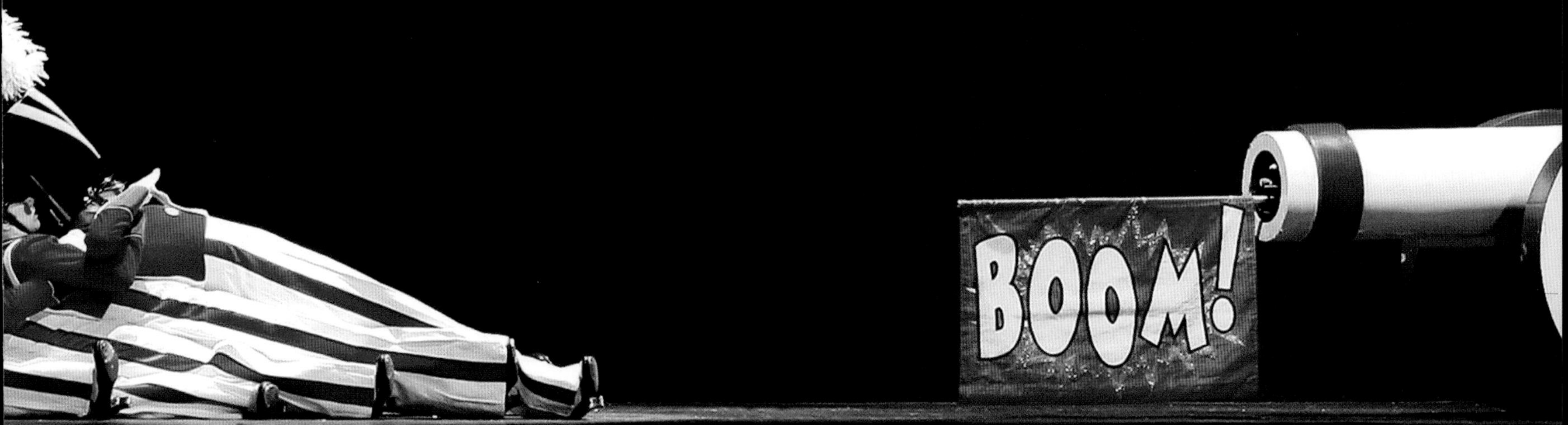
BOOM!

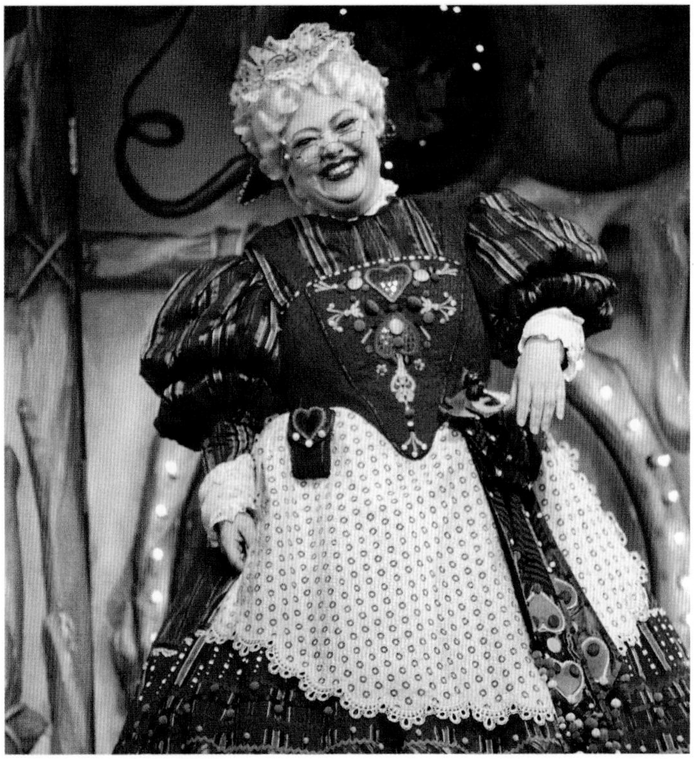

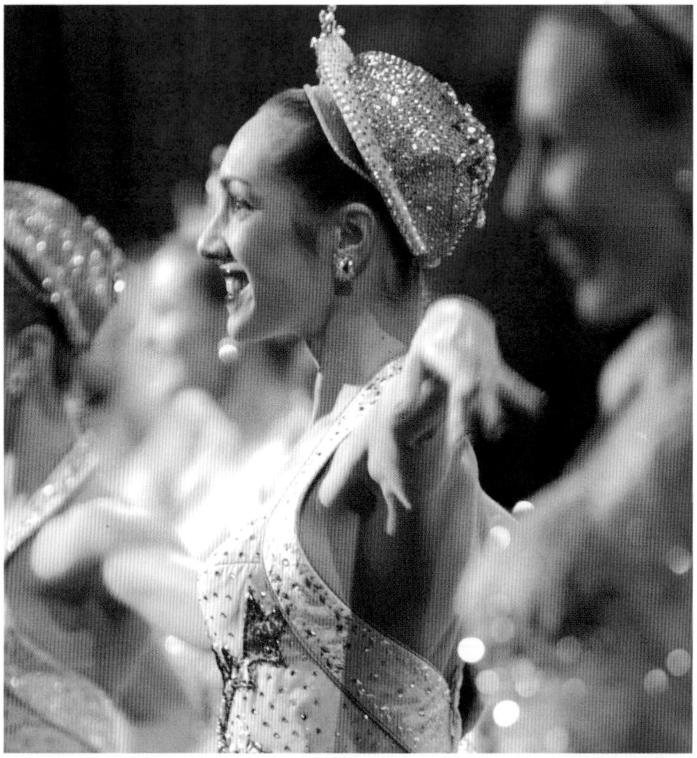

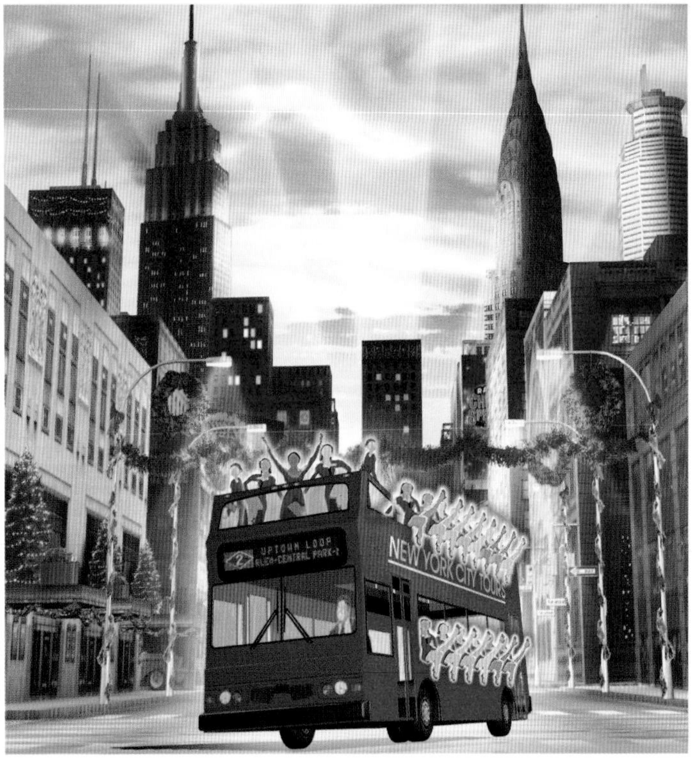
UPTOWN LOOP
NEW YORK CITY TOURS

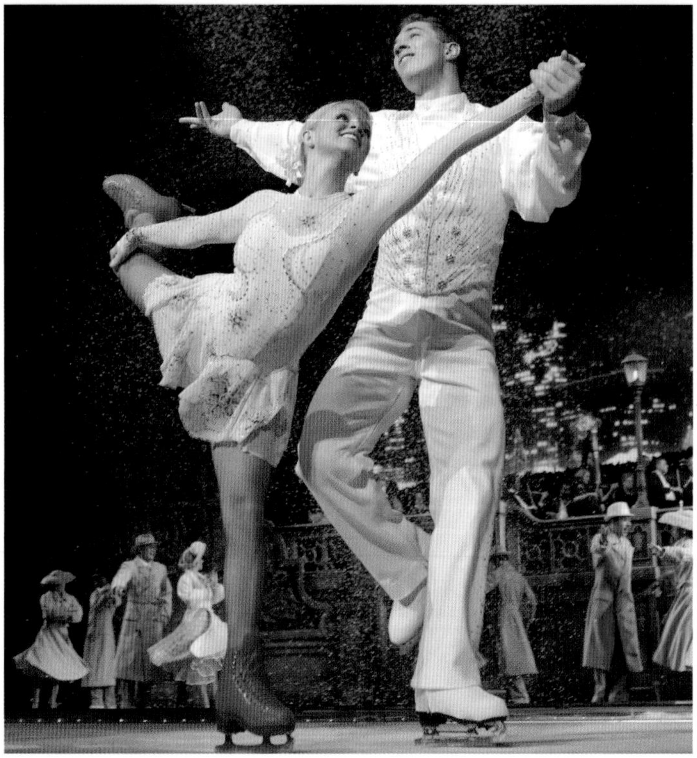

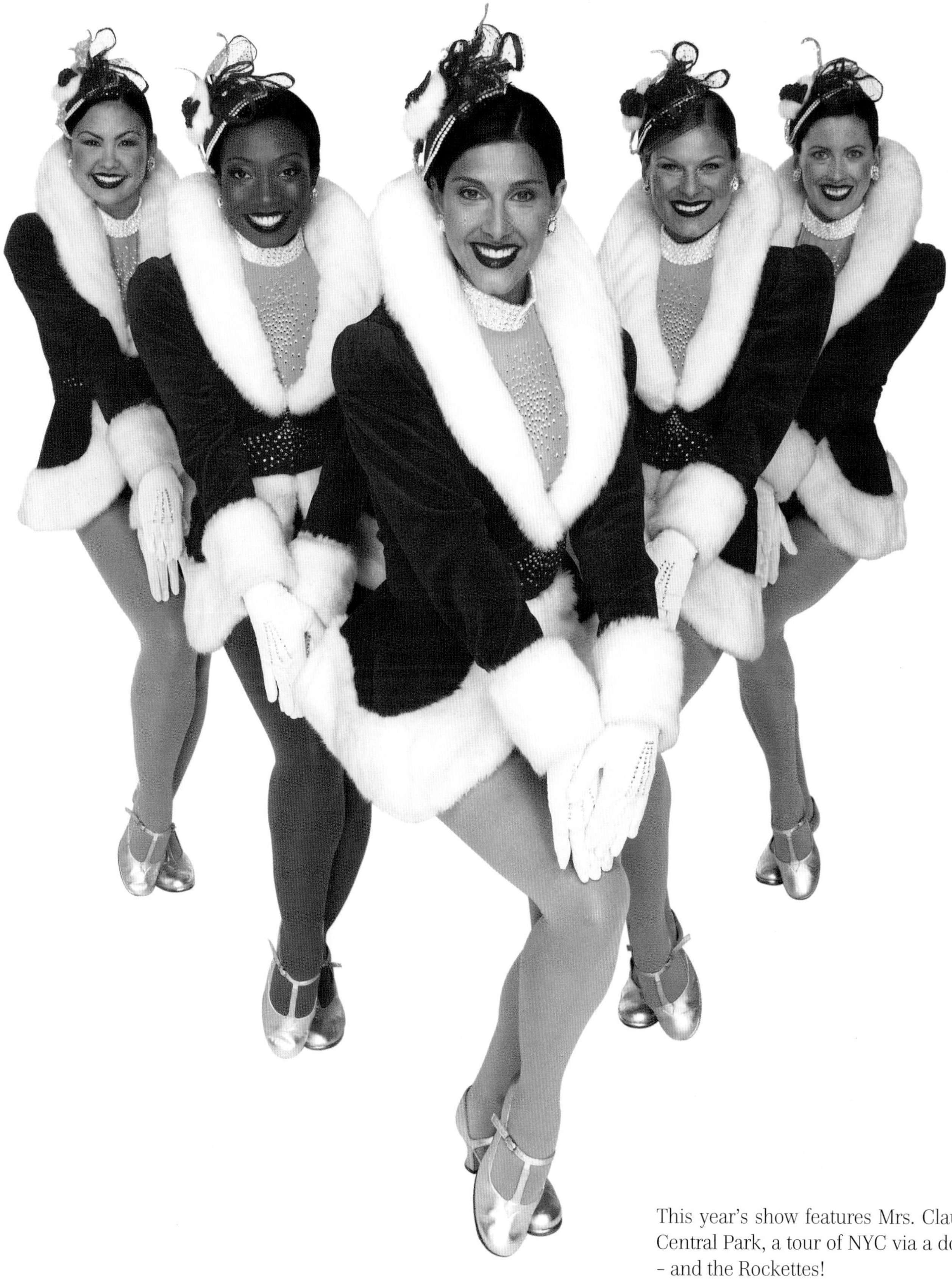

This year's show features Mrs. Claus, ice skaters in Central Park, a tour of NYC via a double-decker bus - and the Rockettes!

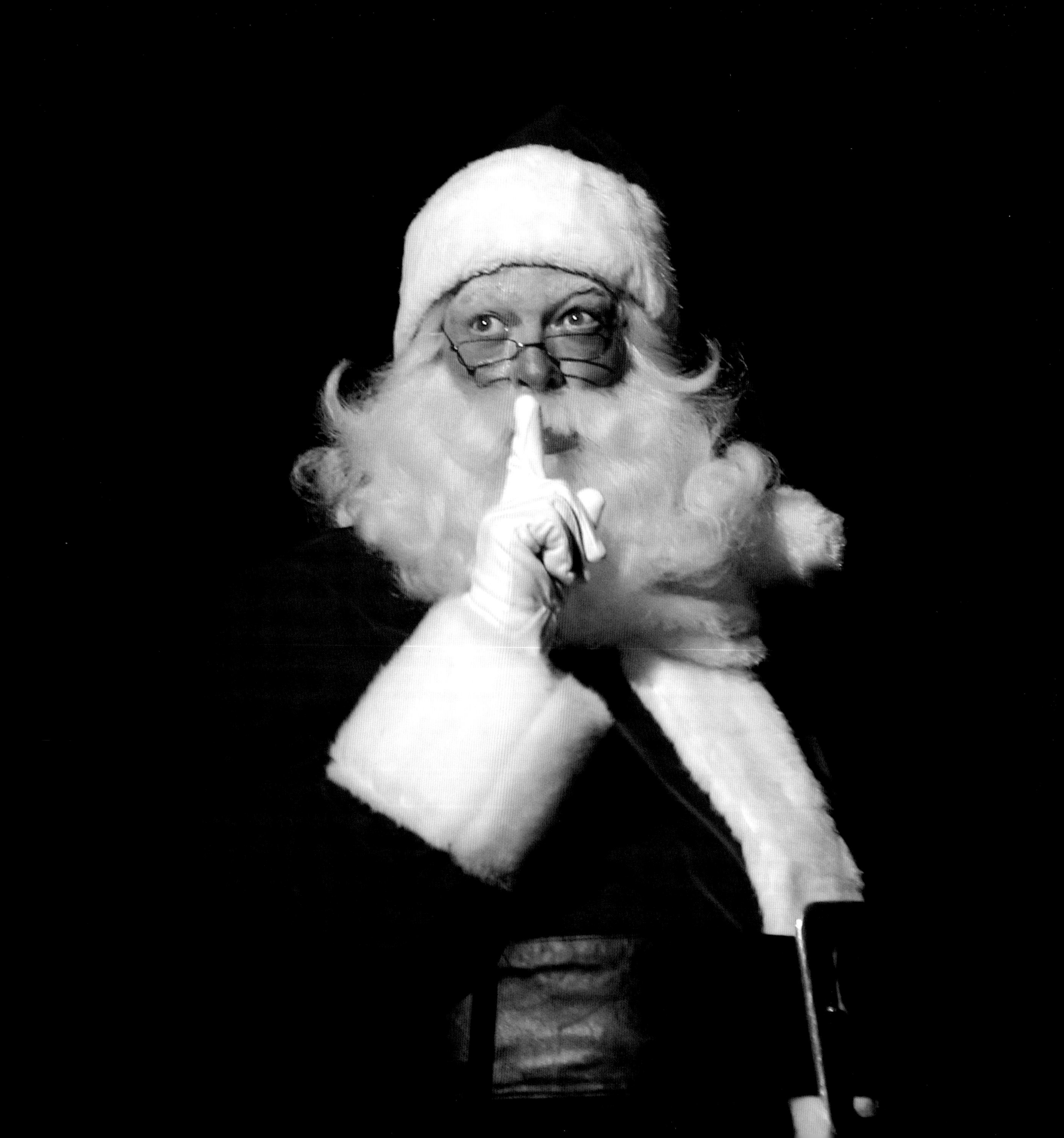

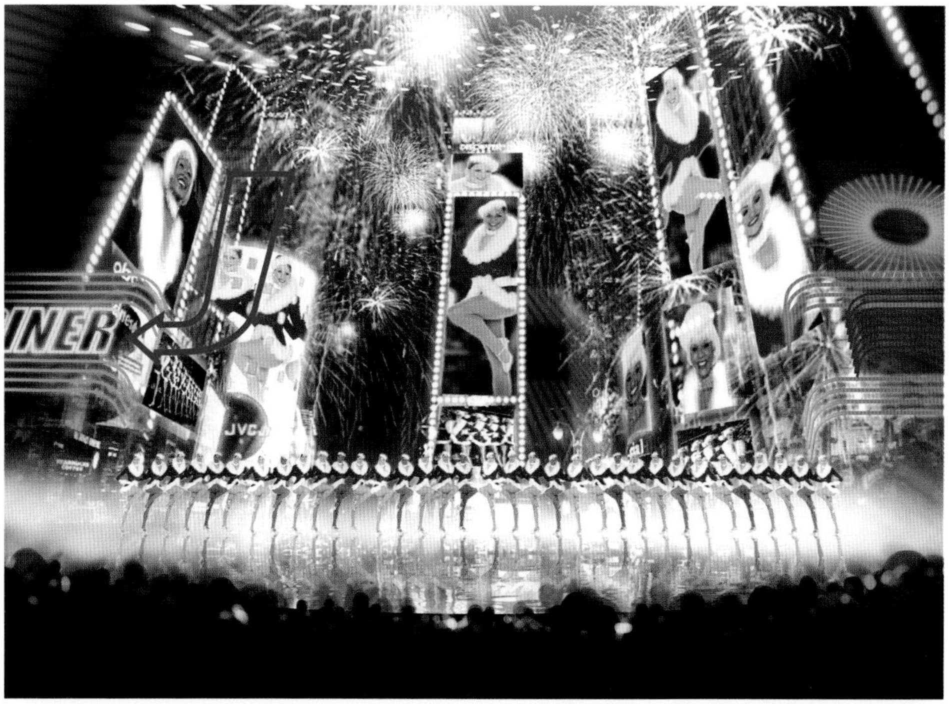

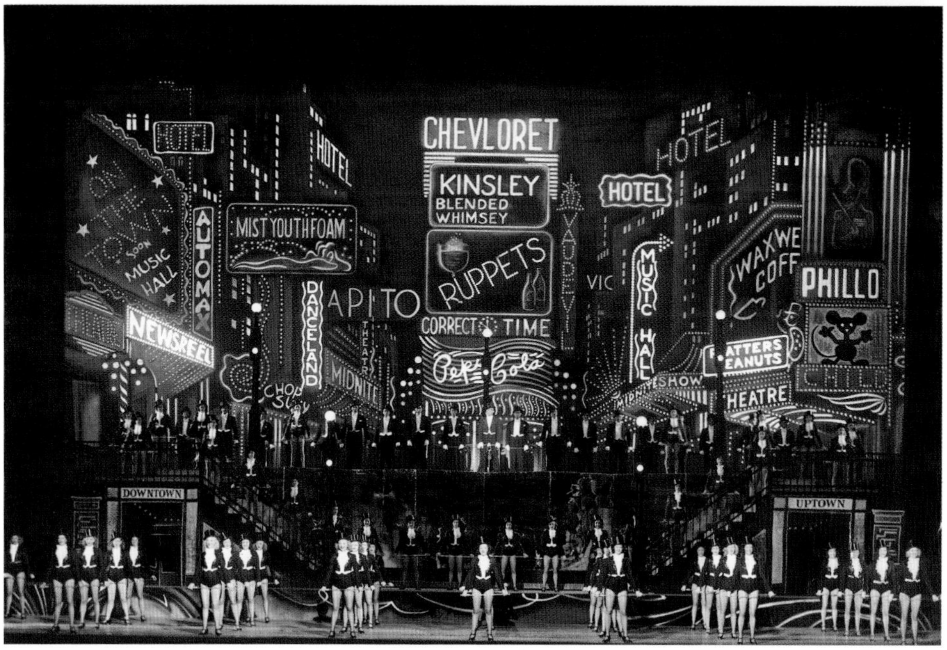

From past designs to current designs, elements of New York stay a part of the stage design.

The 2007 show features the world-famous Rockettes in a dynamic new performance routine within an unforgettable signature production number set in Times Square, lighting up the New York skyline with a glittering fireworks display onstage.

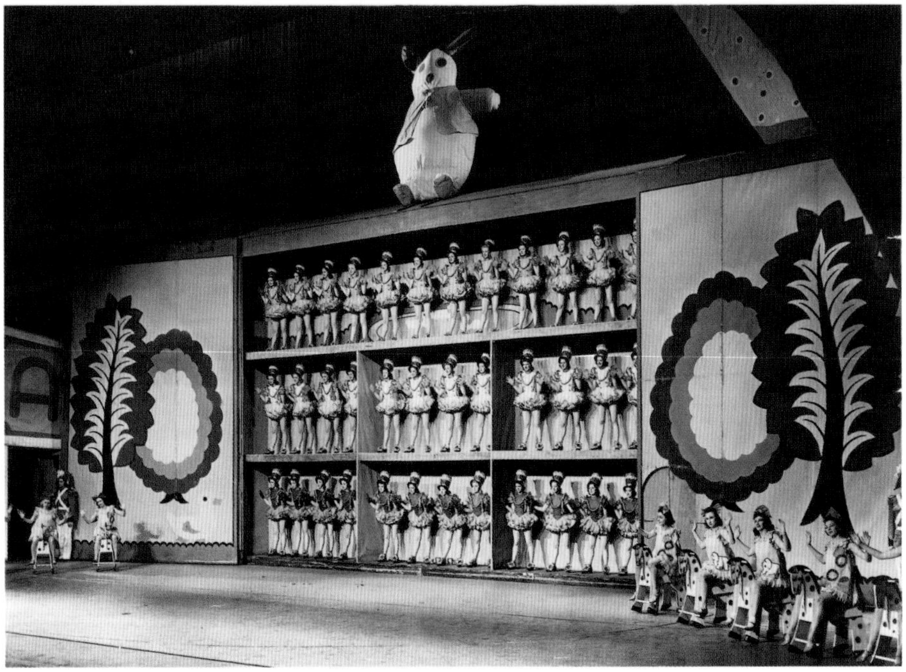

Santa's journey then takes the audience from New York City to the North Pole. A toy workshop unfolds into Santa's gigantic and spectacular 25-foot-high warehouse of Christmas toys.

This larger-than-life production set becomes the backdrop to a high-energy tap routine featuring the Rockettes as rag dolls, a performance re-imagined and inspired by a classic Rockette number that was originally choreographed in 1933 by Russell Markert.

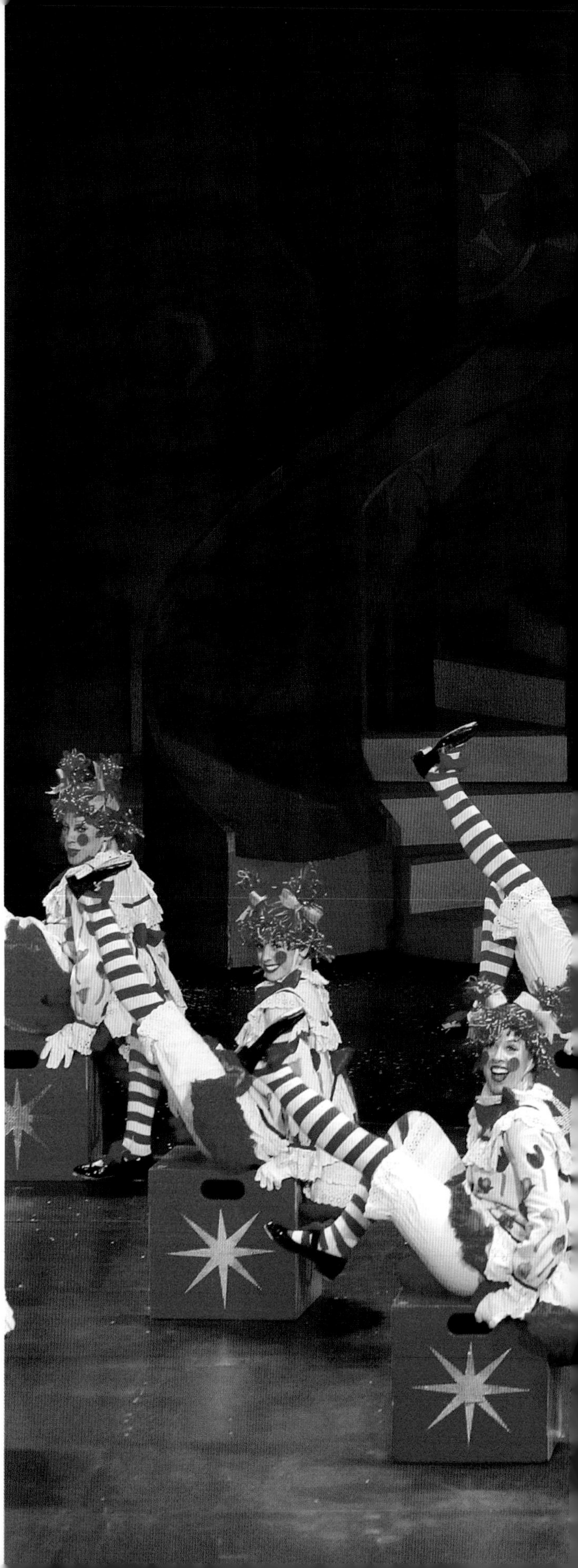

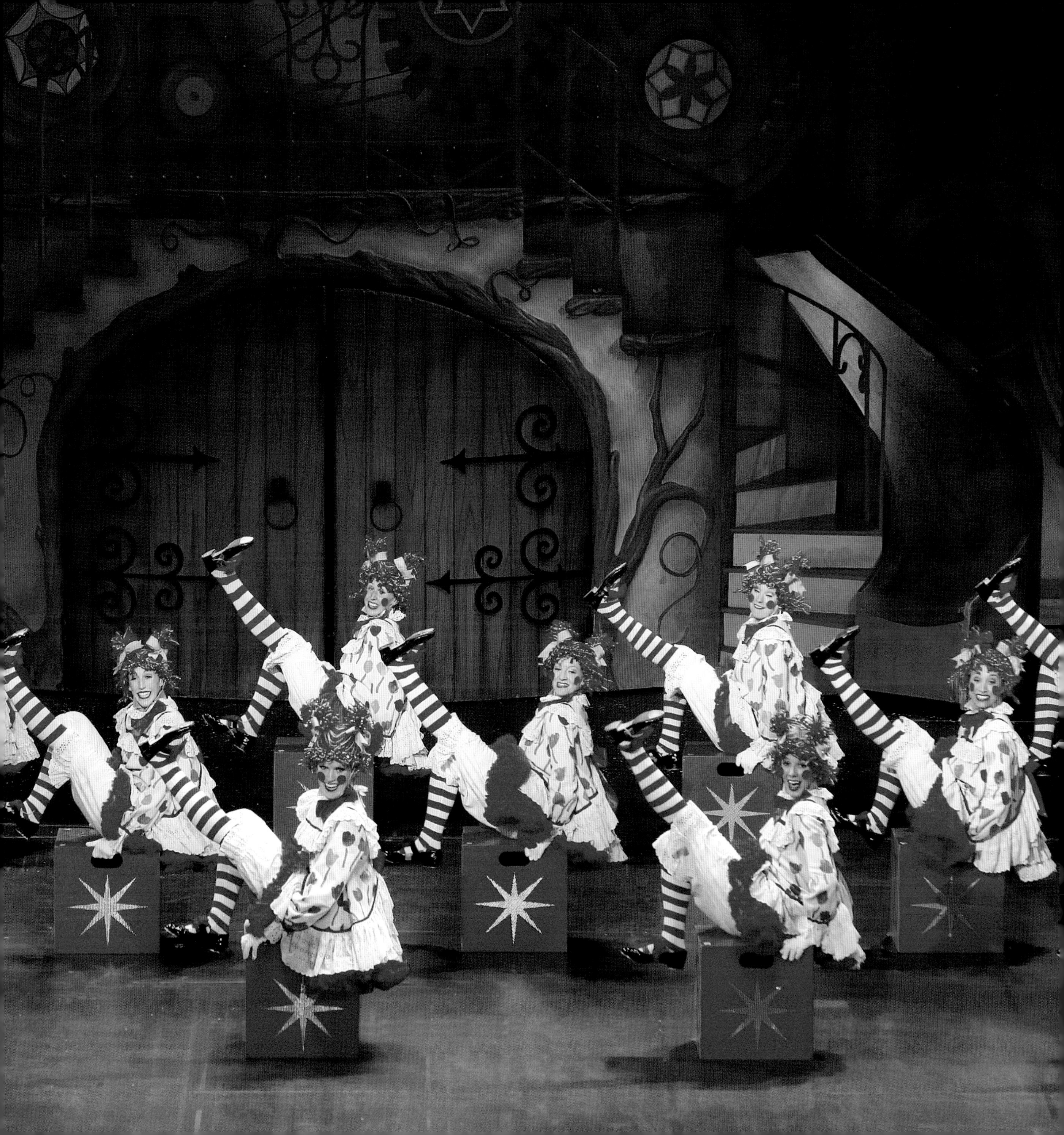

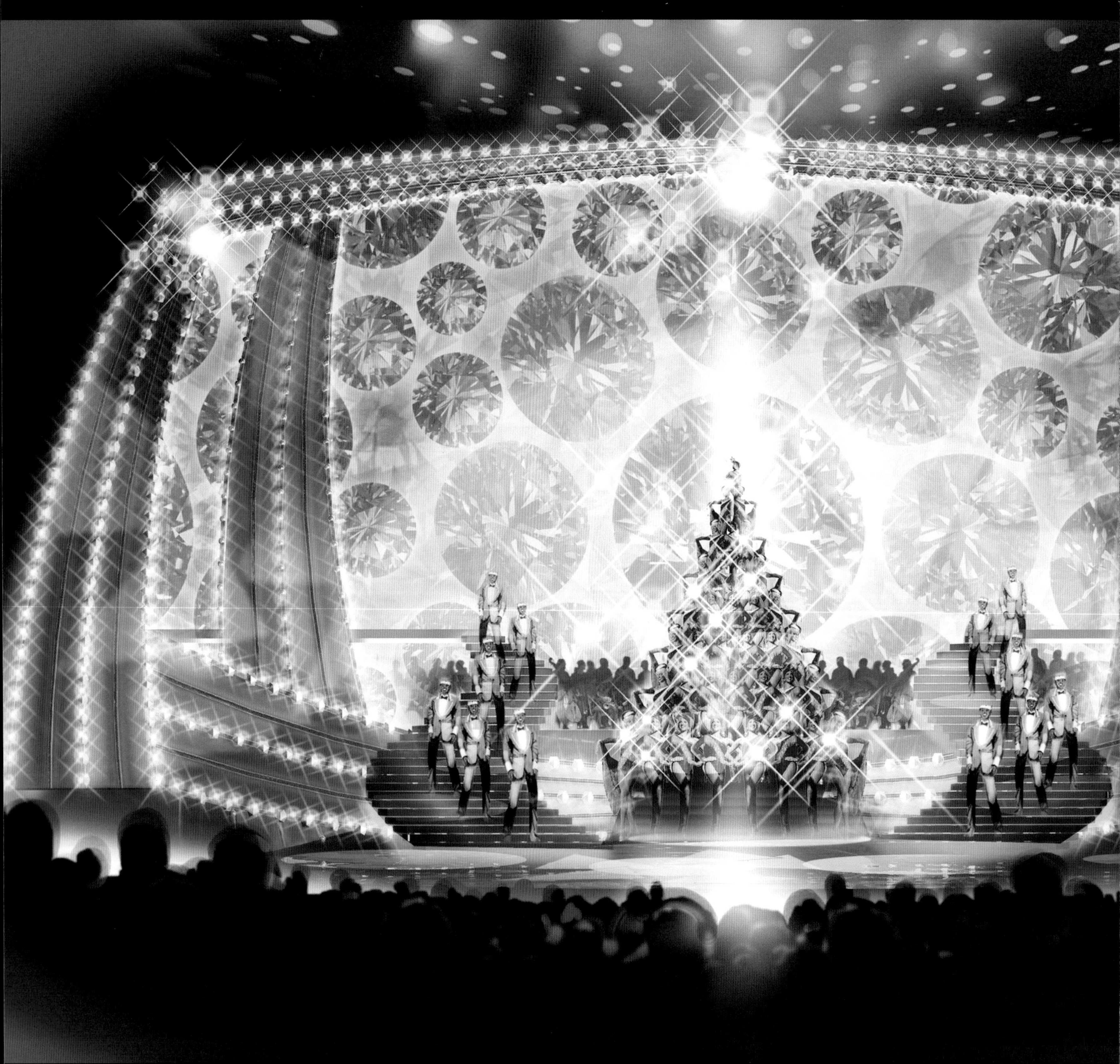

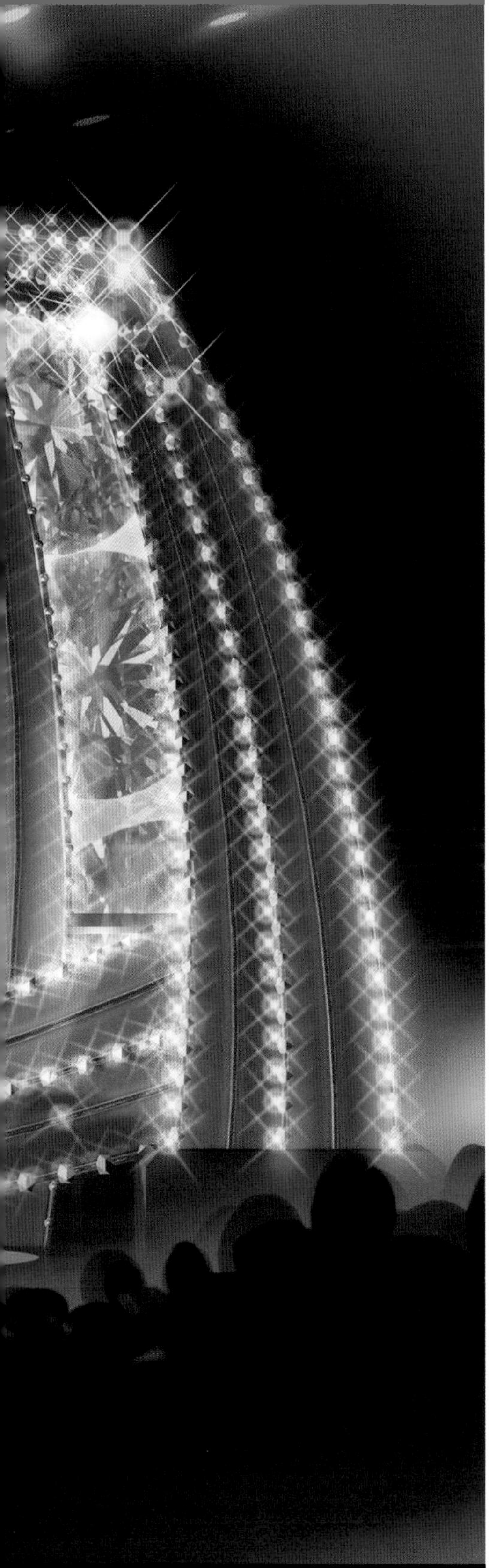

Rockettes will undoubtedly bring the audience to their feet with a Rockette finale "Let Christmas Shine," which honors and celebrates the Rockettes as the stars of the show.

The Rockettes deliver the audience a "Christmas card"-inspired greeting that captures the tradition and grandeur of the holiday spirit and gives the audience an intriguing retrospective look on film at the Christmas Spectacular throughout the past 75 years.

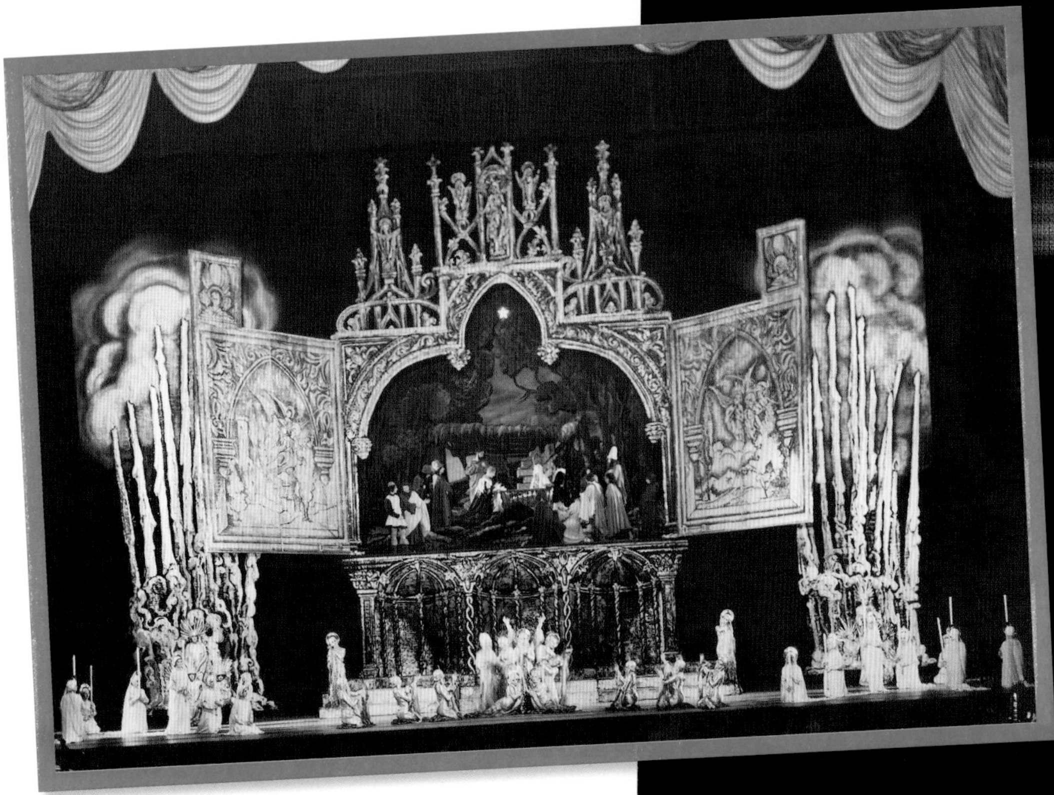

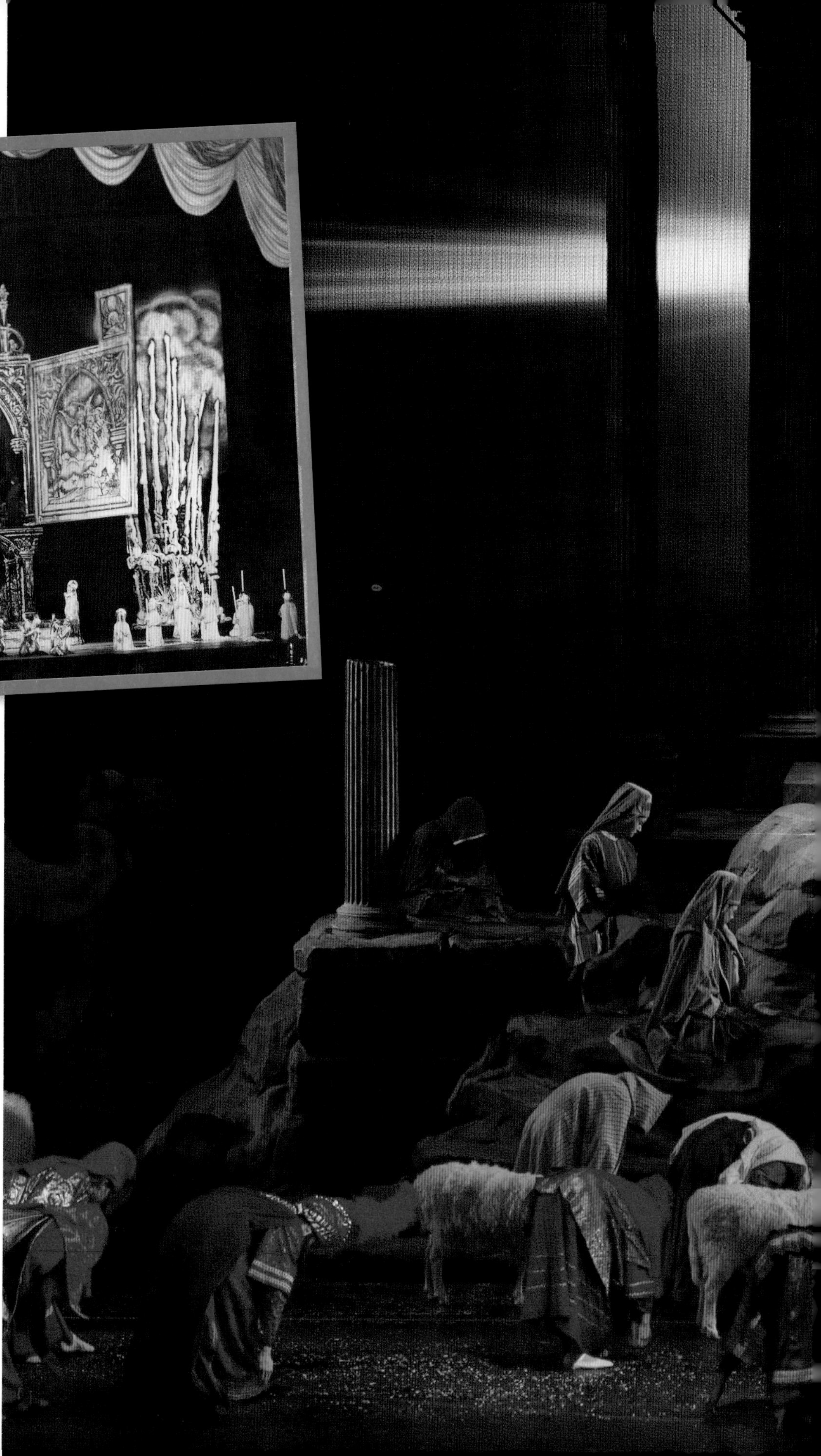

In the "Living Nativity," the Christmas Spectacular presents a moving living tableau of the birth of Christ.

The 2007 edition of the Radio City Christmas Spectacular promises to continue to create memories that audiences have come to treasure. However, this year will truly be a celebration…75 years in the making!

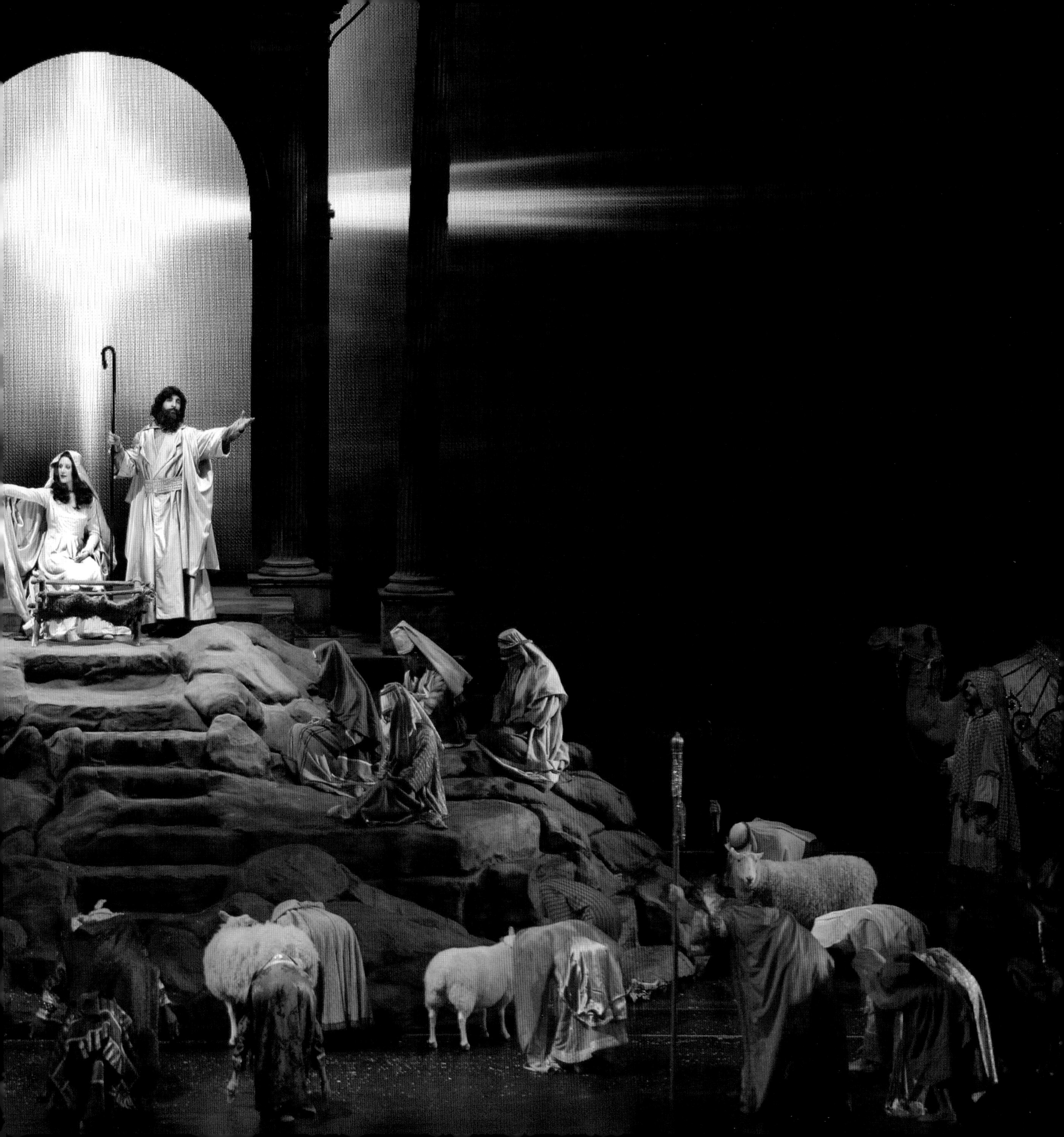

THANK YOU

MSG Entertainment would like to extend its thanks to the following people for contributing their passion and expertise towards the creation of this book:

The amazing staff at Radio City Music Hall: Rich Claffey, Tom Forgione, Darlene Bell, Nef Ruiz, Robert Castronovo, Marty Fuller, Sean Fox, Theodore Wondsel and their crews of experts; Radio City Productions: John Bonanni-Executive Producer, Mark Kaufman-Stage Manager, Anne Snyder-intern and especially Lindsay Bell-Rockette Coordinator; the photo shoot support of Jennifer McCamish- Rockette Make-up consultant, Elizabeth Kamp- Make-up assistant, Lisa Matsuoka- Hair assistant, Karen Keeler- choreographer, Wardrobe: Barbara Vanzandt, Jack McGroder, Marion Wilson, Donna Smith, Ahmeda Ali, Margo Barkdull, Kristin Gardner and Caitlin VanZandt; MSGE Finance: Charlie Groneman, Ray Napoli and Ross Rindner; MSGE Legal: Stephanie Jacqueney and Daria Fessak; MSGE Marketing: Kristina Heney; The folks at HarperCollins - Andrea Rosen, Kathleen Burchell and Denise Dolence; The professionals at James Porto Photography: James Porto, Danielle Bock-Digital Tech, Scott Siken-Producer, Christopher Puente-Lighting Director, Matt Zugale-1st assistant, Matthew La Barbiera-2nd assistant, Lily Mikoski-assistant and Cole Porto-assistant. And a special thanks to Diane Jaust, Radio City Archivist.

2007 RADIO CITY ROCKETTES

Kristin Altfather, Kelly Arne, Ashley Ayer, Lori Barber, Purdie Baumann, Nancy Beard, Danielle Betchel, Miki Berg, Samantha Berger, Emily Blanchard, Torrie Bogda, Nita Borchardt, Elizabeth Bork, Karen Boyd, Erin Boyd-Jellison, Jenee Brown, Nirine Brown, Scarlett Buford, Darci Burke, Teresa Burks, Kimberly Calore-Sedlak, Amber Cameron, Mary Capellas, Audrie Chernauckas, Cassady Fleming Chiarelli, Christina Cichra, Keltie Colleen, Abbie Cooper, Kristine Covillo, Katherine Charlier, Danielle Jolie Dale, Laura Danelski, Gabrielle Del Re Ashley, Ashley DeZeeuw, Stephanie Dolph, Jacquelyn Dowsett, Megan Dragon, Beth Dukleth, Alina Duncan Williams, Tara Dunleavy, Anna Richardson, Jenelle Engleson, Alyssa Epstein, Gretchen Esch, Holly Evans, Mandy Evans-Brown, Melinda Farrell, Jennifer Fiandt, Jaime Fisher, Amanda Fox, Lauren Gaal, Cynthia Muller Geffon, Annie Gibbons-Syke, Sheri Griffith Dague, Michelle Hammar, Andrea Hammond, Katie Hamrah, Cheryl Cutlip, Christina Hedrick, Laura Henning, Andrea Hester, Leah Hofmann, Clare Holmes Tewalt, Melissa Hillmer, Afra Hines, Candace Jablonski, Kristin Jantzie, Sarah Lin Johnson, Kara Jones, Nicole Jones, Angela Kahle, Temple Kane, Rhonda Kaufman Malkin, Karen Keeler, Allyson Kelly, Danielle Kelsey, Chrystie Kenny, Danielle Kimmins, V. Kelly King, Amy Klingler, Toni Rhodus, Sara Kroeger, Krista Kutnick Harvey, Jacey Lambros, Heather Lang, Kristina Larson, Amy Lenhardt, Melissa Lenz, Alison Levenberg, Jocelyne Levesque, Lisa Lewis, Corinna Lindholm, Amy Ling, Synthia Link, Emily Loftiss, Nikki Long, Carissa Lopez, Stephanie Madden, Kara Sandberg, Tiffany Mackrill Tabor, Katie Martin, Danielle Mathews, Lisa Matsuoka, Caitlin McCarthy, Tara Memi, Summyr Whaley, Danelle Morgan, Kenna Michelle Morris, Tina Moya, Rebekah Needham, Alana Niehoff, Jessica Pack, Alison Paterson, Danielle Patrick, Stacy Paydo, Theresa Pelicata, Cheryl Peterson, Talese Peterson, Kimberly Petros, Ami Price, Kristyn Pope, Traci Reszetylo, Joanna Richardson, Sierra Ring, Katie Russell, Krista Saab, Amanda Schoppe, Kelly Sheerins, Margaret Shepherd, Christine Sienicki, Hannah Sides, Carolyn Simpson, Mary Katherine Smartt, Autumn Smith, Elizabeth Sousek, Katharine Steers, Amanda Suchy, Stacey Sund, Karilyn Ashley Surratt, Melissa Sybil, Alexis Thebolt, Melissa Thomas, Corinne Tighe, Julie Tomaino, Stevi Van Meter, Demoya Watson, Gelsey Weiss Mahanes, Sarah Wiechman, Laura Williams, KT Wilson, Jaime Lyn Windrow, Autumn Withers, Tiffany Whitaker, Amy York, Catherine Yurkovich, Melissa Zaremba Crooch, Katherine Raley Zofko.

PHOTO CREDITS

pp. 2-3 image by James Porto, pp. 4-5 image by George Kalinsky for Madison Square Garden, pp. 5-6 image by James Porto, pp. 8-9 images from MSG Entertainment, pp. 10-11 images from MSG Entertainment, p.13 image by James Porto, p. 18 ©New York Times, p. 19 image from MSG Entertainment, pp. 20-21 images from MSG Entertainment, p. 23 image from MSG Entertainment, p. 24 Jimmy Sileo, ©MSG Entertainment, p. 25 image from MSG Entertainment, p. 26 top, Cosmo-Sileo, ©MSG Entertainment; bottom, from MSG Entertainment, p. 27 image from MSG Entertainment, p. 28, Cosmo-Sileo, ©MSG Entertainment, p. 29 images from MSG Entertainment, p. 32 by Cosmo-Sileo, ©MSG Entertainment, p. 33 by Rob Brown, ©MSG Entertainment, p. 34-36, by George Kalinsky for Madison Square Garden, p. 37 top, by George Kalinsky for Madison Square Garden, p. 37 bottom, by Dave Alloca, pp. 39-77 images by James Porto, pp. 78-79 image from MSG Entertainment, pp. 80-81 Cosmo-Sileo, ©MSG Entertainment, p. 81 image from MSG Entertainment, p. 82 image from MSG Entertainment, p. 83 Cosmo-Sileo, ©MSG Entertainment, pp. 84-87 images from MSG Entertainment, p. 88 image by Jon Simon, ©MSG Entertainment; p. 89 image by Mark Kozlowski, ©MSG Entertainment; pp. 90-91 images by James Porto, p. 92 image by David James, p. 94 image by Paul Kolnik ©MSG Entertainment, p. 95 image by James Porto, pp. 96-97 image by Paul Kolnik ©MSG Entertainment, p. 98 Cosmo-Sileo, ©MSG Entertainment, p. 98 image by Vincente Minelli, ©MSG Entertainment; p. 99 image by James Porto, pp. 100-101 images by Paul Kolnik ©MSG Entertainment, p. 102 top left and bottom right images by Paul Kolnik ©MSG Entertainment, top right image by James Porto, bottom left image from MSG Entertainment, pp. 103-104 image by Paul Kolnik ©MSG Entertainment, p. 105 top, image from MSG Entertainment, p. 105 bottom, Cosmo-Sileo, ©MSG Entertainment, pp. 106-107 images by Paul Kolnik ©MSG Entertainment, p. 106 image from MSG Entertainment, pp. 108-110 image from MSG Entertainment, p. 111 image by Paul Kolnik ©MSG Entertainment, p. 112 image by James Porto.

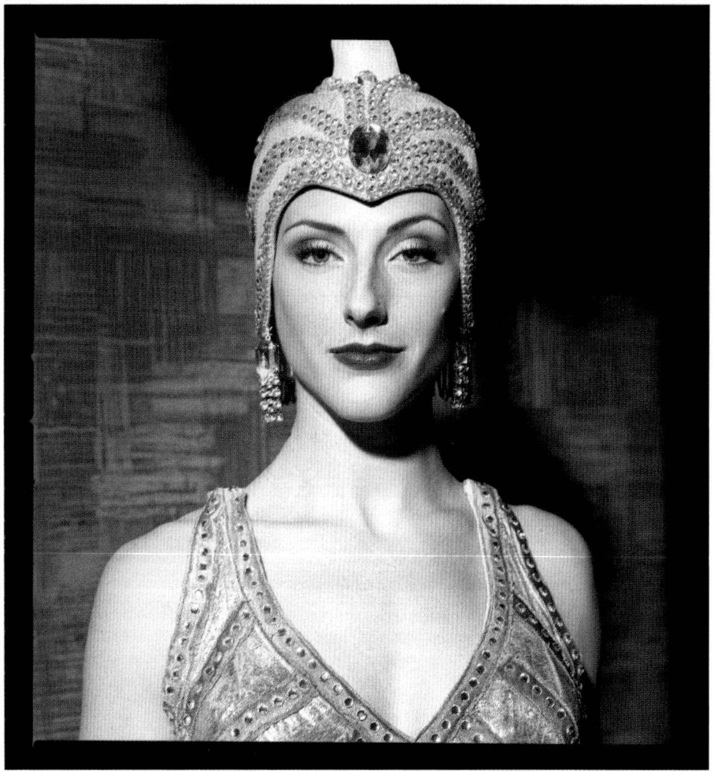

ACKNOWLEDGEMENT

pp. 30-31 The world-famous Radio City Rockettes as featured on the giant Eastman Kodak Colorama display in Grand Central Terminal, New York City.

ENDNOTES

[1] Charles Francisco, *The Radio City Music Hall An Affectionate History of the World's Greatest Theater* (New York: E. P. Dutton, 1979), 49

[2] Charles Francisco, *The Radio City Music Hall An Affectionate History of the World's Greatest Theater* (New York: E. P. Dutton, 1979), VII

[3] Charles Francisco, *The Radio City Music Hall An Affectionate History of the World's Greatest Theater* (New York: E. P. Dutton, 1979), 17

[4] Charles Francisco, *The Radio City Music Hall An Affectionate History of the World's Greatest Theater* (New York: E. P. Dutton, 1979), 69